AF545083

HEALTH CARE ISSUES, COSTS AND ACCESS

PHYSICIAN PRACTICES

CHANGES, TRENDS, AND IMPLICATIONS

HEALTH CARE ISSUES, COSTS AND ACCESS

Additional books in this series can be found on Nova's website
under the Series tab.

Additional E-books in this series can be found on Nova's website
under the E-book tab.

HEALTH CARE ISSUES, COSTS AND ACCESS

PHYSICIAN PRACTICES

CHANGES, TRENDS, AND IMPLICATIONS

ISAAK ANGELIDIS
EDITOR

New York

For permission to use material from this book please contact us:
Telephone 631-231-7269; Fax 631-231-8175
Web Site: http://www.novapublishers.com

Additional color graphics may be available in the e-book version of this book.

Library of Congress Cataloging-in-Publication Data

ISBN: 978-1-62618-184-7

Published by Nova Science Publishers, Inc. † New York

Contents

Preface

A growing number of U.S. physicians are combining their practices; affiliating with hospitals, insurance companies, and specialty management firms; or going to work directly for such organizations. The moves are part of a broader trend toward consolidation in health care, with the overall number of mergers and acquisitions in the sector at the highest level in a decade. Alterations in physician practice appear to be a response to a number of factors. Younger doctors are more eager than their predecessors to work for an outside institution, such as a hospital, to secure a set schedule and salary. Private practices have become more complex to manage, even as physician compensation has been declining. This book provides background on the factors contributing to changes in physician practice organization, including physician supply, lifestyle changes, and government incentives, with a focus on different types of integration, the legal intricacies of affiliation, and the possible implications for consumer and federal policy.

Chapter 1 – A growing number of U.S. physicians are combining their practices; affiliating with hospitals, insurance companies, and specialty management firms; or going to work directly for such organizations. The moves are part of a broader trend toward consolidation in health care, with the overall number of mergers and acquisitions in the sector at the highest level in a decade.

Alterations in physician practice appear to be a response to a number of factors. Younger doctors are more eager than their predecessors to work for an outside institution, such as a hospital, to secure a set schedule and salary. Private practices have become more complex to manage, even as physician compensation has been declining. Doctors see financial advantages to building larger practices, in terms of ability to control expenses and negotiate higher fees with insurers. Further, not all trends are toward consolidation. A small but growing number of doctors are reacting to market incentives by moving in a different direction: creating concierge practices in which they see a limited number of patients who pay an annual retainer.

According to experts, physician practices also may be affected, in part, by provisions of the 2010 Patient Protection and Affordable Care Act (ACA, P.L. 111-148, as amended), designed to spur closer financial and clinical affiliation among health care providers. For example, the ACA creates health care delivery systems called Accountable Care Organizations (ACO), under which providers contract to oversee a patient's total course of care in a bid to manage costs and improve quality. A number of physician practices, insurers, and hospitals have announced affiliations to qualify as ACOs. In another move partly spurred by the ACA, hospitals and health plans have been hiring physicians to ensure they will have adequate staff to treat the millions of Americans projected to gain insurance during the next few years. Several major studies have warned of a looming shortage of physicians, particularly primary care doctors.

Congress is playing dual roles regarding the consolidation. On the one hand, the ACA was designed, in part, to prompt affiliation among doctors and other health care providers in order to reduce fragmentation and help control government and private health spending. At the same time, lawmakers are monitoring the health care system for signs that consolidation is having negative effects on consumer access, prices, and competition. The health care sector went through a similar round of restructuring during the 1980s and 1990s, including mergers and acquisitions of physician practices, ultimately prompting a backlash from some consumers who complained they were being blocked from specialists and procedures. The ACA envisions a different system of "patient-centered care," where doctors and other providers are given incentives to improve quality and efficiency, rather than to limit services. Still, it remains to be seen how the current round of changes will play out as physicians and other providers form larger organizations. This report provides background on factors contributing to changes in physician practice organization, including physician supply, sources of revenue, operating costs, and government incentives. It also examines the different types of integration, the legal intricacies of affiliation, and the possible implications for consumer and federal policy.

Chapter 2 – An adequate physician supply is important for the effective and efficient delivery of health care services and, therefore, for population health and the cost and quality of health care. Assessments of the adequacy of physician supply often focus on three dimensions of the physician population: its size; its composition (e.g., the mix between primary care and specialty physicians); and its geographic distribution. Policies that aim to alter physician supply generally focus on both current and future supply along these three dimensions because physician training is a lengthy process; therefore, changes implemented to alter supply do not have immediate effects.

Each of the three dimensions of physician supply is important for health care spending and for population health because physician clinical decisions affect approximately 90% of each health care dollar spent. In addition, as physicians provide health care services that, with some exceptions, cannot be provided by non-physicians, the size, composition, and geographic distribution of the physician population affects the amount and type of health care services available. A number of studies have found physician shortages overall, in certain specialties, and in certain geographic areas. The federal government pays for physician services, primarily through the Medicare and Medicaid programs, and supports physician training through a number of programs in various departments and agencies. Given current investments in physician services and the physician workforce, the adequacy of the current and future physician supply may be of interest to Congress.

The Patient Protection and Affordable Care Act (PPACA, P.L. 111-148) may affect physician supply because it expands insurance coverage to those previously uninsured. PPACA also includes provisions that may affect the size, composition, and geographic distribution of the physician population by supporting changes to physician training, compensation, and practice. Specifically, provisions targeting the number of physicians trained and their productivity may affect the size of the physician population. The composition of the physician population may be altered by provisions targeting the supply of primary care providers or specialties in shortage. Provisions addressing the diversity of the physician workforce and those incentivizing practice in rural or other underserved areas may affect the geographic distribution of the physician population. Finally, PPACA includes provisions that provide for data collection and evaluation of the adequacy of the workforce in general, and federal workforce programs specifically. Whether and how these provisions will affect physician supply is not yet known because some of these provisions have not been implemented yet, are temporary, will not have immediate effects, or rely on discretionary funding.

This report examines each dimension of physician supply, separately discussing current (and, where appropriate, future) concerns and relevant changes included in PPACA that may affect each dimension. The report then discusses workforce planning activities included in PPACA that may affect all three dimensions of supply.

Chapter 3 – The practice of medicine has always been evolving due to research, but also for technological, societal and legal reasons. For many years, medicine seemed to be a cottage industry, with physicians typically opening or joining a practice after medical school. Over the past ten years, however, increasing numbers of physicians, particularly those in small and solo practices, have found independent practices to be economically unfeasible. For a number of reasons, they are affiliating with larger medical practices or hospitals. The result may be a dramatic shift in the delivery of health care.

This hearing will provide an opportunity for Members to learn more about the reasons for these changes, and some assessments of what they mean.

Chapter 4 – This is the Testimony of Mark Smith, President, Merritt Hawkins.

Chapter 5 – This is the Testimony of Dr. Louis McIntyre, Westchester Orthopedic Associates.

Chapter 6 – This is the Statement of Joseph M. Yasso, Jr., D.O., Heritage Physicians Group.

Chapter 7 – This is the Statement of Scott Gottlieb, M.D., Resident Fellow, American Enterprise Institute.

Chapter 8 – This is the Testimony of Edmund F. Haislmaier, Senior Research Fellow, Center for Health Policy Studies, The Heritage Foundation.

Chapter 9 – This is the Statement of Thomas L. Greaney, Co-Director, Center for Health Law Studies, Saint Louis University School of Law.

Chapter 10 – This is the Statement of Martin Gaynor, Professor, Carnegie Mellon University.

Chapter 11 – This is the Statement of Paul B. Ginsburg, President, Center for Studying Health System Change.

In: Physician Practices
Editor: Isaak Angelidis

ISBN: 978-1-62618-184-7

Chapter 1

PHYSICIAN PRACTICES: BACKGROUND, ORGANIZATION, AND MARKET CONSOLIDATION*

Suzanne M. Kirchhoff

SUMMARY

A growing number of U.S. physicians are combining their practices; affiliating with hospitals, insurance companies, and specialty management firms; or going to work directly for such organizations. The moves are part of a broader trend toward consolidation in health care, with the overall number of mergers and acquisitions in the sector at the highest level in a decade.

Alterations in physician practice appear to be a response to a number of factors. Younger doctors are more eager than their predecessors to work for an outside institution, such as a hospital, to secure a set schedule and salary. Private practices have become more complex to manage, even as physician compensation has been declining. Doctors see financial advantages to building larger practices, in terms of ability to control expenses and negotiate higher fees with insurers. Further, not all trends are toward consolidation. A small but growing number of doctors are reacting to market incentives by moving in a different direction: creating

* This is an edited, reformatted and augmented version of Congressional Research Service, Publication No. R42880, dated January 2, 2013.

concierge practices in which they see a limited number of patients who pay an annual retainer.

According to experts, physician practices also may be affected, in part, by provisions of the 2010 Patient Protection and Affordable Care Act (ACA, P.L. 111-148, as amended), designed to spur closer financial and clinical affiliation among health care providers. For example, the ACA creates health care delivery systems called Accountable Care Organizations (ACO), under which providers contract to oversee a patient's total course of care in a bid to manage costs and improve quality. A number of physician practices, insurers, and hospitals have announced affiliations to qualify as ACOs. In another move partly spurred by the ACA, hospitals and health plans have been hiring physicians to ensure they will have adequate staff to treat the millions of Americans projected to gain insurance during the next few years. Several major studies have warned of a looming shortage of physicians, particularly primary care doctors.

Congress is playing dual roles regarding the consolidation. On the one hand, the ACA was designed, in part, to prompt affiliation among doctors and other health care providers in order to reduce fragmentation and help control government and private health spending. At the same time, lawmakers are monitoring the health care system for signs that consolidation is having negative effects on consumer access, prices, and competition. The health care sector went through a similar round of restructuring during the 1980s and 1990s, including mergers and acquisitions of physician practices, ultimately prompting a backlash from some consumers who complained they were being blocked from specialists and procedures. The ACA envisions a different system of "patient-centered care," where doctors and other providers are given incentives to improve quality and efficiency, rather than to limit services. Still, it remains to be seen how the current round of changes will play out as physicians and other providers form larger organizations. This report provides background on factors contributing to changes in physician practice organization, including physician supply, sources of revenue, operating costs, and government incentives. It also examines the different types of integration, the legal intricacies of affiliation, and the possible implications for consumer and federal policy.

INTRODUCTION

Most Americans enter the health care system through their local physician's office, which is the setting for 84% of primary care visits.[1] Historically, physicians have operated in what the American Medical

Association and others have called a "cottage industry"[2] of small or solo practices around the country. Even now, the majority of the approximately 972,376 doctors and residents[3] in the United States work mainly from smaller, office-based practices.[4] This decentralized network has served to deliver medical services to most Americans, but it has also been cited by analysts as a reason that the health care market is inefficient, with patients seeing duplicate providers who may prescribe overlapping treatments or deliver widely divergent, uncoordinated care.[5]

During the past several years, however, physician practices appear to be changing, as a number of doctors merge their offices into larger practices; sell their practices to hospitals, insurance companies, and physician management firms; contract to provide exclusive services to providers such as hospitals; or go to work for larger providers as salaried employees.[6] While there are no definitive statistics, a 2011 American Hospital Association (AHA) survey found the number of doctors on hospital payrolls had increased by 32% from 2000 to 2010, with the rate of increase accelerating after 2005.[7] According to the AHA, about 20% of practicing physicians now work for hospitals. The Medical Group Management Association (MGMA), which represents larger medical practices and outpatient clinics, has noted an increase in the share of medical groups owned by U.S. hospitals, while other surveys have also found rising hospital employment of doctors, with some regional variations.[8] For example, an American College of Cardiology survey found the share of physician-owned cardiology practices declined to 60% in 2012 from 73% in 2007, while the share of such practices owned by hospitals grew from 8% to an estimated 24%.[9]

The changes appear to be the result of a number of factors, including broad consolidation in the overall health care industry that has created dominant hospitals and insurers in many areas. In order to gain negotiating leverage with large providers and payers, a number of physicians have merged their practices into larger groups or entered into business arrangements with them. Lifestyle preferences are at play, with younger doctors more willing than their predecessors to work for an outside institution to secure a set schedule and salary; about half of doctors hired out of residencies or fellowships in 2010 took jobs at hospitals.[10] Physicians may be having a harder time finding doctors to buy or join a small practice, as management becomes more complex and average compensation declines.[11]

At the same time, hospitals and insurers are eager to hire doctors, given forecasts of a pending physician shortage by the end of the decade (see "Physician Supply"). The shortfall is predicted to occur in the midst of rising demand for medical services by aging baby boomers and millions of Americans who could gain insurance coverage under the 2010 Patient Protection and Affordable Care Act (ACA, P.L. 111-148 as amended).[12] According to some experts, financial incentives in the ACA may provide further incentives for consolidation and integration of services.[13] For example, the health care law creates integrated delivery systems called Accountable Care Organizations (ACO)[14] that contract with payers who agree to be responsible for the entire continuum of care provided to a group of patients. If the treatment costs less than set targets, and certain quality measures are met, the ACO and the payer share in the savings.[15] Hundreds of physician practices, insurers, and hospitals have announced financial and clinical integration to quality as ACOs.[16]

The ongoing changes in practice organization—if they alter the way that physicians deliver care—could help determine whether the U.S. health care system expands access, improves quality of treatment, and addresses the growth of government and private health care spending, according to analysts.[17] Though physician payments account for about 20% of medical spending,[18] studies suggest that physicians direct as much as 90% of total health care spending through referrals, tests, hospital admissions, and other actions.[19]

Congress is playing dual roles regarding the consolidation. On the one hand, lawmakers designed the ACA in part to reduce health delivery fragmentation and help control government and private spending. In addition, Congress and federal regulators have been monitoring, and continue to monitor, the health care system for signs that mergers and acquisitions may be having negative effects on costs, competition, and consumer access such as distorting prices[20] or creating conflicts of interest in provision of services.[21] Analysts and lawmakers are aware that the health care sector went through a similar round of restructuring during the 1980s and 1990s, as physicians sold their practices and managed care insurance plans expanded. The changes ultimately prompted a consumer backlash, and many of the deals were dissolved.[22] In contrast to the previous round of consolidation, where doctors were seen as gatekeepers for managed care plans that attempted to limit services, the ACA envisions "patient-centered" care where doctors and other providers are rewarded for necessary treatment that improves quality of outcomes. Still, it is not clear how the new round of changes ultimately will play out.

This report provides background on factors contributing to changes in physician practice organization, including physician supply, lifestyle changes, and government incentives. Next it examines different types of integration, the legal intricacies of affiliation, and the possible implications for consumer and federal policy.

PHYSICIAN SUPPLY

Most U.S. physicians are MDs, or doctors of medicine, who have completed four years of medical school and a minimum of three years of residency, with specialists undergoing additional training. About 7% of the more than 972,376 physicians and residents[23] are osteopaths, who have completed medical education and additional training in areas including the musculoskeletal system.[24] The physician population is about one-third primary care physicians and two-thirds specialists, a distribution that some experts suggest is not optimal. A quarter of U.S. doctors are graduates of international medical schools. The ratio of physicians to the population varies across the country, with New England and the Middle Atlantic regions having the highest number of doctors per capita, and the West South Central and Mountain regions having the fewest.[25] Rural areas are struggling to attract enough physicians.[26]

In the 1980s, after a congressional effort to fund an expansion of U.S. medical education, experts forecasted a possible surplus of doctors.[27] More recently, however, analysts have predicted that the country faces a potential shortage, particularly in primary care. The federal Health Resources and Services Administration in 2006 predicted a shortfall of 55,000 to 150,000 physicians by 2020, while the nonprofit Association of American Medical Colleges (AAMC) in 2008 said there could be a dearth of 130,600 patient care physicians by 2025.[28] Following up in 2012, the AAMC found that 33 states had documented current physician shortages or were anticipating shortages.[29]

Adding to concerns, nearly a third of physicians are age 55 or older and nearing retirement.[30] In addition, studies indicate that doctors of both sexes and from varying backgrounds are working fewer hours each week, a change more pronounced among younger doctors.[31] A 2010 study found a nearly 6% decrease in hours among nonresident physicians from1996-1998 to 2006-2008. The reduction in hours was akin to a loss of 36,000 doctors, had the number of hours worked not changed.[32] Some analysts have suggested that the combination of retirements and lifestyle changes will put a tremendous stress on the system and hasten the need for doctors to find more efficient ways to practice.[33]

The forecast supply shortage and changes in work patterns are already having impacts, according to analysts. For example, some hospitals have been having increasing difficulty finding physicians to take voluntary duty and have hired more full-time staff doctors, including hospitalists, who oversee patient care in hospitals, and emergency room physicians (see "Hospital Affiliation and Employment"). A number of hospitals are seeking to hire or affiliate with primary care physicians, to ensure supply, staff outpatient centers, gain access to referral networks, and form ACOs. A 2010 survey by the American Hospital Association found 80% of hospitals were looking to hire primary care physicians.[34]

Supporting Practitioners

Mitigating the projected physician shortage somewhat is the growing use of professionals who are not doctors but who have specialized training and can perform some basic functions of physicians, including nurse practitioners and physician assistants. In 2009, nearly half of all office-based physician practices included nurse practitioners, certified nurse midwives, or physician assistants.[35]

However, state laws vary in terms of the scope of services that nurse practitioners and physician assistants are allowed to provide.[36]

Nurse practitioners must complete graduate education beyond the bachelor's degree needed to become a registered nurse. They can work with physicians or separately in such areas as taking case histories, performing basic exams, ordering lab work and prescribing some medications, and providing health education and counseling. There are approximately 155,000 active U.S. nurse practitioners.[37]

Physician assistants complete at least two years of college courses in basic science and behavioral science before applying to one of the 170 accredited physician assistant programs. Most physician assistants have a bachelor's degree, another 27 months of specialized training, and 2,000 hours of clinical rotations.[38]

Physician assistants, once licensed by state boards, generally can take patient medical histories, examine patients, treat minor injuries, order and interpret laboratory tests, and make rounds in medical facilities.[39] There are about 86,000 certified physician assistants in the United States.

PRACTICE CONSOLIDATION

Historically, physicians have operated in small or solo practices,[40] with a number of factors limiting integration with other health care providers. In states such as California, laws designed to bar the corporate practice of medicine complicated efforts at affiliation between physician practices and insurance companies or hospitals.[41] Doctors and hospitals have been paid separately for services, minimizing the need for tight coordination, though physicians benefited from access to and affiliations with hospitals, including serving on voluntary staff or taking call.[42]

There has long been a debate about the efficiency of the decentralized physician practice structure. During the 1930s, for example, a health sector-created blue ribbon "Committee on the Costs of Medical Care" suggested improving health care by moving toward a more coordinated system centered on hospitals, including affiliation between doctors and hospitals. The recommendations created controversy, with some groups concerned that such a change would lead to the corporate practice of medicine, affecting quality and physician independence.[43]

In the 1980s and 1990s, the type of broad system changes that some health experts had advocated appeared to take root, including the growth of managed care plans, where health insurers coordinate use of health care for enrollees by directly arranging for services through affiliated physicians, hospitals, and other providers. A number of physicians sold their practices to hospitals or specialty physician management companies, as health plans were able to pressure providers to accept lower payment rates and assume some financial risk for patient care. [44]

But as consumers protested the managed care restrictions on services, and hospitals and physician management firms found they had overpaid for some physician practices, managed care plans loosened their controls and a number of mergers and acquisitions were dissolved. For example, in California from 1998 to 2002 nearly 150 physician organizations that served millions of patients closed or went into bankruptcy.[45] Though consolidation slowed, it continued (see Table 1).

According to one estimate, the share of doctors with an ownership stake in their practices declined from 62% in 1996-1997 to 54% in 2004-2005.[46] The percentage of office visits to physicians in solo practices declined from 38.7% in 1997 to 30.5% in 2007, while the share visiting physicians in practices of 6 -10 physicians rose from 12.1% in 1997 to 17.7% in 2007.[47]

Table 1. Changes in Physician Practice Over Time

Practice Setting	1996-1997	1998-1999	2000-2001	2004-2005
Solo/Two Physicians	40.7%	37.4%	32.5%	32.5%
Small Group, 3-5 Physicians	12.2%	9.6%	11.7%	9.8%
Medium Group, 6-50 Physicians	13.1%	14.2%	15.8%	17.6%
Large Group, More than 50 Physicians	2.9%	3.5%	2.7%	4.2%
Staff/Group HMO	5.0%	4.6%	3.8%	4.5%
Hospital-Owned, Medical School or Other	26.3%	30.8%	30.8%	31.4%

Source: Center for Studying Health System Change, http://facts.kff.org/chart.aspx?ch=185. Also http://www.hschange.com/CONTENT/941/?topic=topic22.

Note: While the center has 2008 data, the methodology was changed from the 2004-205 survey, meaning that the results cannot be directly compared.

More recently there has been what some analysts call a reconsolidation of physician practices.[48] While there is limited data at the individual office level, general surveys and studies have found a decline in the number of solo practices and an increase in the number of larger practices. There appears to be a rise in the number of practices owned by hospitals and insurers, and in the share of doctors in private practices working under exclusive contract to hospitals and insurance companies.[49] The Center for Studying Health System Change, in a 2010 survey of 12 communities, found rising hospital employment of physicians, with some regional variations.[50] Separately, a 2008 survey by the American Medical Association, which includes more solo and smaller practices than the MGMA data, did not show that the share of physicians working for hospitals had increased significantly since 2000, but did indicate that fewer doctors owned their practices and more were working as employees.[51]

The consulting firm Accenture predicted that just a third of U.S. doctors would be truly independent by 2013, which Accenture defines as physicians who are in a partnership or have an ownership share in a practice.[52] The 33% figure compares to 57% in 2000 and 43% in 2009. A 2012 report by the California Health Care Foundation listed a number of factors for the trends in that state, including the complexity and cost of running a practice; health care providers' concern about a potential shortage of physicians; declining reimbursement for services, including Medicare and Medicaid; and the cost of implementing new systems such as electronic health records.[53]

Market Trends

The practice changes are taking several forms. There is horizontal consolidation, where businesses in the same part of the production process band together for economies of scale and to forestall competition, including mergers of specialty practices. There is vertical consolidation, where different industry segments form financial and clinical affiliations to seek potential efficiency gains. Examples of such consolidation and integration include hospitals buying physician practices or hiring physicians; physicians affiliating with insurers; and formation of ACOs. While not consolidation per say, the growth of concierge practices is another response to economic and other factors, and could affect physician supply and patient care.

Larger Group Practices and Physician Organizations

The share of solo and small practices has been declining, while the number of larger practices is increasing, with some spanning a number of counties or entire states.[54] Larger physician practices, particularly specialty practices, have advantages such as increased leverage in negotiations with insurance companies, greater purchasing power, [55] and efficiencies in overhead and in their ability to use advanced technology and other patient-management tools.[56]

Physicians can organize into different configurations, from mergers to independent practice associations, which are organizations of physicians who maintain their independent corporate status but can integrate financially or clinically and contract as a group.[57] In addition, activity by for-profit practice management companies, which buy and run physician practices, has been growing ,[58] particularly those that contract with hospitals. There is also growth in private equity investment in physician practices.[59]

There are no definitive figures regarding practice consolidation. However, the accounting and consulting firm Moss Adams has documented a doubling of mergers, acquisitions, and private equity investments in specialty physician practices between 2008 and 2012.[60] In 2008 there were 125 mergers, acquisitions, public offerings, or private equity investments involving specialty practices, according to the firm. In 2010 there were nearly 240, and more than 260 were estimated for 2011.[61] Moss Adams says the ACA “is bringing about or accelerating" changes in the health care system, including creation of larger medical group practices and "transactions among specialty physician groups, medical clinics, hospitals, and other organizations looking to take advantage of scale and cost savings."

Some recent examples of growing physician organizations include the 2011 merger of Cogent HMG and the Hospitalists Management Group, which created the largest private hospitalist company in the country.[62] (Hospitalists are physicians who coordinate patient care in hospital settings.) Cogent now contracts with about 130 hospitals around the country. Another example is IPC The Hospitalist Company. The company in 2011 employed or was affiliated with about 1,200 hospitalists, including doctors and other health professionals, and had employment agreements with about 600 additional professionals.[63] Mednax, a physician management firm, oversees 1,400 doctors and nurse practitioners in its Pediatrix division who specialize in neonatal and pediatric care, as well as more than 400 doctors and 500 nurse anesthetists in its American Anesthesiology group.[64]

Hospital Affiliation and Employment

The AHA survey finding a 32% increase in hospital employment of doctors from 2000 to 2010 is one indication of the growing consolidation in this area.[65] In another example, the physician search and consulting firm Merritt Hawkins told the House Committee on Small Business in July 2012 that from April 1, 2011, to March 31, 2012, company employees conducted more than 2,700 physician search assignments for hospitals, medical groups, and small physician practices. Only 2% of those physician searches were on behalf of entities seeking doctors to start a practice in an area or to join a solo practitioner as a partner, compared with 42% in 2004. Overall, 63% of the group's physician search assignments were carried out for hospitals that wanted to hire doctors, compared with 11% in 2004.[66]

Likewise, a 2011 survey by the American College of Cardiology found that 40% of hospital administrators had acquired or considered acquiring a cardiology practice during the previous two years, and 20% were considering a future acquisition.[67] In one example of the changes, the number of hospitalists has risen from less than 1,000 in the late 1990s to nearly 30,000 in 2011.[68]

Physician-hospital affiliation can take a number of forms, from contracts for specific services with physician practices or organizations, such as those outlined above, to full-time employment of doctors (see Figure 1).

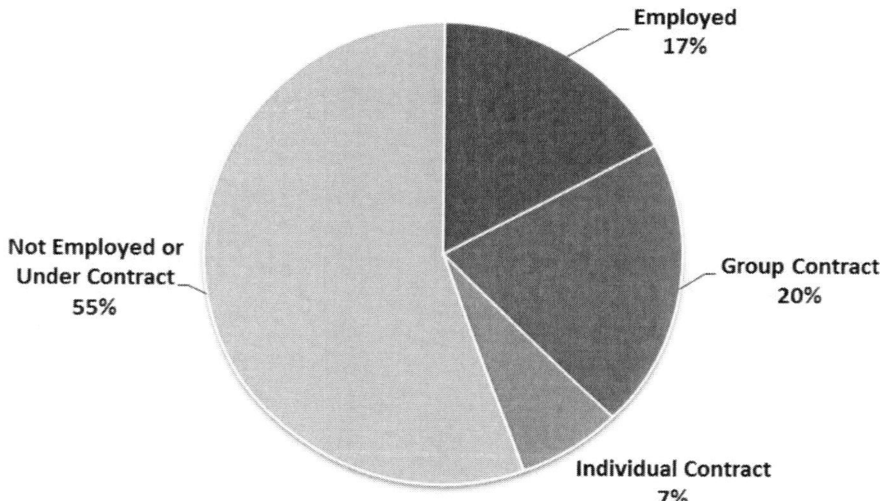

Source: American Hospital Association, *AHA Hospital Statistics 2012 Edition*.
Notes: Survey includes dentists, but few are employed by the community hospitals surveyed.

Figure 1. Physician Medical Staff Arrangements with U.S. Community Hospitals; 2010 data on working arrangements of doctors affiliated with or employed by hospitals.

Over time, physician-hospital arrangements have shifted as financial incentives have changed.[69] Some general examples of possible affiliations include the following:

- Physician practices can contract to provide doctors and other staff for a hospital independently or work through intermediaries like physician management companies.
- Hospitals can directly employ doctors. In states that have laws barring the corporate practice of medicine, some hospitals have created non-profit foundations to secure physician services. [70]
- Doctors and hospitals can form physician-hospital organizations or other forms of joint ventures to provide services, bid for insurance contracts, or achieve financial and clinical integration.

According to the AHA, affiliations involving independent groups of physicians have been declining in prevalence, while arrangements in which physicians are salaried employees have been increasing.[71] For physicians, selling a practice to a hospital or entering into a close financial agreement can reduce overhead, while providing predictable schedules and compensation. For hospitals, buying or affiliating with practices allows development of areas of excellence, ensures staff, provides a network of referrals from physicians, and can give the combined entity more leverage with insurers.[72]

Affiliation in the form of a joint venture such as an outpatient center can be a way for the hospital to increase revenues and ward off competition from independent doctors and practices that open such centers.[73]

Differing Medicare reimbursement based on provider status may also be providing incentives for physician-hospital affiliations. [74] In 2011, Medicare paid more for a 15-minute evaluation and management physician visit in a hospital outpatient setting than it did for a visit in an independent physician's office.

Because hospitals also charge facility fees for physician visits, costs are not only higher costs for payers but also for patients, since the fees are subject to deductibles and coinsurance. In a 2012 report to Congress, Medpac, noting increased outpatient billing as more hospitals employ physicians or buy physician practices, said that if current trends continue, Medicare costs could rise by $2 billion annually by 2020:[75]

> This payment difference creates a financial incentive for hospitals to purchase freestanding physician offices and convert them into (outpatient departments) OPDs without changing their location or patient mix. Indeed, (evaluation and management) clinic visits provided in OPDs increased 6.7% in 2010, potentially increasing Medicare and beneficiary expenditures without any change in patient care.[76]

As the experience of the 1990s showed, hospital employment of physicians has not always been successful. Hospitals may not make as much money as expected, and may incur initial losses. An analysis in *The New England Journal of Medicine* estimated that hospitals lose $150,000 to $250,000 per year for the first three years they employ a doctor, as physicians adapt to the new system.[77]

During the 1990s, some hospitals found that physician productivity declined after practices were purchased by hospitals. Merritt Hawkins data indicate that even though a number of hospitals are now preparing to make the transition to coordinated systems such as ACOs, they are still basing physician compensation on a fee-for-service or volume basis—offering new hires a salary with a productivity bonus.[78]

Affiliation with Insurers and Other Payers

Insurance companies are affiliating with physicians as they attempt to meld coverage and delivery systems to better control costs. Some analysts suggest that physicians may find their financial and professional interests are more aligned with insurers, given that emerging payment systems such as medical homes and ACOs increase pressure to reduce costs and increase quality by improving preventive care and follow-up care to avoid hospitalizations.[79] However, the AMA in a manual for members notes that the success of such arrangements, as with other ACO configurations, depends on a number of factors regarding the amount of decision making insurers are willing to give physicians and other professional and financial concerns.[80]

Some recent examples of affiliation include the following: UnitedHealth Group, a large California insurer, in 2011 bought the management arm of Monarch HealthCare, the largest physician group in Orange County, California.[81] Health insurance firm Cigna has expanded its accountable care network via deals with physician practices in seven states, and now has more than 20 such plans.[82] Pennsylvania-based Highmark Inc., a major insurer in the Blue Cross/Blue Shield system, has been working on an acquisition of the West Penn Allegheny Health System, a physician-led hospital and multi-group practice network. The move is part of a larger effort by Highmark to develop an integrated care system.[83]

Delivery Reforms

Physician practices, hospitals, and other health care providers in recent months have announced affiliations to qualify as accountable care organizations (ACO) under the ACA.[84] Group practices, independent practice associations, and networks or independent practitioners can participate if they meet HHS standards.[85] In the simplest case, an ACO contracts with payers to be accountable for the continuum of care provided to a defined population. If the costs of care provided are less than targeted amounts, and certain quality measures are achieved, the ACO and the payer share the savings. Under the Medicare Shared Savings Program, the government will contract with ACOs that will assume responsibility for improving quality of care and coordinating care across providers. ACOs must be financially and organizationally integrated.

Some industry analysts say the ACOs could have a notable effect on the health care marketplace. Morgan Stanley in a June 2011 analysis predicted the ACA would accelerate health care consolidation, noting that the share of physicians in independent practices was declining by 1% to 3% a year as doctors entered into financial arrangements with hospitals and other providers. While most of the initial ACOs that formed were sponsored by hospitals, however, a growing number are being built around physician practices or insurers.[86]

The ACA includes other provisions intended to increase health system coordination that could help to drive additional integration. One is medical homes, where the primary physician's office assumes the role for coordinating care across other providers to improve outcomes and reduce costs. The ACA also includes Medicare "bundled" payments, where billing is based on the totality of a treatment, and the law gives physicians new ability to form health co-ops or affiliate with insurers and managed care plans.[87] A GAO examination of bundled payments found they are difficult to set up and administer without provider affiliation.[88]

Some analysts predict the market changes now underway will be more long-lasting and pervasive than was the case during the 1990s, given moves toward integrated care.[89] For example, private equity firms looking at investing in health care providers are targeting companies that can capitalize on consolidation by providing management services or physician staff for health care providers. Bain & Co. in a recent report predicted that health care providers and services will become more significant for investors. As Bain analysts wrote: "We expect significant strategic interest in accountable-care oriented investments, including investments that stretch across traditional boundaries (such as UnitedHealth Group's acquisition of Monarch Care)."[90]

Concierge Practices

While the main trends appear to be consolidation, a small but growing number of doctors are responding to pressures to change health care delivery and reimbursement by creating concierge practices, where physicians see fewer patients who pay an annual fee to receive care. In return, patients get enhanced services such as longer office visits, more in-depth physicals, and other preventive and continuous care. Because physicians in concierge practices see fewer patients on average, there have been questions about the potential impact on physician supply. To date, however, the number of such practices remains relatively small.

A 2010 study by researchers at the University of Chicago and Georgetown University for Medpac found there were at least 756 retainer-based physicians providing care (a number the report said probably represented the minimum), with average fees from about $1,500 to $2,000, although the physicians interviewed charged anywhere from $600 to $5,400.[91] The physicians interviewed by the researchers had 100 to 425 patients in their practices, compared to more than 2,000 before starting or joining a concierge practice. Large, regional concierge groups include MDVIP, headquartered in Boca Raton, Florida, and[92] New York-based Concierge Choice Physicians.[93]

Several states have examined whether concierge medicine is in compliance with their insurance laws, and there have also been issues regarding whether the additional fee is in compliance with government and other insurance policies.[94] For example, concierge practices can only include Medicare patients if (1) the physician elects to opt out of Medicare and does not treat any Medicare beneficiaries for two years, or (2) the physician contracts to provide concierge care only for non-Medicare covered services.

LEGAL ISSUES

As physicians seek to affiliate with other practices or providers, through ACOs or other means, they must comply with state and federal laws designed to ensure fair competition and transparency, as well as prevent over-utilization of services in the health care sector. Among the laws are federal antitrust and anti-kickback statutes, state laws barring the corporate practice of medicine, and the Stark law that imposes limitations on physician self-referrals.[95]

Federal antitrust laws are directed at ensuring that markets remain competitive. Antitrust is a means of governing market behavior that is, in essence, the flip side of market regulation accomplished via regulatory oversight. The consolidation or integration of health care entities, or other behavior by them (joint and/or unilateral), even if prompted by or taken in furtherance of achieving some level of joint functioning deemed necessary to achieve the stated goals of the ACA or other improvements in the health care sector, could create cause for antitrust concern. Joint negotiation over fees or terms of reimbursement by physicians or other providers is an example of behavior that might implicate the antitrust laws, for example.

Applicable antitrust or antitrust-related provisions include sections 1 and 2 of the Sherman Act (15 U.S.C. §§1, 2), which prohibit, respectively, "contracts or conspiracies in restraint of trade" and monopolization or attempted monopolization; and §7 of the Clayton Act (15 U.S.C. §18), the so-called "anti-merger" provision; both are enforceable by the antitrust agencies (Antitrust Division of the Department of Justice, FTC), as well as by individual plaintiffs. Section 5 of the FTC Act, which prohibits "unfair methods of competition in or affecting commerce," is enforceable only by the commission. The FTC and the DOJ have issued guidance regarding ACOs and other configurations that could pass antitrust review, and those that might be problematic.[96] The DOJ and FTC have been investigating some hospital physician mergers.[97]

Medicare and Medicaid anti-kickback law (42 U.S.C. §1320a-7b(b)) makes it a felony for a person to knowingly and willfully offer, pay, solicit, or receive anything of value (i.e., "remuneration") in return for a referral or to induce generation of business reimbursable under a federal health care program. The statute prohibits both the offer or payment of remuneration for patient referrals, as well as the offer or payment of anything of value in return for purchasing, leasing, ordering, or arranging for, or recommending the purchase, lease, or ordering of any item or service that is reimbursable by a federal health care program. Persons found guilty of violating the anti-kickback statute may be subject to a fine of up to $25,000, imprisonment of up to five years, and exclusion from participation in federal health care programs for up to one year.[98]

The Stark provisions that impose limitations on physician self-referrals were enacted in 1989 under the Ethics in Patient Referrals Act (42 U.S.C. §1395nn).[99] The Stark law, as amended, and its implementing regulations prohibit certain physician self-referrals for designated health services that may be paid for by Medicare or Medicaid. In its basic application, the Stark law provides that if (1) a physician (or an immediate family member of a physician) has a "financial relationship" with an entity, the physician may not make a referral to the entity for the furnishing of designated health services (for which payment may be made under Medicare or Medicaid), and (2) the entity may not present (or cause to be presented) a claim to the federal health care program or bill to any individual or entity for DHS furnished pursuant to a prohibited referral. The general idea behind the prohibitions in the Stark law is to prevent physicians from making referrals based on financial gain, thus preventing overutilization and increases in health care costs.

The laws include some exceptions for direct employment arrangements, and some legal experts say direct employment of physicians may be the most straightforward way for hospitals and other providers to integrate with physicians, given the legal complexities that can be involved in other arrangements.[100]

There can be financial downsides to direct employment, as hospitals discovered during the 1990s when they did not realize expected financial gains after buying physician practices.

ISSUES FOR CONGRESS

Congress has been paying close attention to consolidation in the health care industry, and specifically in physician practices, including hearings in the Ways and Means Committee and the House Committee on Small Business during the 112th Congress.[101] There are a number of reasons that lawmakers are taking an active interest in the market developments, including physician complaints about federal policies and concerns that a decline in smaller, independent practices could exacerbate existing physician shortages in areas such as rural regions. Lawmakers also want to ensure that the market changes are meeting the goals of expanding access and addressing government and private health care spending. Because health care is highly regulated, and government payments make up an increasing share of physician revenues, congressional action can affect the pace of practice consolidation and other market trends. In general, Congress is monitoring developments in several broad areas:

Medical Spending

Rising health care costs have led to federal, state, and private efforts to rein in medical spending, including controlling physician payments and providing incentives for consolidation to realize greater efficiency. One question surrounding affiliation between physicians and other health organizations such as hospitals is whether they will help to reduce costs. There is concern that such affiliations could instead lead to higher prices for consumers and the government as the larger entities gain negotiating leverage with insurers and can charge more for some Medicare-covered services. To date, studies have provided mixed results on whether closer affiliation improves efficiencies and leads to reduction in prices for health care services.

A study of integration between physician practices and hospitals that took place in California during the 1990s did not find evidence that such affiliations increased prices. There was evidence that such vertical integration may have reduced prices, though the findings were not precise nor statistically significant.[102] Other studies have found differing effects, while a review of research on doctor-hospital affiliation found that such alignments were often designed to increase market power by reducing competition, and that the limited evidence on price impacts was mixed.[103] The study noted that most of the arrangements studied thus far have involved coordination of services, but not clinical integration of the type envisioned in programs such as ACOs.

While the emerging incentives are different, given quality-based initiatives in the ACA and in a number of private insurance plans, some analysts express concerns that large organizations—such as ACOs built around a major regional hospital or large physician group—could gain more market share and negotiating leverage with insurers, which could lead to higher prices.[104] Anecdotally, a growing number of news reports indicate that patients are facing higher charges for services when physicians provide services in hospital outpatient settings, partly due to differences in Medicare payment.[105] Some analysts say pricing concerns can be mitigated with stronger antitrust oversight and have noted an increase in FTC and DOJ investigations of proposed mergers due to concerns about their impact on the competitive landscape.[106]

At the same time, coordinated care delivery systems are in the nascent stage, and health care payments are still mainly based on volume of services rather than quality improvements. As Merritt Hawkins data indicate, many hospitals now hiring physicians or buying practices are basing physician compensation partly on productivity, which, combined with higher Medicare reimbursement for hospital-based services, could result in a higher number of physician services going forward.[107]

Access

According to some experts, the unfolding efforts at physician coordination could improve access to care, by increasing competition in health care markets and creating networks that provide additional services and access to specialists to underserved consumers, such as Medicaid patients.[108]

But lawmakers and analysts have expressed concerns that as more doctors work in larger practices, there could be a change in the traditional doctor-patient relationship and potentially fewer entry points into the health care system if physician offices, outpatient clinics, or other facilities in a local area close.[109] Another open question, as government and private payers base more payments on quality improvement measures, is whether such patient-driven systems could perpetuate disparities in the health care system. For example, some experts have asked whether ACOs and other quality-based systems could have a disincentive to treat sicker, more expensive patients and be more selective in their choice of patients, though HHS has designed the ACOs to make such so-called cherry picking difficult.

Some lawmakers have suggested that consolidation could make it harder for rural areas to attract physicians. Rural areas have long had trouble recruiting doctors. But precisely because there are fewer physicians in rural areas, they may have more individual clout in negotiating with local hospitals during the current market evolution, some analysts say.[110]

The issue of access also goes to the question of whether consumers will have as much freedom to see the doctor of their choice, or visit a specialist, in integrated health care systems where physicians work for insurers or hospitals. In other words, will ACOs and medical homes be managed differently than the managed care plans that created consumer unrest in the 1990s? Some analysts say it will be important to analyze required information on patients' access to primary and specialty physicians in the emerging health organizations.[111]

Access is also linked to the issue of physician supply, such as the potential for growth in concierge practices that accept fewer patients and the projected shortage of primary care doctors. In an effort to increase supply, and possibly reduce prices for certain services, state legislatures and Congress have debated initiatives to expand the scope of allowable care provided by nurse practitioners and physician assistants.

Coordinated Care/Quality

New payment and delivery systems in Medicare and private plans are based on the theory that coordinated care can bring about increased quality, thereby reducing costs and allowing payers to enhance physician reimbursement. Some demonstration programs have shown potential for savings, though the scale is as yet unclear.[112] A Congressional Budget Office analysis of past demonstration programs designed to reduce Medicare spending by implementing quality care initiatives concluded that a number cut hospitalizations and improved measures of patient care, but most did not meet their spending goals. The report also noted that physicians may have incentives to upcode, or increase the severity of an initial diagnosis, in order to show larger quality improvements.[113] A 2012 analysis of a coordinated care pilot study at the University of Washington at St. Louis hospital found notable improvements in quality of care, as well as health savings.[114]

There may also be differences in the ability of smaller versus larger physician practices to experiment with new quality-based systems such as medical homes. Practices bear many of the up-front costs of creating new coordinated care services, while many savings may be dispersed through the broader health care system.[115]

Another potential factor that could affect efforts to improve coordination of care is increased segmentation of physicians as a result of ongoing market changes. A 2012 report on the future of medical practices noted:

> These changes in the practice environment have given rise to a large segment of the physician community that no longer hospitalizes patients, but rather manages them exclusively in ambulatory settings (imaging, surgery, chemotherapy, etc.) ... In an increasing number of places, there are now two non-overlapping physician communities: physicians who never visit the hospital and physicians who never leave it, as is the case in most of Europe.[116]

Under many quality-based systems, primary care physicians are envisioned as the focal point for managing patient care. In some scenarios, coordinating physicians or medical groups can face financial penalties based on the quality of care by other providers whose actions they do not directly control. With the rise of hospitalists, emergency room physicians, and other hospital-based physicians with segmented roles, such coordination can be more challenging, according to some analysts. For example, many lower-income consumers use emergency rooms as their entree to care. The growing use of specialized emergency room doctors and other hospital-based physicians who make the decision to admit patients may mean that primary care physicians are not brought into the decision-making loop in an early fashion. Such issues could be addressed in structured care organizations, analysts say.[117]

APPENDIX. PHYSICIAN INCOME AND PRACTICE COSTS

Although doctors are among the best-paid professionals in the country, they have less ability than some other white collar workers to determine prices for their services, which are largely set by the federal payment rates in the Medicare and Medicaid programs or via negotiations with insurers.[118]

Physician income can be affected by factors, including (1) specialty, (2) source of payment (public vs. private), and (3) productivity, in terms of the volume or range of services offered. General practitioners and pediatricians make less than specialists such as cardiologists and oncologists, [119] for example. Annual survey data from the MGMA provides detailed information on median compensation for physicians in different medical specialties[120] (see Table A-1).

Some studies indicate that physician income has been declining in real terms in recent years. According to one analysis, inflation-adjusted physician fees declined by 25% from 1995 to 2006, a time period during which physicians also worked fewer hours.[121] Income did not appear to decline as much as time worked, however, suggesting that some doctors may have found other ways to earn money, such as performing more tests in their offices, opening outpatient clinics, increasing intensity of services, or providing more expensive services.[122] A second study found that average physician net income declined about 7% after inflation from 1995 to 2003, though there were differences among specialties.[123]

Table A-1. Median Compensation for Select Physician Specialties

Physician Compensation	2010	Change from 2009
Family Practice	$189,402	2.94%
Internal Medicine	$205,379	4.21%
Pediatric/Adolescent Medicine	$192,148	0.39%
Anesthesiology	$407,292	-3.83%
Cardiology: Invasive	$500,993	3.97%
Dermatology	$430,874	4.16%
Emergency Medicine	$277,297	5.65%
Gastroenterology	$463,955	-0.33%
Hematology/Oncology	$382,934	3.78%
Neurology	$249,867	5.02%
Obstetrics/Gynecology	$281,190	-0.51%
Orthopedic Surgery	$514,659	3.71%
Psychiatry	$200,694	3.88%
Pulmonary Medicine	$300,019	4.07%
Radiology: Diagnostic	$471,253	-1.58%
Surgery: General	$343,958	2.34%
Urology	$372,455	-4.66%

Source: Medical Group Management Association.

Notes: Data are based on an annual survey of group practices. The MGMA represents larger medical groups and physician management organizations.

The recession that began in December 2007 and ended in June 2009[124] may have had an impact on physician income. Physician visits by privately insured patients under age 65 declined by 17% from spring 2009 to the end of

2011.[125] The decline in the share of people covered by private insurance during that period was smaller than the decline in visits.

Physician practice operating costs have not been declining in concert with real compensation, according to the MGMA.[126] That may not only make it more financially challenging for some small practices, it may also mean that practices that want to enter into new payment and coordinated care systems such as ACOs or medical homes may have more difficulty raising necessary capital unless they affiliate with other health providers.

Federal Policies Affecting Compensation

Most physicians accept patients insured through the federal Medicare program for the elderly and disabled. Determining the proper level of Medicare physician payments has been a challenge for lawmakers. In the Balanced Budget Act of 1997 (BBA97, P.L. 105-33), Congress created the Medicare Sustainable Growth Rate (SGR) formula, a system for making annual updates to the physician fee schedule.[127] Since 2002, the SGR formula has resulted in spending above targets and mandated annual cuts in physician reimbursement. With the exception of 2002, when a 4.8% cut went into effect, Congress has voted to override the planned cuts.[128] The ACA did not address the SGR issue, but includes financial incentives to increase some primary care, including a 10% bonus for Medicare primary care services from 2011 to 2016. The ACA also introduced new Medicare payment systems such as the Medicare Shared Savings Program, where doctors who are part of ACOs receive a part of any savings to Medicare from higher quality, more efficient care.[129]

Solo and group physician practices face costs for acquiring and using electronic health record (EHR) technology to replace paper-based systems. The transition is being driven by Medicare and Medicaid incentive programs, authorized under the Health Information Technology for Economic and Clinical Health (HITECH) Act,[130] which provide financial assistance to help offset the costs of the systems. In its 2010 final rule establishing the EHR incentive programs, CMS said average EHR implementation costs can be as much as $54,000 per physician, with subsequent annual maintenance costs as much as $20,600 per physician.[131] Physicians who meet certain criteria can receive incentive payments under Medicare of up to $44,000 over five years—plus an additional 10% if practicing in a designated medically underserved area. The payments phase out over time and are replaced by financial penalties. Beginning in 2015, physicians who are not meaningful users of EHR technology will see a slight reduction in Medicare Part B reimbursement.

End Notes

[1] Esther Hing and Sayeedha Uddin, "Visits to Primary Care Delivery Sites: United States, 2008," Centers for Disease Control and Prevention, National Center for Health Statistics, *NCHS Data Brief*, No. 47, October 2010, http://www.cdc.gov/nchs/data/databriefs/db47.htm.

[2] "Virtual Mentor," *American Medical Association Journal of Ethics*, Vol. 13, No. 11, November 2011, p. 750-752, http://virtualmentor.ama-assn.org/2011/11/pdf/fred1-1111.pdf.

[3] Estimates of the U.S. physician supply vary. The American Medical Association estimated there were 972,376 doctors of medicine in 2009, including 792,805 active physicians. Centers for Disease Control and Prevention, *Health, United States, 2011*, Table 111, http://www.cdc.gov/nchs/data/hus/2011/111.pdf. Another estimate, based on information from state medical boards, places the number of active physicians at 850,000. See Aaron Young, Humayun Chaudhry, Janelle Rhyne, and Michael Dugan, "A Census of Actively Licensed Physicians in the United States, 2010," *Journal of Medical Regulation*, Vol. 96, No., 4, 2010-11, pp. 10-20.

[4] U.S. Census Bureau, Industry Statistics Sampler, NAICS 62111, "Offices of Physicians," http://www.census.gov/ econ/industry/hierarchy/i62111.htm; SNR Denton and The Lewin Group for the American Medical Association, "The State-Level Economic Impact of Office-Based Physicians," February 2011, p. A-2, http://www.ama-assn.org/resources/ doc/arc/economic-impact/economic-impact-report.pdf; Centers for Disease Control, *National Ambulatory Medical Care Survey: 2009 Summary Tables*, Table 2, http://www.cdc.gov/nchs/data/ahcd/namcs_summary/ 2009_namcs_web_tables.pdf.

[5] Anthony Shih, Karen Davis, Stephen Schoenbaum, Anne Gauthier, Rachel Nuzum, and Douglas McCarthy, *Organizing the U.S. Health Care Delivery System for High Performance*, The Commonwealth Fund, August 2008, http://www.commonwealthfund.org /usr_doc/Shih_organizingushltcaredeliverysys_1155.pdf.

[6] There is a wide range of evidence that more physician practices are merging or being sold to hospitals and other institutions. See Jeff Goldsmith, Associate Professor, University of Virginia, for the Physicians Foundation, "The Future of Medical Practice: Creating Options for Practicing Physicians to Control Their Professional Destiny," July 2012, http://www.physiciansfoundation.org/uploads/default/Future_of_Medical_Practices__Goldsmith__Final.pdf http://www.physiciansfoundation.org/uploadedFiles/Future of Medical Practices%28Goldsmith%29 Final.pdf; Allison Leibhaber and Joy Grossman, "Physicians Moving to Mid-Sized, Single-Specialty Practices," Center for Studying Health System Change, *Tracking Report*, No. 18, August 2007, http://www.hschange.com /CONTENT/941/?topic=topic22. See also Chad Terhune, "State Investigating Medical Consolidations," *Los Angeles Times*, September 15, 2012, http://articles.latimes.com/2012 /sep/15/business/la-fi-0915- hospital-doctors-review-20120915; and Victoria Stagg Elliott, "More Cardiologists Embrace Working for Hospitals," *American Medical News*, September 24, 2012, http://www.ama-assn.org/amednews/2012/09/24/bisc0924.htm.

[7] American Hospital Association, *AHA Hospital Statistics, 2012 Edition*, p. vii. Includes full- and part-time physicians, interns, residents, and dentists; though dentists are a small number of the overall total. According to the AHA, the number of physicians employed by hospitals

rose to 212,000 in 2010. During the 2007-2009 recession, two-thirds of hospital administrators reported being approached by doctors seeking financial support, including employment.

[8] Medical Group Management Association-American College of Medical Practice Executives, Presentation to Missouri State Medical Association, "Physician/Hospital Integration: Is It In Your Future?" April 17, 2012; Ann O'Malley, Amelia Bond, and Robert Berenson, "Rising Hospital Employment of Physicians: Better Quality, Higher Costs?" Center for Studying Health System Change, *Issue Brief* No. 136, August 2011, http://hschange.org /CONTENT/1230.

[9] American College of Cardiology, "ACC's 2012 Practice Census Shows Continued Changes in Practice Landscape," News Release, September 10, 2012, http://www.cardiosource.org /News-Media/Publications/Cardiology-Magazine/ ACC-Practice-Census-2012.aspx. Survey sent to 2,520 practices with a 42% response rate.

[10] Medicare Payment Advisory Commission, *Report to the Congress, Medicare Payment Policy*, March 2012, p. 18, http://www.medpac.gov/documents/Mar12_EntireReport.pdf. Report cites MGMA data.

[11] Douglas Staiger, David Auerbach, and Peter Buerhaus, "Trends in the Work Hours of Physicians in the United States," *Journal of the American Medical Association*, Vol. 303, No. 8, February 24, 2010, p. 747-753, http://jama.jamanetwork.com/article.aspx? articleid=185433; and Ha Tu and Paul Ginsburg, "Losing Ground: Physician Income, 1995-2003," Center for Studying Health System Change, *Tracking Report*, No. 15, June 2006, http://www.hschange.com/CONTENT/851/851.pdf.

[12] CRS Report R42029, *Physician Supply and the Patient Protection and Affordable Care Act*, by Elayne J. Heisler and Amanda K. Sarata.

[13] Martin Gaynor and Robert Town, "The Impact of Hospital Consolidation – Update," Robert Wood Johnson Foundation, June 2012, http://www.rwjf.org/content/dam/farm /reports /issue_briefs/2012/rwjf73261. The authors point out that there are differences between consolidation, the bringing together of two entities, and integration, which is coordinating services and management. One question is whether the ACA, through ACOs and other efforts, can improve coordinated care and quality of services

[14] The Centers for Medicare & Medicaid Services defines ACOs as "groups of doctors, hospitals, and other health care providers, who come together voluntarily to give coordinated high quality care to their Medicare patients ... When an ACO succeeds both in delivering high-quality care and spending health care dollars more wisely, it will share in the savings it achieves for the Medicare program." A medical home refers to a physician's office or other health care provider serving as the base for coordinating services for a patient. Bundled payments are capped payments for the totality of care of a condition, rather than individual payments for each service.

[15] CRS Report R41474, *Accountable Care Organizations and the Medicare Shared Savings Program*, by Amanda K. Sarata.

[16] Leavitt Partners and KLAS Research, "Leavitt Partners and KLAS Research Release Comprehensive Report on Accountable Care Organizations," November 30, 2012, http://news.leavittpartners.com/newsrelease-cid-1-id-46.html.

[17] Peter Orszag and Ezekiel Emanuel, "Health Care Reform and Cost Control," *The New England Journal of Medicine*. Vol. 363, No. 7, p. 601-603, August 12, 2010; Phil Galewitz, *Kaiser Health News for USA TODAY*, "Obama's Health Law Has Accelerated Marketplace Change," March 26, 2012, http://www.usatoday.com/money/industries/health/story/ 2012-

03-19/health-law-accelerates-marketplace-change/53791744/1. In 2011, about 100 physician groups were sold, mostly to hospitals, up from 63 in 2010.

[18] Centers for Medicare & Medicaid Services, *National Health Expenditures*, Table 4, https://www.cms.gov/ResearchStatistics-Data-and-Systems/Statistics-Trends-and-Reports/NationalHealthExpendData/Downloads/tables.pdf

[19] John Eisenberg, "Physician Utilization: The State of Research About Physicians' Practice Patterns," *Medical Care*, Vol. 40, No. 11, 2002, p. 1016-1035.

[20] House Committee on Ways and Means, Hearing on Health Care Industry Consolidation, September 9, 2011, http://waysandmeans.house.gov/News/DocumentSingle.aspx?DocumentID=272374.

[21] Academy Health, "Integration, Concentration, and Competition in the Provider Marketplace," *Research Insights* paper based on December 2010 meeting for federal policymakers in 2010 funded by the U.S. Agency for Health Care Research and Quality, http://www.academyhealth.org/files/publications/AH_R_Integration%20FINAL2.pdf.

[22] American Medical Association, Practice Management Center, "ACOs, CO-OPs, and Other Options, A How-To Manual for Physicians Navigating a Post-Reform World," Second Edition, http://www.ama-assn.org/resources/doc/psa/ physician-how-to-manual.pdf.

[23] Centers for Disease Control and Prevention, *Health, United States, 2011*, Table 111, http://www.cdc.gov/nchs/data/ hus/2011/111.pdf. The majority of these physicians provided patient care (749,566, or 77%). The remaining physicians were inactive (11%), in administration (2%), conducting research (1%), or teaching (1%). These percentages do not sum to 100% because of rounding or because some physicians are not classified or their professional activity is unknown. See also Derek R. Smart, *Physician Characteristics and Distribution in the US, 2011 Edition*, American Medical Association, 2011.

[24] Osteopaths treat the patient as a whole, rather than focusing on one system or body part. An osteopathic physician will often use a treatment method called *osteopathic manipulative treatment*, described as a hands-on approach to make sure the body is moving freely.

[25] American Medical Association, *Physician Characteristics and Distribution in the U.S., 2011 Edition*, Chapter 3.

[26] Daniel Mareck, "Federal and State Initiatives to Recruit Physicians to Rural Areas," *American Medical Association Journal of Ethics, Virtual Mentor*, Vol. 13, No. 5, May 2011, p. 304-309; http://virtualmentor.ama-assn.org/2011/05/ pfor1-1105.html.

[27] CRS Report R42029, *Physician Supply and the Patient Protection and Affordable Care Act*, by Elayne J. Heisler and Amanda K. Sarata; Robert Wood Johnson Foundation, "Will the United States Have a Shortage of Physicians in 10 Years?" November 2009.

[28] American Association of Medical Colleges, "The Impact of Health Care Reform on the Future Supply and Demand for Physicians, Updated Projections Through 2025," June 2010, https://www.aamc.org/download/158076/data/ updated_projections_through_2025.pdf. The AAMC estimates, which reflect the impact of the ACA on demand, project that the supply of active patient care physicians of all specialties will be 785,400 in 2025, while there will be a demand will be for 916,000 such physicians – meaning a shortfall of 14%.

[29] Association of American Medical Colleges, Center for Workforce Studies, "Recent Studies and Reports on Physician Shortages in the U.S.," August 2012, https://www.aamc.org/download/100598/data/recentworkforcestudies.pdf.

[30] Jeff Goldsmith, Associate Professor, University of Virginia for the Physicians Foundation, "The Future of Medical Practice: Creating Options for Practicing Physicians to Control Their Professional Destiny," July 2012, http://www.physiciansfoundation.org/uploads/default/Future_of_Medical_Practices__Goldsmith__Final.pdf.

[31] Douglas Staiger, David Auerbach, and Peter Buerhaus, "Trends in the Work Hours of Physicians in the United States," *Journal of the American Medical Association*, Vol. 303, No. 8, February 24, 2010, p. 747, http://jama.amaassn.org/content/303/8/747.full.pdf+html; Ha Tu and Paul Ginsburg, "Losing Ground: Physician Income 1995-2003," Tracking Report No. 15, Center for Studying Health System Change, June 2006, http://www.hschange.org/CONTENT/ 851/.

[32] Douglas Staiger, David Auerbach, and Peter Buerhaus, "Trends in the Work Hours of Physicians in the United States," *Journal of the American Medical Association*, Vol. 303, No. 8, February 24, 2010, p. 747, http://jama.amaassn.org/content/303/8/747.full.pdf+html.

[33] Jeff Goldsmith, Associate Professor, University of Virginia for the Physicians Foundation, "The Future of Medical Practice: Creating Options for Practicing Physicians to Control Their Professional Destiny," July 2012, http://www.physiciansfoundation.org/uploads /default/Future_of_Medical_Practices__Goldsmith__Final.pdf.

[34] American Hospital Association, "The State of America's Hospitals: Taking the Pulse," May 24, 2010.

[35] Melissa Park, Donald Cherry, and Sandra Decker, "Nurse Practitioners, Certified Nurse Midwives, and Physician Assistants in Physician Offices," Centers for Disease Control and Prevention, National Center for Health Statistics, *NCHS Brief*, No. 69, August 2011, http://www.cdc.gov/nchs/data/databriefs/db69.htm.

[36] There is a debate in Congress and in state legislatures about whether to expand the scope of practice for such professionals. Julie Fairman, John Rowe, Susan Hassmiller, and Donna Shalala, "Broadening the Scope of Nursing Practice," *New England Journal of Medicine*, Vol. 364, No. 3, January 20, 2011, pp. 193-196; American Medical Association, *Nurse Practitioners*, Scope of Practice Series, October 2009, http://aanp.org/AANPCMS2/public pages/08- 0424%20SOP%20Nurse%20Revised%2010-09.pdf.

[37] American Academy of Nurse Practitioners, Fact Sheet, http://aanp.org/all-about-nps/np-fact-sheet.

[38] Bureau of Labor Statistics, *Occupational Handbook 2010-2011 Edition: Physician Assistants*, http://www bls.gov/oco/ocos081.htm.

[39] American Academy of Physician Assistants, http://www.aapa.org/the_pa_ profession /what_is_a_pa.aspx.

[40] Larger group practices did form early, but represented just a small share of physicians. What is now the Mayo Clinic grew from a multispecialty practice founded in the 1860s in Rochester, Minnesota. The Cleveland Clinic was founded as a group practice in the 1920s by doctors who had served in Europe during World War I. Kaiser Permanente evolved during the 1930s as a prepaid group practice for workers on large public works projects, including the Grand Coulee Dam.

[41] Allegra Kim, *The Corporate Practice of Medicine Doctrine*, California Research Bureau, CRB 07-011, October 2007, http://www.library.ca.gov/crb/07/07-011.pdf. Laws and court cases in California and other states prohibit or limit the corporate practice of medicine, limiting the ability of hospitals to employ doctors for outpatient services, for example. The laws are intended to ensure that medical decisions are based on the needs of a patient. Experts say such laws can limit the ability of physician practices to affiliate with outside organizations or to hire a management team, though doctors can be closely tied to hospitals through other means.

[42] Ann O'Malley, Amelia Bond and Robert Berenson, "Rising Hospital Employment of Physicians: Better Quality, Higher Costs?" Center for Studying Health System Change, *Issue Brief*, No. 136, August 2011, http://www.hschange.com/CONTENT/1230/.

[43] Barbara Bridgman Perkins, "Economic Organization of Medicine and the Committee on the Costs of Medical Care," *American Journal of Public Health*, Vol. 88, No. 11, November 1998, p. 1724, http://www.ncbi.nlm.nih.gov/pmc/ articles/PMC1508565/pdf/amjph00023-0127.pdf. The reasoning behind such laws is that medical decisions should be made by doctors on the basis of medical need.

[44] Testimony of Paul Ginsburg, Center for Studying Health System Change, House Committee on Ways and Means, Hearing on Health Care Industry Consolidation, September 9, 2011, http://waysandmeans.house.gov/uploadedfiles/ ginsburg_testimony_9-9-11_final.pdf.

[45] American Medical Association, Practice Management Center, "ACOs, CO-OPs, and Other Options, A How-To Manual for Physicians Navigating a Post-Reform World," Second Edition, http://www.ama-assn.org/resources/doc/psa/ physician-how-to-manual.pdf.

[46] Allison Liebhaber and Joy Grossman, "Physicians Moving to Mid-Sized, Single-Specialty Practices," Center for Studying Health System Change, Tracking Report, No. 18, August 2007, http://www.hschange.com/CONTENT/941/.

[47] Chun-Ju Hsiao, Donald Cherry, Paul Beatty, and Elizabeth Rechtsteiner, "National Ambulatory Medical Care Survey: 2007 Summary," Centers for Disease Control and Prevention, National Center for Health Statistics, *National Health Statistics Reports*, November 3, 2010, p. 3, http://www.cdc.gov/nchs/data/nhsr/nhsr027.pdf. Visits to groups of two doctors, or those of 11 or more, remained mostly stable.

[48] VMG Health, "Valuing Physician Practices for Acquisitions: Assessing Acquisition Price & Compensation," http://www.vmghealth.com/Downloads/Becker%27sHospitalReview2011.pdf.

[49] David Hilgers and Sidney Welch, "Physicians Post-PPACA: Not Going Bust At The Healthcare Buffet (Conclusion)," *Physicians News Digest*, April 1, 2012, http://www.physiciansnews.com/2012/04/01/physicians-postppaca-not-going-bust-at-the-healthcare-buffet-conclusion/.

[50] Ann O'Malley, Amelia Bond and Robert Berenson, "Rising Hospital Employment of Physicians: Better Quality, Higher Costs?" Center for Studying Health System Change, *Issue Brief*, No. 136, August 2011, http://www.hschange.com/CONTENT/1230/.

[51] Carol Kane, "The Practice Arrangements of Patient Care Physicians 2007-2008: An Analysis by Age Cohort and Gender," American Medical Association, 2009, http://www.ama-assn.org/ama1/pub/upload/mm/363/prp-200906-physprac-arrange.pdf. Supplemented by interview with AMA staff.

[52] Andrew Ziskind, Kristin Ficery, and Richard Fu, "Adapting to a New Model of Physician Employment," Accenture, *Outlook Point of View*, No. 2, August 2011, http://www.accenture.com/SiteCollectionDocuments/PDF/AccentureOutlook-Physician-Trends-August-2011-No2.pdf. Follow up interview with Accenture on April 24, 2012.

[53] Cleo Burtley and Laura Jacobs, The Camden Group for the California Health Care Foundation, *Physician-Hospital Integration 2012: How Health Care Reform Is Reshaping California's Delivery System*, April 2012, chcf.org.

[54] Academy Health, "Integration, Concentration, and Competition in the Provider Marketplace," Research Insights paper based on December 2010 meeting funded by the U.S. Agency for Health Care Research and Quality, p. 4, http://www.academyhealth.org/files /publications/AH_R_Integration%20FINAL2.

[55] Paul Ginsburg, "Wide Variation in Hospital and Physician Payment Rates Evidence of Provider Market Power," Center for Studying Health System Change, *Research Brief*, No. 16, November 2010, http://hschange.org/CONTENT/ 1162/1162.pdf. The ability to

negotiate higher rates for services is more pronounced for hospital groups and provider groups associated with hospitals.

[56] Francis Crosson, “The Delivery System Matters,” *Health Affairs*, Vol. 24, No. 6, November 2005 , pp. 1543-1548.

[57] American Medical Association, Practice Management Center, “ACOs, CO-OPs, and Other Options, A How-To Manual for Physicians Navigating a Post-Reform World,” Second Edition, http://www.ama-assn.org/resources/doc/psa/ physician-how-to-manual.pdf. Practices often contract with management firms to take over their billing and administrative functions. Physician management companies can also buy physician practices and often take the overall company public.

[58] Scott Becker, Kristian Werling, and Holly Carnell, “Private Equity Investing in Healthcare -13 Hot and 4 Cold Areas,” McGuireWoods, 2011, http://www.mcguirewoods.com/news-resources/publications/health_care/privateequity-investing-healthcare.pdf.

[59] Maggie Manning, “Private equity is back and targeting physicians groups,” *Tampa Bay Business Journal*, May 11, 2012, http://www.bizjournals.com/tampabay/print-edition/2012/05/11/private-equity-is-back-and-targeting.html?page= all.

[60] Wiley Kitchell and Robert Hurst, “Specialty Physician Practice Trends,” Moss-Adams, *MANow*, October 2011, http://www.mossadams.com/mossadams/media/Documents /Publications/MA%20Now/MA-Now_HCG_Oct2011.pdf.

[61] Ibid

[62] CogentHMG, http://www.cogenthmg.com/about-us.

[63] IPC The Hospitalist Company, Presentation at 30th Annual J.P. Morgan Healthcare Conference, January 2012, http://files.shareholder.com/downloads/HOSP/1725641096 x0x532414/8d41badc-1c48-4c89-a2e4-67fc90aa3c59/ IPC_Investor_Presentation_JP_Morgan_1_12_Final.pdf.

[64] Mednax Presentation, Bank of America 2012 Health Care Conference, May 16, 2012, http://www.mednax.com/ body_iframe_inv.cfm?id=7&fr=true.

[65] American Hospital Association, *AHA Hospital Statistics, 2012 Edition*, p. vii.

[66] Testimony of Mark Smith, President, Merritt Hawkins, Before the House Committee on Small Business, Subcommittee on Investigations, Oversight, and Regulations, “The Decline of Solo and Small Medical Practices,” July 19, 2012, http://smbiz.house.gov/UploadedFiles/7-19_Smith_Testimony.pdf.

[67] American College of Cardiology, “Hospital Administrators Identify Recruitment of Cardiology Team Among Biggest Challenges,” News Release, March 20, 2012, http://www.cardiosource.org/News-Media/Media-Center/NewsReleases/2012 /03/Hospital AdminRecruitment.aspx. The group surveyed 300 hospital executives and cardiovascular professionals representing 291 hospitals and medical facilities.

[68] Victor Fuchs, “Major Trends in the U.S. Health Economy since 1950,” *The New England Journal of Medicine*, Vol. 366, March 15, 2012, http://www.nejm.org/doi /full/10.1056 /NEJMp1200478.

[69] Lawton Burns and Ralph Muller, “Hospital-Physician Collaboration: Landscape of Economic Integration and Impact on Clinical Integration,” *The Milbank Quarterly*, Vol., 86, No. 3, 2008, http://www.milbank.org/publications/the-milbank-quarterly/featured-articles/article /2918/hospital-physician-collaboration-landscape-of-economic-integration and-impact-on-clinical-integration.

[70] “Hospital/Physician Integration, Three Key Models,” Member Briefing, American Health Lawyers Association, October 2011, http://www.wilentz.com/Files/Articlesand Publications

FileFiles/308/ArticlePublicationFile/HospitalPhysician_Integration_Three_Key_Models_MB.pdf.

[71] American Hospital Association, *AHA Hospital Statistics, 2012 Edition*, p. ix.

[72] Rob Grannum and Nancy Schauer, "Achieving Success in New Era of Hospital Physician Alignment," Moss-Adams, *MANow*, February 2011, http://www.mossadams.com /mossadams/media/Documents/Publications/Health%20Care/MA-Now_HCG_Feb2011. Pdf ?ext=.pdf.

[73] Robert Zasa, "Physician-Hospital Joint Ventures; Alignment of Physicians With Hospitals," *Becker's Hospital Review*, September 8, 2011, http://www.beckershospitalreview.com /hospital-physician-relationships/physicianhospital-joint-ventures-alignment-of-physicians-with-hospitals.html.

[74] There is growing attention to the potential for increased consumer costs when some physician practices operate in a hospital setting. For example, see Dave Davis, "Medical Billing, A World Of Hurt: Costs Rise For Patients On High Deductible Insurance Plans As Hospital Health Centers Replace Private Practice Doctors," *The Plain Dealer*, September 22, 2012.

[75] Medicare Payment Advisory Commission, *Report to the Congress, Medicare Payment Policy*, March 2012, p. 75, http://www.medpac.gov/documents/Mar12_EntireReport.pdf.

[76] Ibid., Executive Summary, p. xiv. MedPAC suggested that Congress equalize payments by gradually reducing reimbursement for certain hospital-based physician visits.

[77] Robert Kocher and Nikhil Sahni, "Hospitals' Race to Employ Physicians—The Logic Behind a Money-Losing Proposition," *The New England Journal of Medicine*, No. 364, May 12, 2011, pp. 1790-1793. For hospitals to break even, newly hired primary care doctors must generate at least 30% more visits, and new specialists 25% more referrals, than they do at the outset of the business arrangement, according to the article.

[78] Merritt Hawkins, "2011 Review of Physician Recruiting Incentives, Summary Report," http://www.merritthawkins.com/uploadedfiles/mha2011incentivesurveypreview.pdf. The report was based recruiting and placement activity between April 1, 2010 to March 31, 2011.

[79] Christopher Weaver, "Managed Care Enters The Exam Room As Insurers Buy Doctor Groups," *Kaiser Health News*, July 1, 2011, http://www.kaiserhealthnews.org /Stories/2011 /July/01/unitedhealth-insurers-buy-doctors-groups.aspx; Rebecca Vesley, "Marriage of Convenience," *Modern Healthcare*, January 2, 2012, http://www.modern healthcare.com/article/20120102/MAGAZINE/301029918#.

[80] American Medical Association, Practice Management Center, "ACOs, Co-ops, and Other Options, A How-to Manual for Physicians Navigating a Post-Reform World," Second Edition, p. 8, http://www.ama-assn.org/resources/ doc/psa/physician-how-to-manual.pdf.

[81] The deal led to complaints by Blue Shield of California that the Monarch doctor network was steering patients away from Blue Shield plans.

[82] Cigna Corporation, "Cigna Works with Physicians to Bring Accountable Care to 94,000 More Individuals From Maine to California," News Release, July 19, 2012, http://newsroom.cigna.com/NewsReleases/cigna-works-withphysicians-to-bring-accountable-care-to-94-000-more-individuals-from-maine-to-california.htm. Wellpoint is changing its reimbursement for primary care providers by offering incentive payments for medical home-type programs to increase coordination of care and preventive care.

[83] Highmark and West Allegheny Health System Affiliation Agreement, News Release, October 31, 2011, https://www.highmark.com/hmk2/about/newsroom/2011/hmwp/ Affiliation_Agreement_Exhibits_and_Schedules_redacted.pdf.

[84] CRS Report R41474, *Accountable Care Organizations and the Medicare Shared Savings Program*, by Amanda K. Sarata; and The Centers for Medicare & Medicaid Services, "First Accountable Care Organizations Under the Medicare Shared Savings Program," News Release, April 10, 2012, http://www.cms.gov/apps/media/press /factsheet.asp?Counter= 4334&intNumPerPage=10&checkDate=&checkKey=&s rchType=1&numDays=3500&srchOpt=0&srchData=&keywordType=All&chkNewsType= 6&intPage=&showAll=&p Year=&year=&desc=&cboOrder=date.

[85] Department of Health and Human Services, "HHS Announces New Incentives For Providers To Work Together Through Accountable Care Organizations When Caring For People With Medicare," October 20, 2011, http://www.hhs.gov/news/press/2011pres /10/20111020a. html.

[86] David Muhlestein, Andrew Croshaw, Tom Merrill and Christian Pena, "Growth and Dispersion of Accountable Care Organizations, June 2012 Update" Leavitt Partners, http://leavittpartners.com/wp-content/uploads/2012/06/Growthand-Dispersion-of-ACOs-June-2012-Update.pdf; and Victoria Stagg Elliott, ACO Growth Driven Fastest By Physicians, *American Medical News*, July 2, 2012, http://www.ama-assn.org/amednews /2012/07/02/bisa0702.htm.

[87] CRS Report R42029, *Physician Supply and the Patient Protection and Affordable Care Act*, by Elayne J. Heisler and Amanda K. Sarata.

[88] Government Accountability Office, "Subject: Medicare: Private Sector Initiatives to Bundle Hospital and Physician Payments for an Episode of Care," January 31, 2011, p.9, http://www.gao.gov/new.items/d11126r.pdf.

[89] Merritt Hawkins for The Physicians Foundation, *Health Reform and the Decline of Physician Private Practice*, October 2010, http://www.physiciansfoundation.org/uploadedFiles/Health Reform and the Decline of Physician Private Practice.pdf.

[90] Bain & Co., "Global Healthcare Private Equity Report 2012," http://www.bain.com/Images/ BAIN_REPORT_Global_Healthcare_Private_Equity_Report_2012.pdf.

[91] Elizabeth Hargrave, Ayesha Mahmud, Kate Quirk, Laura Summer, and Jack Hoadley, "RetainerBased Physicians: Characteristics, Impact, and Policy Considerations," MedPAC, October, 2010, http://www.medpac.gov/documents/oct10_retainerbasedphysicians_ contractor_cb.pdf.

[92] MDVIP, http://www.mdvip.com/pressreleases/mdvipgrowthistransformingprimarycare.aspx.

[93] Concierge Choice Physicians, http://choice.md/about.

[94] *Knowledge@Wharton*, "Concierge Medicine: The Doctor Is (Always) In, If You Pay Enough," November 22, 2011, http://knowledge.wharton.upenn.edu/article.cfm?articleid=2884.

[95] CRS Report RS22743, *Health Care Fraud and Abuse Laws Affecting Medicare and Medicaid: An Overview* , by Jennifer Staman. The Stark law includes exceptions applicable to compensation arrangements that include office space and equipment rental arrangements, physician recruitment, as well as bona fide employment relationships. See 42 U.S.C. § 1395nn (e) and implementing regulations.

[96] Federal Trade Commission and the U.S. Department of Justice, "Federal Trade Commission, Department of Justice Issue Final Statement of Antitrust Policy Enforcement Regarding Accountable Care Organizations," October 20, 2011, http://www.ftc.gov/opa/2011 /10/aco.shtm and "Statement of Antitrust Enforcement Policy Regarding Accountable Care Organizations Participating in the Medicare Shared Savings Program," http://www.justice.gov/atr/public/ health_care/276458.pdf.

[97] Joe Carlson, "Picking up the Scent Wave of practice acquisitions by hospitals has antitrust regulators on notice," *Modern Healthcare*, June 9, 2012, http://www.modernhealthcare.com

/article/20120609/MAGAZINE/306099971/ picking-up-the-scent#; and Letter from Idaho Attorney General to St. Luke's Health System, http://bloximages.chicago2.vip. townnews. com/idahopress.com/content/tncms/assets/v3/editorial/a/41/a41ca640-7091- 11e1-9ee2-0019bb2963f4/4f652d6450012.pdf.pdf.

[98] CRS Report RS22743, *Health Care Fraud and Abuse Laws Affecting Medicare and Medicaid: An Overview* , by Jennifer Staman.

[99] Ibid. and Centers for Medicare & Medicaid Services, "Physician Self-Referral," https://www.cms.gov/ PhysicianSelfReferral/.

[100] American Medical Association, *Competing in the Marketplace, How Physicians Can Improve Quality and Increase Their Value in the Health Care Market Through Medical Practice Integration*, March 2008, http://www.ama-assn.org/ resources/doc/psa/competing-in-market.pdf.

[101] House Committee on Ways and Means, Hearing on Health Care Industry Consolidation, September 9, 2011, http://waysandmeans.house.gov/news/documentsingle. aspx?DocumentID=272374; and House Committee on Small Business, Subcommittee on Investigations, Oversight, and Regulations, "Health Care Realignment and Regulation: The Demise of Small and Solo Medical Practices?" July 19, 2012, http://smallbusiness.house.gov/calendar/ eventsingle.aspx?EventID=302953.

[102] Frederico Ciliberto and David Dranove, "The Effect of Physician-Hospital Affiliations on Hospital Prices in California," *Journal of Health Economics*, Vol. 25, 2006, p. 29-38, http://people.virginia.edu/~fc3p/papers/ CilibertoDranove.pdf.

[103] Martin Gaynor and Robert Town, "The Impact of Hospital Consolidation—Update," Robert Wood Johnson Foundation, Synthesis Project, June 2012, http://www.rwjf.org/content /dam/farm/reports/issue_briefs/2012/rwjf73261.

[104] Robert Berenson, Paul Ginsburg, Jon Christianson, and Tracy Yee, "The Growing Power of Some Providers to Win Steep Payment Increases from Insurers Suggests Policy Remedies May Be Needed," *Health Affairs*, Vol. 31, No. 5, May 2012, p. 973-981.

[105] Anna Wilde Matthews, "Same Doctor Visit, Double the Cost," *The Wall Street Journal*, August 27, 2012.

[106] Kristiana Garcia and Toby Singer, "Pennsylvania Attorney General Challenge to Physician Group Consolidation: Lessons for the Future," American Health Lawyers Association, Antitrust Practice Group, November 2011.

[107] Conversely, cuts in Medicare reimbursement may affect hospitals that hire more doctors based partly on financial analyses including differences in payment rates.

[108] Thomas Greaney, "Health Care Consolidation and Competition after PPACA," House Committee on the Judiciary Subcommittee on Intellectual Property, Competition, and the Internet, May 18, 2012, http://judiciary.house.gov/ hearings/Hearings%202012/Greaney %2005182012.pdf.

[109] Cleo Burtley and Laura Jacobs of the Camden Group, "Physician-Hospital Integration 2012: How Health Reform is Shaping California's Delivery System," California Healthcare Foundation, April 2012, http://www.chcf.org/~/media/ MEDIA%20LIBRARY%20Files /PDF/P/PDF%20PhysicianHospIntegration.pdf.

[110] American Medical Association, Practice Management Center, "ACOs, Co-ops, and Other Options, A How-to Manual for Physicians Navigating a Post-Reform World," Second Edition, p. 8, http://www.ama-assn.org/resources/ doc/psa/physician-how-to-manual.pdf.

[111] Cleo Burtley and Laura Jacobs of the Camden Group, "Physician-Hospital Integration 2012: How Health Reform is Shaping California's Delivery System," California Healthcare

Foundation, April 2012, http://www.chcf.org/~/media/ MEDIA%20LIBRARY%20Files /PDF/P/PDF%20PhysicianHospIntegration.pdf.

[112] John Iglehart, "Assessing an ACO Prototype—Medicare's Physician Group Practice Demonstration," New England Journal of Medicine, 364:198-200, January 20, 2011.

[113] Congressional Budget Office, "Lessons from Medicare's Demonstration Projects on Disease Management, Care Coordination, and Value-Based Payment," Issue Brief, January 2012, http://cbo.gov/sites/default/files/cbofiles/ attachments/01-18-12-MedicareDemoBrief.pdf.

[114] Deborah Peikes, Greg Peterson, Randall Brown, Sandy Graff, and, John Lynch, "How Changes In Washington University's Medicare Coordinated Care Demonstration Pilot Ultimately Achieved Savings," *Health Affairs*, Vol. 31, No. 6, June 2012, p. 1216-1226.

[115] Robert Reid, "Financial Implications of the Patient-Centered Medical Home," *Journal of the American Medical Association*, Vol. 308, No. 1, July 4, 2012.

[116] Jeff Goldsmith, Associate Professor, University of Virginia for the Physicians Foundation, "The Future of Medical Practice: Creating Options for Practicing Physicians to Control Their Professional Destiny," July 2012, http://www.physiciansfoundation.org /uploadedFiles/ Future%20of%20Medical%20Practices%20%28 Goldsmith%29%20Final. pdf.

[117] Emily Carrier, Tracy Yee, Rachel A. Holzwart, "Coordination Between Emergency and Primary Care Physicians," National Institute for Health Care Reform, *Research Brief* , No. 3, February 2011, http://www.nihcr.org/EDCoordination.html.

[118] Paul Ginsburg, "Wide Variation in Hospital and Physician Payment Rates Evidence of Provider Market Power," Center for Studying Health System Change, *Research Brief*, No. 16, November 2010, http://www.hschange.com/ CONTENT/1162/; American medical Association (Medicare Physician Fee Schedule), http://www.cardiosource.org/ Science-And-Quality/Quality-Programs/PINNACLE-Network/~/media/Files/Science%20and%20Quality/ Quality%20Programs/feeschedulesrbrvs.ashx.

[119] Thomas Bodenheimer, Mina Matin, and Brian Yoshio Laing, "The Specialist–Generalist Income Gap: Can We Narrow It?," *Journal of General Internal Medicine*, Vol. 23, No. 9, September 2008, p. 1477–1481. http://www.ncbi.nlm.nih.gov/pmc/articles/PMC2518004. The ACA includes provisions to boost the number of primary care doctors, including increasing medical school loan forgiveness, reserving more slots in medical schools for primary care doctors and providing financial incentives to such doctors who work in underserved or rural areas.

[120] The MGMA survey includes a number of hospital-centered integrated delivery systems. In addition, about 40% of the physicians are in practices of more than 150 doctors and only 6% are in practices of four full-time physicians or fewer, which may affect the data. Physicians in large specialty practices tend to earn more on average.

[121] Douglas Staiger, David Auerbach, and Peter Buerhaus, "Trends in the Work Hours of Physicians in the United States," *Journal of the American Medical Association*, Vol. 303, No. 8, February 24, 2010, p. 750.

[122] Ibid. "The evidence on the relationship between fees and work hours is mixed, with some studies finding that lower fees encourage physicians to work more hours to achieve a target income. Because fees have decreased, some physicians have undertaken other activities to offset the loss in income, such as reducing the proportion of time spent in non-patient care activities, increasing ownership stake in ancillary services, and increasing the intensity of services providers, or spending less time per patient." A number of specialty physician groups operate ambulatory care clinics in areas such as urology, ophthalmology, or plastic

surgery, helping to fuel the movement of such services from inpatient hospital settings. Physicians also offer ancillary services such as imaging, which they say improves efficiency and is a convenience for patients. The GAO in a 2008 report said such services may increase costs to the federal government, noting that as more doctors provided in-house imaging to patients, the number of procedures increased.

[123] Ha Tu and Paul Ginsburg, "Losing Ground: Physician Income, 1995-2003," Center for Studying Health System Change, Tracking Report, No. 15, June 2006, http://www. hschange. com/CONTENT/851/.

[124] National Bureau of Economic Research, http://www.nber.org/cycles.html.

[125] Study by Stanford University for the Henry J. Kaiser Family Foundation, "The Economy and Medical Care," November 15, 2011; http://healthreform.kff.org/notes-on-health-insurance-and-reform/2011/november/the-economyand-medical-care.aspx.

[126] Data for CRS from MGMA.

[127] CRS Report R40907, *Medicare Physician Payment Updates and the Sustainable Growth Rate (SGR) System*, by Jim Hahn and Janemarie Mulvey.

[128] Ibid.

[129] Centers for Medicare & Medicaid Services, http://www.cms.gov/Medicare/Medicare-Fee-for-Service-Payment/ sharedsavingsprogram/index.html?redirect=/sharedsavingsprogram/.

[130] The HITECH Act was incorporated in the American Recovery and Reinvestment Act (ARRA; P.L. 111-5), the economic stimulus package enacted in February 2009. In addition to creating the Medicare and Medicaid EHR incentive programs, the HITECH Act expanded the duties of the HHS Office of the National Coordinator for Health Information Technology, authorized and provided funding for several HIT grant programs, and expanded the health information privacy and security standards under the Health Insurance Portability and Accountability Act (HIPAA).

[131] 75 *Federal Register* 44492, July 28, 2010.

In: Physician Practices
Editor: Isaak Angelidis

ISBN: 978-1-62618-184-7

Chapter 2

PHYSICIAN SUPPLY AND THE PATIENT PROTECTION AND AFFORDABLE CARE ACT*

Elayne J. Heisler and Amanda K. Sarata

SUMMARY

An adequate physician supply is important for the effective and efficient delivery of health care services and, therefore, for population health and the cost and quality of health care. Assessments of the adequacy of physician supply often focus on three dimensions of the physician population: its size; its composition (e.g., the mix between primary care and specialty physicians); and its geographic distribution. Policies that aim to alter physician supply generally focus on both current and future supply along these three dimensions because physician training is a lengthy process; therefore, changes implemented to alter supply do not have immediate effects.

Each of the three dimensions of physician supply is important for health care spending and for population health because physician clinical decisions affect approximately 90% of each health care dollar spent. In addition, as physicians provide health care services that, with some exceptions, cannot be provided by non-physicians, the size, composition, and geographic distribution of the physician population affects the amount and type of health care services available. A number of studies have found physician shortages overall, in certain specialties, and in

* This is an edited, reformatted and augmented version of Congressional Research Service, Publication No. R42029, dated September 26, 2011.

certain geographic areas. The federal government pays for physician services, primarily through the Medicare and Medicaid programs, and supports physician training through a number of programs in various departments and agencies. Given current investments in physician services and the physician workforce, the adequacy of the current and future physician supply may be of interest to Congress.

The Patient Protection and Affordable Care Act (PPACA, P.L. 111-148) may affect physician supply because it expands insurance coverage to those previously uninsured. PPACA also includes provisions that may affect the size, composition, and geographic distribution of the physician population by supporting changes to physician training, compensation, and practice. Specifically, provisions targeting the number of physicians trained and their productivity may affect the size of the physician population. The composition of the physician population may be altered by provisions targeting the supply of primary care providers or specialties in shortage. Provisions addressing the diversity of the physician workforce and those incentivizing practice in rural or other underserved areas may affect the geographic distribution of the physician population. Finally, PPACA includes provisions that provide for data collection and evaluation of the adequacy of the workforce in general, and federal workforce programs specifically. Whether and how these provisions will affect physician supply is not yet known because some of these provisions have not been implemented yet, are temporary, will not have immediate effects, or rely on discretionary funding.

This report examines each dimension of physician supply, separately discussing current (and, where appropriate, future) concerns and relevant changes included in PPACA that may affect each dimension. The report then discusses workforce planning activities included in PPACA that may affect all three dimensions of supply.

INTRODUCTION

An adequate physician supply is important for the effective and efficient delivery of health care services and, therefore, for population health and the cost and quality of health care. Assessments of the adequacy of physician supply often focus on three dimensions of the physician population: its size; its composition (e.g., the distribution of primary care and specialty physicians); and its geographic distribution. Policies that aim to alter physician supply generally focus on both current and future supply along these three dimensions because physician training is a lengthy process; therefore, changes implemented to alter supply do not have immediate effects.[1]

Each of the three dimensions of physician supply is important for health care spending because physician clinical decisions affect approximately 90% of each health care dollar spent.[2] The size of the physician population partially determines the volume of health services provided and therefore costs, as physicians provide health care services that generally cannot be provided by non-physicians.[3] The composition may affect spending because, as some researchers have found, areas with more specialists have higher health care spending.[4] Similarly, the geographic distribution of the physician population can affect spending since in areas with too few physicians, there may be higher utilization of potentially costly emergency room services because more appropriate physician services are unavailable. In contrast, in areas with more physicians, individuals may receive unnecessary services, which can increase health care spending.[5] The three dimensions of physician supply are also important for population health. Too few physicians—overall or in specific geographic areas—may result in delayed or foregone care that can worsen health conditions or lead to premature death because adequate and timely services were not obtained. Too many physicians can mean that additional health services are provided, which may increase the risk of adverse events or medical errors.[6] The composition of the physician population also affects population health. A number of studies have found that areas with more primary care physicians have better health outcomes, including, for example, all-cause mortality, life expectancy, and self-rated health.[7]

The federal government supports physician services and training, which may make the adequacy of the current and future physician supply of interest to Congress. Specifically, the federal government pays for physician services, primarily through the Medicare and Medicaid programs. The federal government also supports physician training through a number of programs in various departments and agencies.[8]

On March 23, 2010, President Obama signed the Patient Protection and Affordable Care Act (PPACA, P.L. 111-148), which may affect the demand for physician services; therefore, the new law may increase congressional interest in physician supply.[9] PPACA may expand the demand for physician services by expanding insurance coverage to those previously uninsured and by expanding Medicaid eligibility to individuals who were previously ineligible. PPACA may specifically increase the demand for primary care physicians through increased coverage of preventive services by Medicare, Medicaid, and private insurance. PPACA also (1) authorizes increased funding or program changes for a number of programs that support physician training, (2) includes provisions to increase support for primary care,; and (3) appropriates funds to expand programs that encourage physicians to practice in certain geographic areas.[10] This report examines each dimension of physician supply, separately discussing current (and, where appropriate, future) concerns and changes included in PPACA that may affect each dimension. The report then discusses workforce planning activities included in PPACA that may affect all of these dimensions of supply. The **Appendix** presents relevant PPACA provisions, summarizes them, and indicates which of the dimensions of physician supply each may affect.

SIZE OF THE PHYSICIAN POPULATION

An appropriately sized physician population is necessary for an effective and efficient health care system. As noted above, too few physicians may mean delayed care, which can worsen health conditions and increase costs through greater hospital and emergency department use.[11] Too many physicians can mean that individuals receive unnecessary health services, which may increase the risk of adverse events and increase costs.[12] This section provides an overview of how the physician population is measured, considerations in determining its appropriate size, and debate around the appropriateness of its current and future size. It concludes with a discussion of PPACA's potential effect on the size of the physician population, including a discussion of provisions in the law that aim to increase the number of physicians or to improve physician productivity.

Measuring the Physician Population

The number of physicians in the United States may be measured in two ways: (1) absolute counts of practicing physicians and (2) ratios of physicians providing services to a specified population (e.g., per 10,000 or 100,000). For ratios, the population served may refer to the population receiving services at a given health care facility or the population residing in a specified geographic area.[13] According to both of these measures, the physician population has increased since 1970. Specifically, according to the American Medical Association (AMA) Physician Masterfile, the major source of data on the physician population,[14] there were 972,376 physicians in the United States in 2009.[15] This represents a 191% increase from 1970 (see **Table 1**). The AMA also calculates physician-to-population ratios and found that this ratio increased by 97% from 1970 to 2009 (from 161 per 100,000 to 317 per 100,000).[16] Despite the wide use of physician counts and physician-to-population ratios, some have criticized these measures because they do not take into account physicians' specialties or their geographic distribution, both of which may affect access to, and quality of, care.[17]

Table 1. Measuring the U.S. Physician Population, 1970 to 2009

Year	Total Physicians	Percent Change from Prior Decade	Physicians/100,000 Population	Percent Change from Prior Decade
1970	334,028	—	161	—
1980	469,679	41%	202	25%
1990	615,421	31%	244	21%
2000	813,770	32%	288	18%
2009	972,376	17%	317	10%
Total Change 1970 to 2009		*191%*	—	*97%*

Source: Adapted by CRS from Derek R. Smart, *Physician Characteristics and Distribution in the US*, 2011 Edition (American Medical Association, 2011).

Determining the Appropriate Size of the Physician Population

When the volume of physician services available and the demand for physician services are equal, the size of the physician population is generally considered to be appropriate. Determining whether the size of the physician population is appropriate requires accurate measures of the number of physicians and the volume of services they provide, as well as demand for their services (see text box). The volume of physician services is based on the number of practicing physicians and their productivity. The number of physicians can be altered by changing the number of physicians trained, the number of physicians retiring, or both. Physician productivity is affected by factors such as the hours that physicians work, available technology, and the use of physician extenders.[18] The demand for physician services is affected by the size, age, health, and insurance status of the population receiving services, among other factors.[19] Policies that support the development of an appropriately sized physician population rely on measuring all of these components accurately, which can be challenging. In addition, as demand-side factors are often less amenable to policy intervention, many policies that aim to support the development of an appropriately sized physician population do so by targeting either the number of physicians or their productivity. PPACA includes provisions taking both of these approaches, and these are discussed later in the report.

Determinants of the Size of the Physician Population

Volume of Physician Services: Number of Physicians (e.g., number of medical schools and their class size, residency slots) x Productivity (e.g., hours worked, technology available, use of physician extenders)

Demand for Physician Services: A function of, for example, the age of the population, population health, insurance status, and patient preference.

Appropriate Size of Physician Population: Where Volume = Demand, the size of the physician population is appropriate.

Source: CRS Analysis of *The Physician Workforce: Projections and Research into Current Issues Affecting Supply and Demand,* U.S. Department of Health and Human Services, Health Resources and Services Administration, Bureau of Health Professions, December 2008.

Experts debate whether the size of the current physician population is appropriate; that is, whether the volume of services made available is equal to demand for those services (see text box for description of expert groups).[20] The Association of American Medical Colleges (AAMC) and the U.S. Government Accountability Office (GAO) have both studied this issue. AAMC released a report in 2011 that compiled state workforce reports and found that 33 states documented current physician shortages or were anticipating future physician shortages.[21] In another report, AAMC found that there were 7,400 too few physicians in 2008.[22] In contrast, in 2009, GAO[23] examined the physician population serving Medicare beneficiaries and concluded that approximately 97% of beneficiaries had access to physician services and that between 2000 and 2008, the number of Medicare beneficiaries using physician services and the number of services per beneficiary increased.[24] Some of the differences between AAMC and GAO estimates may result from differences in methodologies used to assess the adequacy of the physician population or because the GAO study focuses only on the Medicare population. Other experts have suggested that the current size of the physician population is appropriate, and maintain that concerns about access to care result instead from the inefficient composition and geographic distribution of the physician population.[25]

Expert Groups That Evaluate Physician Supply

American Association of Medical Colleges (AAMC): Private, non-profit organization that represents U.S. accredited medical schools and some teaching hospitals. AAMC, through its Center for Workforce Studies, makes physician population projections and publishes studies that evaluate the physician workforce. See www.aamc.org.

Council on Graduate Medical Education (COGME): Federal executive branch advisory council that provides ongoing assessment of physician workforce trends and training. Group does not make physician population projections, but will evaluate existing projects and may make recommendations about federal policies affecting the physician workforce. See http://www.hrsa.gov/advisorycommittees/bhpradvisory/cogme/index.html.

Government Accountability Office (GAO): Federal legislative branch agency that evaluates federal programs including those that finance health care and support the physician workforce. Agency may make recommendations regarding the effectiveness of federal programs. Agency does not make physician population projections, but may evaluate existing projections. See www.gao.gov.

Health Resources and Services Administration (HRSA): Federal executive branch agency that administers health workforce programs including the National Center for Health Care Workforce Analysis that makes physician population projections and evaluates existing projections. See http://bhpr.hrsa.gov/healthworkforce/index.html.

Medicare Payment Advisory Commission (MedPAC): Federal legislative branch advisory commission that evaluates Medicare payment policy, including Medicare's financing of physician training. Agency does not make physician population projections, but may make recommendations about Medicare physician payment policy or Medicare's role in financing physician training. See www.medpac.gov.

National Health Care Workforce Advisory Commission: Federal executive branch advisory commission that evaluates and makes recommendations about the health care workforce. Commission uses data from the National Center for Health Care Workforce Analysis and evaluates health workforce programs across the federal government. See "PPACA and Workforce Planning."

In general, over the past 30 years, concerns about the appropriateness of the size of the physician population have been cyclical. For example, in the 1980s and early 1990s, experts predicted that physician surpluses would emerge by 2000[26] based on the expectation that health reform would occur in 1993 and that the increased use of managed care organizations would restrict patients' access to physician services.[27] Instead, when these conditions did not occur, concerns about physician shortages resulted based on the aging of the U.S. population, the aging of the physician workforce, and advances in medical technology that increased the demand for physician services.

Experts also debate whether, and to what extent, the size of the future physician population will be appropriate. The Health Resources and Services Administration (HRSA) and AAMC both predict future physician shortages. Specifically, in 2006, HRSA predicted that there will be between 55,000 and 150,000 too few physicians by 2020,[28] while, in 2008, AAMC predicted that there will be nearly 124,400 too few physicians by 2025.[29] As with differences in estimates of the appropriateness of the size of the current physician population, differences in estimates of the appropriateness of the size of the future physician population may result from the models' assumptions and limitations. These limitations include both models' assumption that, in the base year, supply is appropriate, an assumption which is debated. Both sets of projections also draw conclusions about the future demand for physician services based on assumptions about changes in medical technology, changes in physician productivity, and the aging population.[30] Both HRSA and AAMC note that policy changes may affect the future demand for physician services, which may alter the direction or magnitude of their projections. However, predicting the timing, content, and effect of policy changes is difficult, which adds to the uncertainty of the projections.

PPACA and the Size of the Physician Population

PPACA may affect both the demand for physician services as well as the volume of physician services available, and therefore may influence determinations of the appropriate size of the physician population. PPACA contains a number of provisions aimed at increasing access to insurance coverage, which could, in turn, increase the demand for physician services.[31] HRSA notes that physician use varies by insurance status, with those who are insured using more services.[32] This increase in demand for physician services would affect models assessing the appropriateness of the current and future size of the physician population (discussed above). Specifically, AAMC suggests that changes in PPACA created a shortfall of 13,700 physicians in 2010 and predicts that by 2025, an additional 130,600 physicians will be needed.[33]

As mentioned previously, PPACA also includes a number of provisions that aim to increase the volume of physician services available. In general, these provisions may achieve this goal by targeting (1) methods to increase the number of physicians trained or (2) methods to increase physician productivity by providing incentives to coordinate care or by increasing the number of non-physician providers trained.[34] Coordinated care may increase the volume of physician services available by decreasing physicians' administrative duties and by increasing efficiencies in care delivery.[35] Increasing the number of non-physician providers trained may increase the volume of physician services available because non-physician providers may substitute for, or augment, physician services.[36]

PPACA Provisions Targeting the Number of Physicians Trained

PPACA includes three types of provisions that may increase the number of physicians trained, provisions that (1) modify federal Medicare payments for medical residency training, (2) authorize additional HRSA funding for medical residency training, and (3) authorize funding for additional medical residency training programs. The number of medical school graduates completing residency training determines the number of physicians because residency training is required to be a licensed physician able to practice independently.[37] Therefore, because the federal government is the major source of residency funding, increased federal payments for medical residency training may increase the number of physicians.[38] The Medicare program is the largest source of support for medical residency training, through Graduate Medical Education (GME) payments[39] to teaching hospitals for residents training in accredited training programs.[40]

Medicare makes approximately $9.5 billion in payments to teaching hospitals annually, supporting about 90,000 residents and providing payments of more than $100,000 per resident in 2009.[41] Medicaid, the Department of Veterans Affairs (VA), and HRSA also provide support or GME payments for medical residency training.[42]

Individual hospitals determine the types of training programs offered and receive Medicare payments based on the number of Medicare-approved residency training slots for residents in training and the size of the Medicare population the hospital serves. Medicare restricts the number of approved training slots (often called the Medicare GME Cap; see text box).

The Medicare GME "Cap"

The Balanced Budget Act of 1997 (P.L. 105-33) restricted the number of residency slots the Medicare program would subsidize. This restriction, also referred to as a "cap," is placed on each hospital that operates residency programs. Some believe that the cap limits the number of medical residents a hospital will train because hospitals at their cap must use non-Medicare sources of funding to support these residents. The evidence that it restricts the number of residents trained is mixed because the number of residency positions has grown since the cap was enacted; however, there is evidence that it slowed the growth of residency positions. There is stronger evidence that the cap affected the specialty composition of the physician population, because hospitals have generally created new positions at the fellowship level or positions in medical specialties.

Source: Edward Salsberg et al., "U.S. Residency Training Before and After the 1997 Balanced Budget Act," *Journal of the American Medical Association*, vol. 300, no. 10 (September 10, 2008), pp. 1174-1180.

Although PPACA does not remove this restriction,[43] it does contain two provisions that may increase the number of residents trained by redistributing unused Medicare-funded residency training slots from hospitals not using them, or from hospitals that have closed, to hospitals seeking to train additional residents.[44] Section 5503 of PPACA redistributes 65% of unused residency positions to hospitals that meet a number of criteria (e.g., are located in a state with a low resident-to-population ratio or a state that has a high proportion of its population living in Health Professional Shortage Areas [HPSAs]).[45] As 75% of these redistributed residency positions must be used in primary care or general surgery, this section may also affect the composition of the physician population. Section 5506 requires the Secretary of HHS to develop a procedure to redistribute residency slots from closed hospitals.[46]

PPACA also includes provisions that may increase the number of non-Medicare-funded residents, specifically including residents funded by HRSA and through PPACA's Prevention and Public Health Fund (PPHF). Section 5508 provides grants to establish or expand primary care residency training in community-based settings (called teaching health centers) and appropriates GME payments for residents trained in these settings.[47] In addition, Section 4002 establishes the PPHF to support investments in prevention and public health programs.[48] This fund, which receives indefinite appropriations, received $750 million in FY2010, of which $167.3 million was used to fund an additional 889 primary care residents.[49]

PPACA Provisions Targeting Physician Productivity

PPACA includes two types of provisions to increase physician productivity and thereby increase the volume of physician services available. The first type encourages care coordination, while the second type expands the non-physician provider workforce that may augment or substitute for physician services.

PPACA's care coordination provisions encourage health care providers to join accountable care organizations[50] or to establish or expand medical homes, among other things. Medical homes, which provide integrated care to eligible patients, aim to better manage patients' chronic conditions by coordinating care across primary care physicians, specialists, and non-physician providers. PPACA includes many provisions to encourage care coordination including, among others:

- Section 3502 establishes a grant program to support care coordination through medical homes;[51]
- Section 2703 establishes a Medicaid option for states to permit Medicaid beneficiaries with chronic conditions to designate a medical home;[52]
- Section 3021 establishes a Center for Innovation within CMS to test a number of innovative physician payment approaches including the medical home;[53]
- Section 3022 establishes the Medicare Shared Savings Program to pilot Accountable Care Organizations (ACOs) in the Medicare program;[54]
- Section 3023 creates a pilot program in Medicare to provide payment incentives—through payment bundling or other methods—for coordinated care for hospitalized Medicare beneficiaries; and
- Section 3024 requires a demonstration program, within Medicare, to test payment incentives and service delivery models that use home-based primary care teams designed to reduce costs and improve health outcomes for Medicare beneficiaries.

As noted above, PPACA also includes provisions to increase the number of non-physician providers trained[55] whose services may substitute for, or augment, physician services, thereby increasing the volume of physician services.[56] For example, Section 5301, in addition to providing support for primary care physician training, provides support for physician assistant training.[57] Other examples include Section 5509, which establishes a new program to support the clinical training of advanced practice nurses, and Section 10501(e), which authorizes a new program to support Family Nurse Practitioner training.

Composition of the Physician Population

The composition of the physician population is an important determinant of access to care and health care costs. There are two main concerns about the composition of the physician population: (1) that the distribution of primary care and specialty physicians has resulted in primary care shortages and an oversupply of specialty physicians, and (2) that, despite excess specialists overall, there are shortages in certain specialties. In 2009, the physician population consisted of two-thirds specialists and one-third primary care physicians.[58] Some experts suggest this composition is not optimal, a suggestion that is generally consistent with research that examines the effects of the composition of the physician population on health. Research suggests that primary care is correlated with improved health outcomes and decreased costs. For example, researchers have found that each additional primary care physician lowers the risk of death and that patients who have a regular primary care physician have lower overall health care costs.[59] Similarly, in more targeted studies of the Medicare population, the supply of primary care physicians was found to correlate with reduced mortality (although associations with other health outcomes were weaker).[60] Internationally, those countries with more primary care physicians have better overall population health as measured by indicators such as infant mortality, child health, and all-cause mortality.[61] In contrast, research on the effects of more specialists on health outcomes is less clear. For example, a meta-analysis comparing specialty to primary care found that while some studies concluded that specialists provide better care for certain diseases, others found no differences or better outcomes from primary care physicians.[62] Other studies have found that specialty supply has little effect on infant mortality or on all-cause mortality.[63] Researchers have suggested that the current distribution of specialists and primary care physicians may be linked with a number of adverse health outcomes, including higher mortality rates in areas with more specialists.[64] With respect to shortages in certain specialties, several have been documented (e.g., in anesthesiology, cardiology, and neurosurgery), often by studies conducted by specialty professional associations. These associations may have an interest in publicizing shortages and minimizing oversupply;[65] therefore, determining which specialties are in shortage based only on these studies may be challenging. However, some specialties, such as general surgery, geriatrics,[66] the pediatric subspecialties,[67] and psychiatry,[68] have more widely acknowledged shortages[69] and have targeted federal programs to address these shortages.[70]

This section discusses primary care supply, as well as factors deterring entry into primary care practice. It then summarizes PPACA provisions that aim to address these factors through a number of mechanisms. It concludes with an overview of PPACA provisions targeting shortages in specialty areas.

Primary Care Supply and Factors Influencing Primary Care Supply[71]

As noted previously, the U.S. physician population presently is approximately one-third primary care physicians (see text box for a discussion of primary care definitions)[72] and two-thirds specialists, a distribution that experts suggest is not optimal. In 2009, the most recent year for which data on the physician population are available, there were 334,509 primary care physicians (34% of all physicians)[73] practicing in the United States, which HRSA has estimated is approximately 7,000 too few primary care physicians.[74] The Council on Graduate Medical Education (COGME) recommends that the percentage of U.S. primary care physicians be raised "to at least 40 percent."[75] This rate would be more comparable to that of other industrialized nations such as Australia, Canada, and France, which have closer to a 50-50 split between primary care and specialty physicians.[76] COGME also recommends changing the composition to help avert predicted *future* primary care shortages.[77]

Altering the composition of primary care physicians and specialists would require an increase in the number of primary care physicians. Experts have identified three main barriers to primary care entry and practice:

- The majority of medical school and residency training occurs in hospital settings, where there are fewer primary care role models and a greater orientation toward specialty care. Role models and exposure are important factors in specialty choice;[78] therefore, hospital-based training may influence medical students toward specialties. Prior research has found that medical students exposed to federal programs that promote primary care, such as those authorized by PHSA Title VII, during their training are more likely to enter primary care.[79]

What Is Primary Care?

- GAO and COGME define primary care as family medicine, internal medicine, and pediatrics.
- HRSA uses different definitions of primary care. For the National Health Service Corps (NHSC)—the loan and scholarship program that places providers in shortage areas—it defines primary care as family medicine; general internal medicine; general pediatrics; geriatrics; obstetrics and gynecology; and psychiatry. However, for the primary care loan program, it defines primary care as family medicine; internal medicine; osteopathic general practice; pediatrics; combined medicine/pediatrics; and preventive medicine.
- CMS, for GME funds, and MedPAC define primary care as family medicine, geriatrics, internal medicine, obstetrics and gynecology, and pediatrics.

Sources:
GAO: U.S. Government Accountability Office, Primary Care Professionals: Recent Supply Trends, Projections, and Valuation of Services, 08-472T, February 12, 2008.
COGME: COGME 20th Report.
HRSA: NHSC definition at http://nhsc.hrsa.gov/ loanrepayment/pdf/2011 nhsclrpguidance.pdf, and primary care loans definition at http://www.hrsa. gov loanscholarships/loans/primarycare.html.
CMS: Section 1886(h) of the Social Security Act. MedPAC: 2009 MedPAC Report.

- There are large and growing salary differences between primary care physicians and specialists. The average salary for a primary care physician was $193,000 in 2009, while the average specialist salary was $302,000.[80]

- Primary care physicians often have uncompensated care coordination duties and other administrative burdens that specialty physicians do not have. For example, in managed care, primary care physicians serve as gatekeepers determining access to specialists. Studies have also found that these responsibilities distract primary care physicians from providing patient care[81] and deter students from entering primary care specialties.[82]

In general, policy options included in PPACA that aim to alter the composition of primary care and specialty physicians seek to do so by increasing primary care supply through mitigation of one or more of these three barriers.

PPACA and the Composition of the Physician Population

A number of provisions in PPACA may influence the composition of the physician population, and specifically primary care supply, by (1) authorizing programs that may increase exposure to primary care content in physician training, (2) requiring increased Medicare and Medicaid payments for primary care providers, and (3) providing incentives to coordinate care. In general, these provisions aim to remove or lessen some of the factors noted above that deter physicians from entering and practicing primary care.[83] In addition, PPACA includes provisions that provide support for training of specialists identified as being in shortage. This part summarizes these provisions.

PPACA Provisions Targeting Primary Care Supply

Primary Care Content in Physician Training

PPACA targets primary care content in physician training through changes to (1) PHSA Title VII programs that support physician training in primary care and (2) the Medicare GME program.

PPACA Section 5301 reauthorizes PHSA Section 747, "Primary Care Training and Enhancement," which provides grants or contracts to support medical students, residents, and faculty in primary care.[84] PPACA amends this program to increase support for primary care training programs; to provide traineeships to students, residents, and faculty; and to support the development of innovative academic units in primary care.[85] Under this program's authority, HHS, through the PPHF, is supporting additional primary care resident training beginning in July of 2011 for five years (see "PPACA Provisions Targeting the Number of Physicians Trained").

In addition, PPACA authorizes a new program that may encourage physician training in community-based settings. Section 5508(a) authorizes grants to support the development or expansion of teaching health centers—community-based, ambulatory, patient care centers that operate a primary care residency program.[86] Section 5508(b) permits National Health Service Corps (NHSC) providers,[87] who often fulfill their service commitment in teaching health centers, to count teaching time toward their NHSC service requirement. Section 5508(c) appropriates GME payments for teaching health centers, which are in addition to GME payments received from other sources (e.g., Medicare or the Children's Hospital GME program).[88] Although HRSA did not provide funding to operate teaching health centers in FY2011, it awarded GME funds to 11 teaching health centers in FY2011.[89]

PPACA also makes a number of changes to Medicare GME payments that may encourage primary care training. Section 5503 of PPACA redistributes 65% of unused residency positions to hospitals that meet a number of criteria and requires that 75% of these redistributed residency positions be used in primary care or general surgery. It further requires that hospitals receiving additional positions maintain their pre-redistribution level of primary care residents. PPACA requires changes to how the Medicare program counts time spent by residents in non-hospital (i.e., community-based) settings to increase payment for time spent in these settings, which may remove a barrier experts have identified as reducing primary care exposure in training.[90] Section 5504 amends Medicare GME payment rules to count resident time spent in non-hospital settings for direct and indirect GME payments, provided that the hospital incurs most of the costs of the residents' stipends and other benefits while in the non-hospital setting. Section 5505 permits hospitals to count resident time spent at conferences and seminars in non-hospital settings for GME payments.

Primary Care Physician Payment

As noted above, primary care physicians, on average, earn less than specialty physicians, and these pay differentials may discourage entry into primary care practice. PPACA contains two provisions that require increased payments for certain primary care physicians providing specific primary care services to Medicare and Medicaid beneficiaries. Section 5501 establishes a new Medicare 10% bonus payment for physicians who meet specific requirements and provide certain primary care and general surgery services.[91] These new payments were effective January 1, 2011, and will remain in effect for five years. Section 1202 of HCERA requires increased Medicaid payments to primary care physicians in 2013 and 2014, to the generally higher Medicare payment rate.[92]

Care Coordination by Primary Care Physicians

As discussed above (see "PPACA Provisions Targeting Physician Productivity"), PPACA includes a number of provisions to encourage care coordination, for example, through medical homes. Relevant PPACA provisions include Sections 3502, 2703, 3021, 3023, and 3024 and have been summarized previously (see "PPACA Provisions Targeting Physician Productivity"). PPACA Section 5405 may also facilitate care coordination by authorizing a new grant program to educate and support primary care providers about care coordination, chronic disease management, and preventive medicine. In addition, Section 3503 authorizes a new program to establish medication management programs that involve a multidisciplinary group of providers (including physicians) in order to improve the treatment of chronic disease and to reduce costs.

PPACA Provisions Targeting Shortages in Specialties

PPACA includes a number of provisions to increase the number of physicians practicing in specialties that have identified shortages. PPACA Section 5203 authorizes loan repayments for pediatric medical, surgical, and mental health subspecialists (including psychiatrists) in return for providing care in a medically underserved or health professional shortage area (HPSA).[93] As noted previously, pediatric subspecialists are a group of specialists generally considered to be in shortage.[94] PPACA includes two provisions that may encourage training and practice in general surgery—a specialty in shortage because an increasing number of medical residents training in general surgery are pursuing subspecialty training in a surgical subspecialty.[95] Section 5501 establishes a new 10% Medicare bonus payment for general surgeons who perform certain surgeries in a HPSA.[96] Section 5503, discussed above, redistributes 65% of unused Medicare residency positions to hospitals that meet certain criteria, and requires that 75% of the redistributed residency positions be used in primary care or general surgery.[97] PPACA also includes provisions that authorize training in geriatrics and behavioral health, two areas where experts agree there are shortages.[98] Section 5305 authorizes grants to increase physician training in geriatrics, including grants for fellowship training, training in chronic care management, and short-term training in geriatric-related topics. Section 5306 authorizes grants for programs to increase the mental and behavioral health workforce, including psychiatrists. Grants may be used to support internship and residency training in child and adolescent psychiatry or behavioral pediatrics.

GEOGRAPHIC DISTRIBUTION OF THE PHYSICIAN POPULATION

The geographic distribution of physicians is an important determinant of health care access, quality, and cost. Physicians are distributed differently across the United States; specifically, researchers have found large regional variations in physician supply, with some areas having a 50% surplus of physicians and others having a 10% deficit.[99] Experts suggest that both over- and undersupply may be problematic. In high-supply areas, the population may receive unnecessary and excess care,[100] whereas in low-supply areas, the population may receive little or no care because of long wait times or long travel distance to providers.[101] Rural areas, in particular, experience physician shortages; however, some urban areas, specifically areas with economically disadvantaged populations, may have shortages as well.[102]

This section discusses physician shortages in specific geographic areas. It begins with a discussion of Health Professional Shortages Areas (HPSAs) and Medically Underserved Populations/Areas (MUA/Ps). The federal government uses these designations to determine areas and populations that have heath professional shortages (including physician shortages). Designated areas are eligible for a number of programs—some of which were amended or created by PPACA—that aim to increase the number of health professionals in a specific geographic area. Given the use of HPSA and MUA/Ps for guiding federal policies that seek to lessen geographic shortages of health professionals, it is necessary to understand this designation when discussing the geographic distribution of the physician population. The section also discusses some reasons why geographic areas may have physician shortages, and PPACA provisions that may affect the geographic distribution of the physician population. Although areas with an excess of physicians are of concern, federal policies tend to focus on increasing access in shortage areas, and in rural areas in particular.

Health Professional Shortage Areas and Medically Underserved Areas/Populations

The federal government designates some areas as HPSAs or areas or populations as medically underserved (MUAs/MUPs) because these areas/populations have physician or other health provider shortages. These designations make an area eligible for federal programs that may lessen these shortages. This section discusses the definition of HPSAs and MUP/As and some of the federal programs for which these areas are eligible.

HPSAs are areas with less than 2.86 providers per population of 10,000. These areas can be designated as such based on having a shortage of primary medical care, dental, or mental health providers, and may be located in urban or rural areas. Specific population groups (e.g., populations with unusually high needs for health services, as indicated by measures such as the poverty rate and the infant mortality rate) and specific facilities (e.g., a community health center, or a facility operated by the Indian Health Service) may also be designated as HPSAs.[103] The HPSA designation is considered to be the most restrictive designation of physician undersupply;[104] therefore, it is possible that areas, populations, or facilities may have physician shortages without being designated a HPSA. The federal government also designates areas and populations as being MUAs or MUPs. This designation takes into account both the services available in a given area and population characteristics, such as the economic, linguistic, and cultural barriers a population may face.

Policies that aim to change the geographic distribution of the physician population often do so by trying to reduce the number of HPSAs or MUA/Ps. As the number of primary care physicians is one of the criteria used to designate HPSAs and MUA/Ps, one way to reduce their number is to increase primary care supply.[105] In addition, the majority of physicians in underserved areas (and, in particular, in rural areas) are family medicine physicians who provide primary care to individuals of all ages. However, there are documented family medicine shortages,[106] and fewer medical school graduates are choosing to enter this field.[107] Given the relationship between the HPSA/MUA/P definition and primary care, policies and programs that encourage primary care, and in particular, family medicine, may be of greater benefit to areas with few physicians.

Areas designated as HPSAs are eligible for a number of federal programs that seek to bring providers to shortage areas and lessen the costs associated with providing medical care in a shortage area. For example, HPSAs are eligible for NHSC providers. The NHSC provides scholarships and loan repayments to health professionals (including physicians) in return for service in a HPSA for a specific period of time.[108] Physicians in HPSAs are also eligible for Medicare bonus payments,[109] and certain facilities in MUAs may be designated as federally qualified health centers (FQHCs) that are eligible for higher Medicare and Medicaid reimbursements.[110] Areas and populations designated as MUA/Ps may be eligible for, or given preference in, certain federal programs, such as health workforce programs authorized by Title VII of the PHSA.[111]

Why Geographic Shortages May Exist

Physician shortages in certain geographic areas may result from aspects of physician training. As discussed above, aspects of physician training may also influence specialty choice. This section discusses how the content of physician training may influence where physicians choose to practice. Specifically, the majority of medical training occurs in teaching hospitals, which are usually located in urban areas. The location of training may thereby influence the geographic distribution of physicians because students generally practice near their training site.[112] There is also evidence that student and resident educational experiences ultimately influence individuals' career choices;[113] therefore, training concentrated in teaching hospitals may discourage practicing in non-hospital settings. Researchers have found that medical residents who spend part of their training in community health centers—a type of FQHC—are more likely to practice in these settings after completing their residency.[114] Some researchers have also suggested that medical students' racial and ethnic and geographic (i.e., rural, urban, or suburban) origin may influence where these students choose to practice after residency.[115] These researchers have suggested that medical students from underrepresented groups and those from rural areas are more likely to provide care to the medically underserved. They recommend that medical schools consider these characteristics in their admission policies and that educational programs be developed to recruit and retain students more likely to provide care to the underserved.[116] Recent research has found that medical students are increasingly considering lifestyle factors, such as the amount of on-call time, when choosing where (and which specialty) to practice.[117] Physicians practicing in shortage areas may face lifestyle challenges not present in areas with more physicians. For example, physicians in shortage areas may be more isolated (either geographically or from colleagues to collaborate with), may care for a large population, and may feel the strain of always having to be available for emergencies (i.e., may have more on-call time). These lifestyle considerations make practicing in a shortage area less attractive to newer physicians, thereby contributing to the geographic maldistribution of the physician population.

PPACA and the Geographic Distribution of the Physician Population

PPACA includes provisions that may expand the number of NHSC providers available to serve in shortage areas, increase the diversity of the physician workforce, and increase physician training in shortage areas. It also includes provisions to revise the criteria used to designate HPSAs and MUPs, which may affect the geographic distribution of providers by changing the areas eligible for incentives such as the NHSC.

PPACA Provisions Targeting the NHSC[118]

PPACA authorizes program changes to the NHSC that may encourage NHSC providers to serve as faculty at teaching health centers, increase loan repayment amounts, and increase provider flexibility. As previously discussed, Section 10501(n) permits NHSC clinicians to count teaching time as part of their NHSC service requirement, increases loan repayment amounts, and permits NHSC clinicians to work-part time in exchange for an extended service requirement. Teaching time at NHSC sites may be important for teaching health centers (see "PPACA Provisions Targeting the Number of Physicians Trained") because many teaching health centers rely on NHSC clinicians who might be reluctant to participate in resident training if this time did not count toward their NHSC service requirement. Part-time service may make NHSC participation more attractive to younger providers who are interested in achieving work-life balance, which may help recruit or retain NHSC providers.[119] PPACA also increases amounts authorized for appropriation for the NHSC. Specifically, Section 5207 authorizes increased discretionary appropriations for the NHSC. In addition, Section 10503 requires that $1.5 billion be transferred—between FY2011 and FY2015—from the Community Health Center Fund (created in this section of PPACA) to support the NHSC. These transferred funds are in addition to the program's annual appropriation and are required to be used to increase NHSC appropriations over FY2008 levels.[120]

PPACA Provisions Targeting the Diversity of the Physician Workforce

PPACA includes provisions that authorize programs that aim to increase the diversity of the physician workforce. Prior research has found that the current physician population is less diverse than the U.S. population. In addition, research has found that individuals from racial and ethnic minorities are more likely to practice in underserved areas.[121] Consequently, the federal government supports programs to increase the racial and ethnic diversity of medical students and faculty.

Section 5401 reauthorizes the Centers of Excellence program funded in Section 736 of the PHSA. The program supports activities related to increasing the diversity of the health professions workforce, including efforts that encourage underrepresented minorities to enter health professional education and programs to assist these individuals during their studies. Section 5402 authorizes increased appropriations for scholarship, loan repayment, and fellowship programs that provide funding to students and faculty from disadvantaged backgrounds to pursue health professions education.

PPACA Provisions Targeting Rural Practice

PPACA includes provisions to encourage training in rural areas specifically, and in HPSAs or MUAs in general. The law also authorizes a new program to recruit medical students from rural areas and to provide training in rural settings in order to encourage rural practice. Prior research has found that medical students who have participated in similar programs are more likely to practice in rural areas after completing their training.[122]

PPACA authorizes programs that may connect physicians in HPSAs and MUAs, which may reduce isolation and increase contact with colleagues. As isolation and lack of colleagues are commonly cited barriers to practice in underserved and shortage areas, programs to reduce these barriers may affect the geographic distribution of physicians. Section 5403 amends the Area Health Education Center (AHEC) program. These centers aim to address workforce shortages by supporting physician recruitment and retention from medically underserved populations and those from rural and medically underserved areas. AHECs sponsor programs for students, faculty, and providers, including programs for medical students and medical residents. PPACA authorized an expansion of the AHEC program to include new grants to medical and nursing schools to develop these programs. PPACA also authorized increased appropriations for the AHEC program and noted that it is the sense of Congress that every state have an AHEC. In addition, Section 5403 authorizes new grants to provide continuing educational support to health providers in underserved communities. Such efforts may involve distance learning, conferences, and telehealth. The content and location of training are important determinants of where physicians ultimately practice. Programs that encourage rural and community-based training may influence the geographic distribution of the physician population; therefore, PPACA includes a new program that trains students who are likely to practice in rural settings.[123] Section 10501(l) authorizes a new program to award grants to medical schools to recruit and provide focused training and experiences to students likely to practice medicine in underserved rural communities. The program aims to recruit students most likely to enter into rural practice[124] and includes rural-focused training experiences while in medical school. PPACA also authorizes teaching health centers, which may increase medical residency training in underserved areas (see "PPACA Provisions Targeting the Number of Physicians Trained").

PPACA Provisions Amending HPSA and MUP Designation Criteria

PPACA requires that the criteria used to designate HPSAs and MUPs be updated in response to concerns that these criteria were outdated and that some areas designated as HPSAs may no longer have shortages.[125] Section 5602 requires the HHS Secretary to establish new methodology for designating MUPs and HPSAs and to publish a final rule by July 1, 2011.[126] Although HHS has been working since 1998 to develop new methodology, it has not been implemented.[127]

PPACA AND WORKFORCE PLANNING

Some experts have argued that lack of workforce planning has contributed to current physician supply concerns and that federal programs supporting the physician workforce are not coordinated.[128] GAO has also noted that lack of data hamper efforts to evaluate programs funded under PHSA Title VII.[129] Such data may be necessary for comprehensive workforce planning. Concerns about lack of planning and coordination and lack of data to evaluate programs existed prior to PPACA, but PPACA may exacerbate these concerns because it expands federal support for the health care workforce. PPACA includes provisions to increase workforce planning and collect data needed to support these efforts. PPACA includes provisions that may increase workforce planning at the federal and state levels. Section 5101 establishes the National Health Workforce Commission to evaluate and make recommendations about the health care workforce (including physicians). The commission was appointed by GAO in September of 2010 and is required to review health care workforce supply and demand and make recommendations on national priorities and policies. Commission members are required to make reports to Congress and to review reports from the state workforce development planning grants and from the National Center for Health Workforce Analysis (see below).[130] Section 5102 authorizes grants for states to undertake health care workforce development.[131] PPACA also requires additional data collection on health workforce programs and establishes a federal center to undertake health workforce analysis to support the new commission. Section 5103 requires HHS to establish a National Center for Health Care Workforce Analysis[132] and to establish State and Regional Centers for Health Workforce Analysis. Section 5103 also requires longitudinal evaluations of individuals who have received support (education, training, or financial assistance) from grants awarded under PHSA Title VII. The section authorizes increased grant amounts for this purpose and requires PHSA Title VII advisory groups to develop performance measures and guidelines for longitudinal evaluations for the programs they advise.

CONCLUSION

The current and future physician supply may be inadequate. Some experts suggest that there are too few physicians overall, too few primary care physicians specifically, and that physicians are inadequately distributed throughout the United States. PPACA may intensify some of these concerns; specifically, although PPACA includes a number of provisions that aim to alter physician supply, it is not yet known whether and how these provisions will affect physician supply. Many of the programs established by PPACA have not yet been implemented, and others may not have immediate effects. In addition, some PPACA programs are temporary, and many rely on discretionary funding.[133]

APPENDIX. PPACA PROVISIONS THAT MAY AFFECT PHYSICIAN SUPPLY

Table A-1. Physician Supply and PPACA

PPACA Section Number	PPACA Section Description	Section May Affect the Size of the Physician Population	Section May Affect the Composition of the Physician Population	Section May Affect the Geographic Distribution of the Physician Population
2703	Section permits state Medicaid programs to offer the option for Medicaid beneficiaries with chronic conditions to designate a medical home.	√	√	
3021	Section establishes a Center for Medicare and Medicaid Innovation within the Centers for Medicare & Medicaid Services (CMS) to test innovative physician payment approaches including the medical home.	√	√	
3022	Section establishes the Medicare Shared Savings Program to pilot Accountable Care Organizations in the Medicare program.	√	√	
3023	Section creates a pilot program in Medicare to provide payment incentives—through payment bundling or other methods—for coordinated care for hospitalized Medicare beneficiaries.	√	√	
3024	Section requires a demonstration program, within Medicare, to test payment incentives and service delivery models that use home-based primary care teams designed to reduce costs and improve health outcomes for Medicare beneficiaries.	√	√	
3502	Section requires the Secretary of the Department of Health and Human Services (HHS) to provide grants or contracts to establish care coordination through medical homes for Medicare beneficiaries.	√	√	
3503	Section authorizes grants for medication management programs that involve a multidisciplinary group of providers (including physicians) in order to improve the treatment of chronic disease and reduce costs.		√	

Table A-1. (Continued)

PPACA Section Number	PPACA Section Description	Section May Affect the Size of the Physician Population	Section May Affect the Composition of the Physician Population	Section May Affect the Geographic Distribution of the Physician Population
5101	Section establishes the National Health Workforce Commission to evaluate and make recommendations about the health care workforce (including physicians).	√	√	√
5102	Section authorizes grants for states to undertake health care workforce development.	√	√	√
5103	Section requires HHS to establish the National Center for Health Care Workforce Analysis and to establish State and Regional Centers for Health Workforce Analysis. The section also requires longitudinal evaluations of individuals who have received support (education, training, or financial assistance) from grants awarded under the authority of Title VII of the Public Health Service Act (PHSA).	√	√	√
5203	Section authorizes loan repayments for pediatric medical subspecialists and pediatric mental health subspecialists who provide care to a medically underserved or health professional shortage area (HPSA).		√	√
5207	Section permanently authorizes the National Health Service Corps (NHSC) program and authorizes discretionary appropriations for the program.			√
5301	Section authorizes the HHS Secretary to make grants to support primary care training including primary care residency training and programs to increase primary care content in medical school and residency training. Section also authorizes programs to support physician assistant training.a	√	√	
5305	Section authorizes grants or contracts for geriatric workforce development including support for fellowship training in geriatrics and support for training in chronic care management. Section also authorizes support for short-term training programs in geriatrics.		√	

PPACA Section Number	PPACA Section Description	Section May Affect the Size of the Physician Population	Section May Affect the Composition of the Physician Population	Section May Affect the Geographic Distribution of the Physician Population
5306	Section authorizes grants for internship and residency training programs in child and adolescent psychiatry and behavioral pediatrics that are establishing or expanding internships or other field placements.		√	
5401	Section authorizes the Center of Excellence programs that provide grants to support activities related to increasing the diversity of the health professions workforce, including efforts that encourage underrepresented minorities to enter health professional education and programs to assist these individuals during their studies.			√
5402	Section authorizes increased appropriations for scholarship, loan repayment, and fellowship programs that provide funding to students and faculty from disadvantaged backgrounds to pursue health professions education.			√
5403	Section amends the Area Health Education Program (AHEC) to authorize new grants to medical and nursing schools to develop new AHECs. AHECs aim to address workforce shortages by supporting physician recruitment and retention in rural and medically underserved areas. Section also authorizes grants to provide continuing education programs to support health providers in underserved communities.			√
5405	Section authorizes a new grant program to educate and support primary care providers about care coordination, chronic disease management, and preventive medicine.		√	
5501	Section requires the Medicare program to increase payments to primary care physicians that provide certain primary care procedures by 10%. The section also requires that the Medicare program provide a 10% bonus payments to general surgeons that perform certain surgeries in a HPSA. Both payment increases are effective between January 1, 2011 and January 1, 2016.		√	√

Table A-1. (Continued)

PPACA Section Number	PPACA Section Description	Section May Affect the Size of the Physician Population	Section May Affect the Composition of the Physician Population	Section May Affect the Geographic Distribution of the Physician Population
5503	Section requires CMS to redistribute 65% of unused Medicare-funded residency positions to hospitals that meet a number of criteria (e.g., are located in a state with a low resident-to-population ratio or a state that has a high proportions of its populations living in a HPSA). The section further requires that 75% of these redistributed residency positions be filled by residents training in primary care or general surgery,	√	√	√
5504	Section requires that CMS count resident time spent in community based settings for purpose of Medicare Graduate Medical Education (GME) payments.		√	
5505	Section requires that CMS permit hospital to count resident training time spent in conferences and seminars while in community-based settings for Medicare GME payments.		√	
5506	Section requires the Secretary of HHS to develop a procedure to redistribute residency slots from closed hospitals.[b]	√	√	√
5508	Section authorizes grants to establish or expand primary care residency training in community-based settings—such as federally qualified health centers (FQHCs)—called teaching health centers. Section also appropriates GME payments for residents trained in these settings.	√	√	√
5509	Section requires the HHS Secretary to establish a Medicare-funded graduate nurse education demonstration project to provide clinical training of advance practice nurses.	√		
5602	Section requires the HHS Secretary to establish new methodology for designating medically underserved populations (MUPs) and HPSAs.			√

PPACA Section Number	PPACA Section Description	Section May Affect the Size of the Physician Population	Section May Affect the Composition of the Physician Population	Section May Affect the Geographic Distribution of the Physician Population
10501(e)	Section requires the HHS Secretary to establish a demonstration program to train family nurse practitioners to serve as primary care providers at outpatient facilities such as FQHCs.	√	√	√
10501(l)	Section authorizes grants to medical schools to recruit and provide focused training and experiences to students likely to practice medicine in underserved rural communities.			√
10501(n)	Section permits NHSC providers to count teaching time in teaching health centers (see Sec. 5508 above) towards their NHSC service requirement. Section also increases annual loan repayment amounts and permits NHSC providers to work part-time in exchange for an extended service requirement.	√	√	√
10502	Section creates the multi-billion dollar Community Health Center Fund and transfers $1.5 billion, to be appropriated from FY2011 to FY2015, to the NHSC.			√

Source: CRS Analysis of the Patient Protection and Affordable Care Act (PPACA, P.L. 111-148) as amended by the Health Care and Education Reconciliation Act (HCERA, P.L. 111-152). The two laws are collectively referred to in this table as "PPACA."

Notes: The table only includes section summaries that relate to physician supply. More complete section summaries can be found in the series of CRS reports related to PPACA at http://www.crs.gov/Pages/subissue.aspx?cliid=3746&parentid=13. HHS has promulgated regulations to implement a number of provisions in the table; however, the table does not list all regulations. Rather, regulations are only noted in this table if these regulations affect the three dimensions of physician supply.

[a] FY2010 funds appropriated by the Prevention and Public Health Fund (PPACA Sec. 4002) will be used to support additional primary care residency training and additional physician assistant training.

[b] The regulations promulgated to implement this section, 75 C.F.R. § 72129, may redistribute residency positions from closed hospitals in ways that may affect the composition and geographic distribution of the physician population.

[c] Section number refers to the HCERA.

End Notes

[1] Training time to become a physician varies between 11 and 19 years and varies by specialty chosen. See Figure 1.1. (p. 8) in the Medicare Payment Advisory Commission's June 2009 Report to Congress: Improving Incentives in the Medicare Program, Chapter 1, at http://www.medpac.gov/chapters/Jun09_Ch01.pdf; hereafter *2009 MedPAC Report*.

[2] Sager, Alan, and Deborah Socolar, "Health Costs Absorb One-Quarter of Economic Growth, 2000–2005," Data Brief No. 5, Boston University School of Public Health (February 9, 2005); and Eisenberg, John, "Physician Utilization: The State of Research About Physicians' Practice Patterns," *Medical Care*, vol. 40, no. 11 (2002), pp. 1016-1035.

[3] As discussed below, factors such as the number of hours that physician work may also determine the amount of health services available.

[4] Peter J. Cunningham, "What Accounts for Differences in the Use of Hospital Emergency Departments Across U.S. Communities?" *Health Affairs*, vol. 25 (July 18, 2006), pp. w324-w336.

[5] Elliott Fisher, et al., *Health Care Spending, Quality, and Outcomes: More Isn't Always Better*, The Dartmouth Institute for Health Policy and Clinical Practice, A Dartmouth Atlas Project Topic Brief, Hanover, NH, February 27, 2009, http://www.dartmouthatlas.org/downloads/reports/Spending_Brief_022709.pdf.

[6] Ibid.

[7] See review in Barbara Starfield, Leiyu Shi, and James Macinko, "Contribution of Primary Care to Health Systems and Health," *The Milbank Quarterly*, vol. 83, no. 3 (2005), pp. 457-502.

[8] For example, see Health Resources and Services Administration, Bureau of Health Professions at http://bhpr.hrsa.gov.

[9] Some provisions of PPACA were subsequently amended by the Health Care and Education Reconciliation Act of 2010 (HCERA, P.L. 111-152). The two laws are collectively referred to in this report as "PPACA."

[10] Provisions in the Patient Protection and Affordable Care Act are described in a series of CRS reports available at http://www.crs.gov/Pages/subissue.aspx?cliid=3746&parentid=13. Several reports track PPACA's implementation and funding (see CRS Report R41180, *Rulemaking Requirements and Authorities in the Patient Protection and Affordable Care Act (PPACA)*, by Curtis W. Copeland, CRS Report R41301, *Appropriations and Fund Transfers in the Patient Protection and Affordable Care Act (PPACA)*, by C. Stephen Redhead, and CRS Report R41390, *Discretionary Funding in the Patient Protection and Affordable Care Act (PPACA)*, coordinated by C. Stephen Redhead,); both topics are beyond the scope of this report.

[11] Barbara Starfield, Leiyu Shi, and James Macinko, "Contribution of Primary Care to Health Systems and Health," *The Milbank Quarterly*, vol. 83, no. 3 (2005), pp. 457-502.

[12] Elliott Fisher, et al., *Health Care Spending, Quality, and Outcomes: More Isn't Always Better*, The Dartmouth Institute for Health Policy and Clinical Practice, A Dartmouth Atlas Project Topic Brief, Hanover, NH, February 27, 2009, http://www.dartmouthatlas.org/downloads/reports/Spending_Brief_022709.pdf.

[13] There are other health professionals who contribute to the health care workforce; however, for purposes of this report, the focus is on physician supply. Potential substitution effects and the role of other professions in augmenting the health care workforce are discussed as appropriate.

[14] Despite being widely used and the major source of data on the physician population, these data have been criticized by some because, for example, they do not adequately track retired

physicians and because they do not count hours worked by physicians. For example, see Diane R. Rittenhouse et al., "No Exit: An Evaluation of Measures of Physician Attrition," *Health Services Research*, vol. 39, no. 5 (October 2004), pp. 1571-1588, and Chiang-Hua Chang et al., "Primary Care Physician Workforce and Medicare Beneficiaries' Health Outcomes," *Journal of the American Medical Association*, vol. 305, no. 20 (May 25, 2011), pp. 2096-2105.

[15] The majority of these physicians provided patient care (749,566, or 77%). The remaining physicians were inactive (11%), in administration (2%), conducting research (1%), or teaching (1%). These percentages do not sum to 100% because of rounding or because some physicians are not classified or their professional activity is unknown. Derek R. Smart, *Physician Characteristics and Distribution in the US*, 2011 Edition (American Medical Association, 2011); hereafter, *Physician Characteristics and Distribution*.

[16] Ibid.

[17] Sean Nicholson, *Will the United States Have a Shortage of Physicians in 10 Years?* Robert Wood Johnson Foundation, November 2009.

[18] Physician extenders refer to health professionals whose services can substitute for, or augment, physician services. Such health professionals include physician assistants and nurse practitioners.

[19] U.S Department of Health and Human Services, Health Resources and Services Administration, Bureau of Health Professions, *The Physician Workforce: Projections and Research into Current Issues Affecting Supply and Demand,* December 2008, http://bhpr.hrsa.gov/healthworkforce/reports/physwfissues.pdf; hereafter *HRSA Physician Workforce Report*.

[20] As discussed below, there is greater concern among experts about the specialty composition and geographic distribution of the current physician population.

[21] Association of American Medical Colleges, Center for Workforce Studies, *Recent Studies and Reports on Physician Shortages in the U.S.*, Washington, DC, May 2011, http://www.aamc.org/workforce/stateandspecialty/recentworkforcestudiesnov09.pdf. A number of state studies use HRSA or AAMC projection methodology; therefore, concerns about the methodology used in these projections would also apply to a number of state studies. For discussion, see Sean Nicholson, *Will the United States Have a Shortage of Physicians in 10 Years?* Robert Wood Johnson Foundation, November 2009.

[22] Association of American Medical Colleges, "Physician Shortages to Worsen Without Increases in Residency Training," September 30, 2010, http://www.aamc.org/newsroom/presskits/mdShortage1.pdf. As discussed below, AAMC has altered its 2010 projections to reflect new changes to the health care system made by PPACA. In doing so, it found that the physician shortage increased by 46% between 2008 and 2010 (from 7,400 to 13,700).

[23] GAO, formerly the U.S. General Accounting Office, has conducted several studies on this topic. See discussion in U.S. Government Accountability Office, *Medicare Physician Services: Utilization Trends Indicate Sustained Beneficiary Access with High and Growing Levels of Service in Some Areas of the Nation*, 09-0559, August 28, 2009, http://www.gao.gov/new.items/d09559.pdf. The Medicaid population also faces a number of challenges accessing providers; however, these challenges may be less about the availability of providers and more about providers unwilling to accept Medicaid. See Peter J. Cunningham and Ann S. O'Malley, "Do Reimbursement Delays Discourage Medicaid Participation by Physicians?" *Health Affairs*, vol. 28, no. 1 (November 18, 2008), pp. w17–w28, for discussion.

[24] U.S. Government Accountability Office, *Medicare Physician Services: Utilization Trends Indicate Sustained Beneficiary Access with High and Growing Levels of Service in Some Areas of the Nation*, 09-0559, August 28, 2009, http://www.gao.gov/new.items/d09559.pdf.

[25] Sean Nicholson, *Will the United States Have a Shortage of Physicians in 10 Years?* Robert Wood Johnson Foundation, November 2009.

[26] *HRSA Physician Workforce Report.*

[27] In particular, managed care is thought to limit access to specialty care.

[28] U.S. Department of Health and Human Services, Health Resources and Services Administration, Bureau of Health Professions, *Physician Supply and Demand: Projections to 2020*, October 2006.

[29] Michael J. Dill and Edward S. Salsberg, *The Complexities of Physician Supply and Demand: Projections Through 2025*, Association of American Medical Colleges, Washington, DC, November 2008, http://services.aamc.org/ publications/showfile.cfm?file=version122.pdf &prd_id=244&prv_id=299&pdf_id=122; hereafter referred to as *AAMC Supply Report.*

[30] Ibid., and HRSA Physician Workforce Report.

[31] For more information about PPACA generally, see CRS Report R41664, *PPACA: A Brief Overview of the Law, Implementation, and Legal Challenges*, by Hinda Chaikind et al.

[32] HRSA Physician Workforce Report.

[33] *AAMC Supply Report* and Association of American Medical Colleges, "Physician Shortages to Worsen Without Increases in Residency Training," September 30, 2010, http://www.aamc.org/newsroom/presskits/mdShortage1.pdf. The Alliance for Health Reform also summarized a number of reports detailing health workforce shortages; see Alliance for Health Reform, *Health Care Workforce: Future Supply vs. Demand*, Washington, DC, April 2011, http://www.allhealth.org/publications/Medicare/ Health_Care_Workforce_104.pdf.

[34] The stated purpose of PPACA Title V "Health Care Workforce" is to improve access to and the delivery of health care services for all individuals, particularly low income, underserved, uninsured, minority, health disparity, and rural populations. Title V includes four mechanisms to achieve this purpose, one of which is to "increase the supply of a qualified health care workforce." The provisions discussed in this report are not an exhaustive list of all PPACA provisions that may influence physician supply. In addition, to avoid redundancy, provisions that include programs that may affect the composition or the geographic distribution of the physician workforce are discussed below. For further information on PPACA workforce provisions, see CRS Report R41278, *Public Health, Workforce, Quality, and Related Provisions in PPACA: Summary and Timeline*, coordinated by C. Stephen Redhead and Erin D. Williams.

[35] Advisory Committee on Training In Primary Care Medicine and Dentistry, *The Redesign of Primary Care with Implications for Training*, Health Resources and Services Administration, Eighth Annual Report to the Secretary of the U.S. Department of Health and Human Services and to the U.S. Congress, Rockville, MD, May 2010, http://www.hrsa.gov/advisorycommittees/bhpradvisory/actpcmd/Reports/8threport.pdf.

[36] HRSA Physician Workforce Report.

[37] Graduates of U.S. medical schools, Canadian medical schools, U.S. schools of osteopathic medicine, and international medical schools who meet certain requirements are eligible to apply for residency training. For additional information, see *2009 MedPAC Report* and U.S. Government Accountability Office, *Graduate Medical Education: Trends in Training and Student Debt*, 09-438R, May 4, 2009, http://www.gao.gov/new.items/d09438r.pdf; hereafter, *GAO GME Report.*

[38] This is debated by some because hospitals receive revenue from residents' work, and this revenue may exceed the cost of resident training. If this is true, hospitals should not require additional federal funds to train more residents, because training more residents would be in a hospital's financial interest without these additional funds. See Jerry Cromwell, Walter Adamache, and Edward R. Drozd, "BBA Impacts on Hospital Residents, Finances, and Medicare Subsidies," *Health Care Financing Review*, vol. 28, no. 1 (fall 2006), pp. 117-129.

[39] Medicare provides two types of GME payments to teaching hospitals: direct and indirect. Direct payments are for costs directly related to medical training, such as salary and administration. Indirect payments are made to hospitals to defray the hospital's increased costs due to the inefficiencies in patient care associated with medical training (see 2009 MedPAC report).

[40] To receive Medicare GME payments, a residency program must be accredited by either the American Osteopathic Association (AOA) or the Accreditation Council for Graduate Medical Education (ACGME).

[41] Medicare Payment Advisory Commission, *Graduate Medical Education Financing: Focusing on Educational Priorities*, Report to the Congress: Aligning Incentives in Medicare, Washington, DC, June 2010, http://www.medpac.gov/documents/Jun10_EntireReport.pdf.

[42] See 2009 MedPAC Report for more information.

[43] Some groups advocate an increase in Medicare funding for residency training; see for example, Association of American Medical Colleges, "Physician Shortages to Worsen Without Increases in Residency Training," September 30, 2010, http://www.aamc.org/newsroom/presskits/mdShortage1.pdf, and American Osteopathic Association, *Physician Workforce and Graduate Medical Education,* Washington, DC, http://www.osteopathic.org/inside-aoa/advocacy/ Documents/talking-points-physician-workforce-and-graduate-medical-education.pdf. Others, such as MedPAC and COGME, recommend changes to how Medicare GME is funded by linking payments to specific training goals or outcomes. PPACA does not include either of these changes.

[44] PPACA defines closed as a hospital that closed within two years of PPACA's enactment (i.e., between March 23, 2008, and March 23, 2010).

[45] These areas are defined and discussed later in the report, see "Health Professional Shortage Areas and Medically Underserved Areas/Populations."

[46] The Centers for Medicare and Medicaid Services, the agency that administers the Medicare program, issued regulations implementing these provisions; see *Federal Register,* August 3, 2010, (75 CFR 46390-46432).

[47] As noted above, most residency training occurs in teaching hospitals. This section requires new training programs to train primary care physicians; therefore, it will likely also affect the specialty composition of the physician population. HRSA has awarded funds for FY2011 teaching health center GME payments (see http://www.hrsa.gov/about/news/pressreleases/110125teachinghealthcenters.html).

[48] H.R. 1217 would repeal the Public Health and Prevention Fund.

[49] These residents will enter three-year primary care training programs beginning in July of 2011 continuing through July of 2015; therefore, these additional residents will complete their training in 2018 or earlier. U.S. Department of Health and Human Services, "HHS Awards $320 Million to Expand the Primary Care Workforce," press release, September 27, 2010, http://www.hhs.gov/news/press/2010pres/09/20100927e.html.

[50] For more information, see CRS Report R41474, *Accountable Care Organizations and the Medicare Shared Savings Program*, by David Newman.

[51] See description in CRS Report R41278, *Public Health, Workforce, Quality, and Related Provisions in PPACA: Summary and Timeline*, coordinated by C. Stephen Redhead and Erin D. Williams.

[52] CRS Report R41210, *Medicaid and the State Children's Health Insurance Program (CHIP) Provisions in PPACA: Summary and Timeline*, by Evelyne P. Baumrucker et al.

[53] CRS Report R41196, *Medicare Provisions in the Patient Protection and Affordable Care Act (PPACA): Summary and Timeline*, coordinated by Patricia A. Davis.

[54] CRS Report R41474, *Accountable Care Organizations and the Medicare Shared Savings Program*, by David Newman.

[55] CRS Report R41278, *Public Health, Workforce, Quality, and Related Provisions in PPACA: Summary and Timeline*, coordinated by C. Stephen Redhead and Erin D. Williams.

[56] HRSA Physician Workforce Report.

[57] In 2010, HHS awarded $30 million from the Prevention and Public Health Fund (PPHF) to support the training of an additional 700 physician assistants. U.S. Department of Health and Human Services, "HHS Awards $320 Million to Expand the Primary Care Workforce," press release, September 27, 2010, http://www.hhs.gov/news/press/2010pres/09/20100927e.html.

[58] *Physician Characteristics and Distribution*. According to these data, 34% of physicians were practicing in the specialties of family medicine, internal medicine, or pediatrics.

[59] Council on Graduate Medical Education, *Twentieth Report*, Advancing Primary Care, Rockville, MD, December 2010; hereinafter, *COGME 20th Report*. Specifically, for each incremental primary care physician, there are 1.44 fewer deaths per 10,000 persons (COGME 20th Report, p. 4).

[60] Chiang-Hua Chang et al., "Primary Care Physician Workforce and Medicare Beneficiaries' Health Outcomes," *Journal of the American Medical Association*, vol. 305, no. 20 (May 25, 2011), pp. 2096-2105.

[61] Barbara Starfield, Leiyu Shi, and James Macinko, "Contribution of Primary Care to Health Systems and Health," *The Milbank Quarterly*, vol. 83, no. 3 (2005), pp. 457-502.

[62] Gerald W. Smetana et al., "A Comparison of Outcomes Resulting From Generalist vs Specialist Care for a Single Discrete Medical Condition," *Archive of Internal Medicine*, vol. 167 (January 8, 2007), pp. 10-20.

[63] Barbara Starfield, Lieyu Shi, and Atul Grover, et al., "The Effects of Specialist Supply on Populations' Health: Assessing the Evidence," *Health Affairs*, 2005, pp. w597-w5107.

[64] Barbara Starfield, Leiyu Shi, and James Macinko, "Contribution of Primary Care to Health Systems and Health," *The Milbank Quarterly*, vol. 83, no. 3 (2005), pp. 457-502.

[65] Specifically, specialty societies may be reluctant to examine or publicize that their specialty is in oversupply for fear that it may result in declining interest in their specialty or declining hospital support for residency positions in their specialty. For a discussion of specific specialty studies and findings, see Center for Workforce Studies, *Recent Studies and Reports on Physician Shortages in the U.S.*, Association of American Medical Colleges, Washington, DC, April 2009.

[66] Committee on the Future Health Care Workforce for Older Americans, Institute of Medicine, Retooling for an Aging America: Building the Health Care Workforce, Institute of Medicine, Washington, DC, April 14, 2008, http://www.iom.edu/CMS/3809/40113/53452.aspx.

[67] Note that pediatric subspecialties refers to a number of specialists and subspecialists that focus on children (e.g., pediatric cardiologists or pediatric surgeons).

[68] Institute of Medicine, Improving the Quality of Health Care for Mental and Substance-Use Conditions: Quality Chasm Series, Washington, DC, 2006, http://books.nap.edu/openbook.php?record_id=11470.

[69] See discussion in COGME 20th Report.

[70] See "PPACA Provisions Targeting Shortages in Specialties."

[71] This discussion was adapted from "Letter from The Council on Graduate Medical Education to The Honorable Kathleen Sebelius, Secretary of Health and Human Services," May 5, 2009, http://www.cogme.gov/cogmeletter.htm. The COGME 20th Report reiterates and expands on these factors as deterrents from primary care practice.

[72] Although pediatricians are generally included in definitions of primary care physicians, recent studies have found that the total number of general pediatricians is adequate (or possibly in surplus), but state that there are concerns about the geographic distribution of pediatricians. *COGME 20th Report.*

[73] *Physician Characteristics and Distribution.* Includes general practice, the specialty now known as family medicine.

[74] U.S. Department of Health and Human Services, Health Resources and Services Administration, Bureau of Health Professions, *Physician Supply and Demand: Projections to 2020*, October 2006.

[75] COGME 20th Report, p. 5.

[76] U.S. Congress, Senate Committee on Finance, *Witness Testimony Fitzhugh Mullan, MD*, Workforce Issues in Health Care Reform: Assessing the Present and Preparing for the Future, 111th Cong., 1st sess., March 12, 2009, http://finance.senate.gov/hearings/testimony/2009test/031209fmtest.pdf.

[77] COGME 20th Report. For example, some researchers have predicted that in 2025 there will be between 35,000 and 44,000 too few primary care physicians to care for the adult population. See Jack M. Colwill, James M. Cultice, and Robin L. Kruse, "Will Generalist Physician Supply Meet Demands of An Increasing and Aging Population," *Health Affairs*, vol. 27, no. 3 (April 28, 2008), pp. w232-w241.

[78] GAO GME Report.

[79] COGME 20th Report.

[80] Medical Group Management Association, *Physician Compensation and Productivity Survey*, 2010 Report Based on 2009 Data, 2010, p. 3. These data are for physicians practicing in multispecialty practices. The average compensation for primary care physicians in single specialty practices is $183,000, while the average compensation for specialty physicians in single specialty practice is $385,000 in 2008. The 20th COGME report reports the average specialty compensation as $340,000 using the Medical Group Management Association specialty average in 2008. See COGME 20th Report, p. 22.

[81] The Physician's Foundation, The Physicians' Perspective: Medical Practice in 2008 Survey Summary and Analysis, October 2008, http://www.physiciansfoundations.org/usr_doc/PF_Survey_Report.pdf.

[82] Dale A. Newton and Martha Grayson, "Trends in Career Choice by U.S. Medical School Graduates," *Journal of the American Medical Association*, vol. 290, no. 9 (September 3, 2003).

[83] In addition to the types of provisions noted above, PPACA encourages additional training of non-physician providers (see "PPACA Provisions Targeting Physician Productivity"). Non-physician providers can increase the amount of primary care services available and lessen the need for primary care physicians.

[84] PHSA Section 747 had previously expired.

[85] PPACA also requires that 15% of the amount appropriated under this program be used for Physician Assistant training.

[86] These include community health centers, rural health clinics, and community mental health centers, among others.

[87] The NHSC and its role in altering the geographic distribution of physician supply is discussed below. Additional information about the NHSC program can also be found in CRS Report R40533, *Health Care Workforce: National Health Service Corps*, by Bernice Reyes-Akinbileje.

[88] H.R. 1216, which passed the House on May 26, 2011, would convert this funding from a direct appropriation to a discretionary authorization and would repeal any unobligated appropriations for this program.

[89] U.S. Department of Health and Human Services, Health Resources and Services Administration, "HHS announces new Teaching Health Centers Graduate Medical Education Program," press release, January 25, 2011, http://www.hrsa.gov/about/news/pressreleases/110125teachinghealthcenters.html.

[90] 2009 MedPAC Report and COGME 20th Report.

[91] For more information, see CRS Report R41196, *Medicare Provisions in the Patient Protection and Affordable Care Act (PPACA): Summary and Timeline*, coordinated by Patricia A. Davis.

[92] See discussion in CRS Report R41210, *Medicaid and the State Children's Health Insurance Program (CHIP) Provisions in PPACA: Summary and Timeline*, by Evelyne P. Baumrucker et al.

[93] Given this requirement, Section 5203 may also affect the geographic distribution of physicians. COGME, among others, has found shortages of pediatric subspecialists; see COGME 20th Report and Kevin O'Leary, Gerald Katz, and Fred Hollander, "The Shortage of Pediatric Subspecialists," *Children's Hospitals Today*, Winter 2003.

[94] COGME 20th Report.

[95] Edward Salsberg et al., "U.S. Residency Training Before and After the 1997 Balanced Budget Act," *Journal of the American Medical Association*, vol. 300, no. 10 (September 10, 2008), pp. 1174-1180.

[96] For more information, see CRS Report R41196, *Medicare Provisions in the Patient Protection and Affordable Care Act (PPACA): Summary and Timeline*, coordinated by Patricia A. Davis.

[97] The Centers for Medicare and Medicaid Services, the agency that administers the Medicare program, issued regulations implementing these provisions; see *Federal Register,* August 3, 2010, (75 CFR 46390-46432).

[98] Committee on the Future Health Care Workforce for Older Americans, Institute of Medicine, Retooling for an Aging America: Building the Health Care Workforce, Institute of Medicine, Washington, DC, April 14, 2008, http://www.iom.edu/CMS/3809/40113/53452.aspx and Institute of Medicine, Improving the Quality of Health Care for Mental and Substance-Use Conditions: Quality Chasm Series, Washington, DC, 2006, http://books.nap.edu/ openbook.php?record_id=11470.

[99] David C. Goodman and Elliot S. Fisher, "Physician Workforce Crisis? Wrong Diagnosis, Wrong Prescription," *New England Journal of Medicine,* vol. 358, no. 16 (April 17, 2008), pp. 1658-1661

[100] U.S. Government Accountability Office, *Medicare Physician Services: Utilization Trends Indicate Sustained Beneficiary Access with High and Growing Levels of Service in Some Areas of the Nation*, 09-559, August 28, 2009, http://www.gao.gov/new.items/d09559.pdf.

[101] Centers for Disease Control and Prevention, National Center for Health Statistics, *Health United States, 2007*, Figure 22, Data from the Area Resource File.

[102] See this report's discussion of HPSAs and MUA/Ps, in the section titled "Health Professional Shortage Areas and Medically Underserved Areas/Populations."

[103] See http://bhpr.hrsa.gov/shortage/index.htm.

[104] David C. Goodman, "Twenty-Year Trends in Regional Variation in The U.S. Physician Workforce," *Health Affairs*, October 7, 2004, pp. VAR 90-VAR96.

[105] The converse is also true, whereby policies that aim to affect primary care supply may also affect the geographic distribution of the physician population.

[106] See COGME 20th Report.

[107] Frederick Chen et al., "Which Medical Schools Produce Rural Physicians? A 15-Year Update," *Academic Medicine*, vol. 85, no. 4 (April 2010), pp. 594-598, and GAO GME Report.

[108] CRS Report R40533, *Health Care Workforce: National Health Service Corps*, by Bernice Reyes-Akinbileje.

[109] See http://bhpr.hrsa.gov/shortage/.

[110] Note: community health centers are automatically designated as federally qualified health centers (FQHCs). For more information about FQHCs, see http://bphc.hrsa.gov/policies regulations/policies/index.html.

[111] See http://bhpr.hrsa.gov/shortage/.

[112] Laurence Baker, "Efforts to Expand Physician Supply," *Health Services Research*, vol. 43, no. 4 (July 18, 2008), pp. 1121-1127.

[113] GAO GME Report.

[114] Carl G. Morris et al., "Training Family Physicians in Community Health Centers: A Health Workforce Solution," *Health Services Research*, vol. 40, no. 4 (April 2008), pp. 271-276.

[115] See, for example, Institute of Medicine, Committee on Institutional and Policy-Level Strategies, *In the Nation's Compelling Interest: Ensuring Diversity in the Health Care Workforce* (Washington, DC: National Academy Press, 2004). This study also notes that a student's racial, ethnic, and geographic origin may also influence the choice to pursue medical education; therefore, some suggest that programs need to focus on students prior to college to encourage them to consider a career in medicine.

[116] Ibid. Howard K. Rabinowitz et al., "Critical Factors for Designing Programs to Increase the Supply and Retention of Rural Primary Care Physicians," *Journal of the American Medical Association*, vol. 286, no. 9 (September 5, 2001), pp. 1041-1048.

[117] E. Ray Dorsey, David Jarjoura, and Gregory W. Rutecki, "Influence of Controllable Lifestyle on Recent Trends in Specialty Choice by US Medical Students," *Journal of the American Medical Association*, vol. 290, no. 9 (September 3, 2003), pp. 1173-1178; and Association of American Medical Colleges, Division of Medical Education, GQ Student, Survey Priorities in Medical Education: All Schools Summary Report Final, Association of American Medical Colleges, Washington, DC, 2010, https://www.aamc.org/download/140716/data/2010_gq_all_schools.pdf. The majority of this research focuses on specialty choice; however, student preference for greater work/life balance would also extend to a preference to practice in settings where on-call hours can be spread across colleagues.

[118] In addition to physicians, National Health Service Corps scholarships and loan repayments are available to other health professionals such as dentists, nurses, psychologists, and social workers.

[119] GAO GME Report and HRSA Physician Supply report.

[120] P.L. 112-10 removed this requirement. The HHS FY2011 Operating Plan, required by P.L. 112-10, reduced NHSC discretionary funding by $117 million (from $141 million in FY2010 to $25 million in FY2011). However, the NHSC received a $290 million direct appropriation under PPACA; therefore, FY2011 funding for this program is higher than FY2010 funding.

[121] Institute of Medicine, Committee on Institutional and Policy-Level Strategies, *In the Nation's Compelling Interest: Ensuring Diversity in the Health Care Workforce* (Washington, DC: National Academy Press, 2004).

[122] Howard K. Rabinowitz et al., "Critical Factors for Designing Programs to Increase the Supply and Retention of Rural Primary Care Physicians," *Journal of the American Medical Association*, vol. 286, no. 9 (September 5, 2001), pp. 1041-1048.

[123] 20th COGME Report.

[124] Individuals from a rural area are more likely to enter rural practice. For example, see Howard K. Rabinowitz, James J. Diamond, Fred W. Markham, et al., "Critical Factors for Designing Programs to Increase the Supply and Retention of Rural Primary Care Physicians," *Journal of the American Medical Association*, vol. 286, no. 9 (September 5, 2001), pp. 1041-1048. This program was not funded in FY2011 and is not proposed for FY2012 funding.

[125] U.S. Government Accountability Office: (1) *Health Care Shortage Areas: Designation Not A Useful Tool for Directing Resources to the Underserved*, GAO/HEHS-95-200, Washington, DC, September 8, 1995; (2) *Health Workforce: Ensuring Adequate Supply and Distribution Remains Challenging*, GAO-01-1042T, Washington, DC, August 1, 2001; and (3) *Health Professional Shortage Areas*, GAO-07-84 Washington, DC, October 2006.

[126] Section 5602 also includes interim deadlines, such as establishing a rulemaking committee and publishing an interim final rule. More information about this process can be found at http://www.hrsa.gov/advisorycommittees/ shortage/index.html. As of this writing, the final rule has not been published.

[127] In 1998, the Secretary published a proposal to revise the HPSA methodology (Department of Health and Human Services, "Designation of Medically Underserved Populations and Health Professional Shortage Areas; Proposed Rule," 63 *Federal Register* 46583-46555, September 1, 1998). The proposal was subsequently withdrawn. In February 2008, HHS proposed a new rule (Department of Health and Human Services, "Designation of Medically Underserved Populations and Health Professional Shortage Areas; Proposed Rule," 73 *Federal Register* 11232-11281, February 29, 2008). In response to extensive comments, in July 2008, the Secretary announced that HHS would issue a new notice of public rulemaking for further review and public comment prior to issuing a final rule.

[128] David C. Goodman, "Improving Accountability for the Public Investment in Health Profession Education: It's Time to Try Health Workforce Planning," *Journal of the American Medical Association*, vol. 300, no. 10 (September 10, 2008), pp. 1205-1207.

[129] U.S. Government Accountability Office, *Health Professions Education Programs: Action Still Needed to Measure Impact*, 06-55, February 28, 2006.

[130] The Commission did not receive funding in FY2011, see Amy Goldstein, "Partisan Fights in Congress Stall Panel on Primary-Health-Care Shortage," *Washington Post*, May 13, 2011, National Edition.

[131] In September of 2010, HHS announced that it had awarded grants to 26 states under this program. Grants were awarded for either workforce planning activities (e.g., data collection and analysis) or for implementing development plans to address previously identified workforce needs. See U.S. Department of Health and Human Services, "HHS Awards $320

Million to Expand the Primary Care Workforce," press release, September 27, 2010, http://www.hhs.gov/ news/press/2010pres/09/20100927e.html.

[132] This center had existed previously within HRSA, but was renamed in accordance with this PPACA section.

[133] Ongoing efforts to reduce the budget deficit may also affect PPACA-authorized programs and their funding levels. For more information, see CRS Report R41965, *The Budget Control Act of 2011*, by Bill Heniff Jr., Elizabeth Rybicki, and Shannon M. Mahan.

In: Physician Practices
Editor: Isaak Angelidis

ISBN: 978-1-62618-184-7

Chapter 3

OFFICIAL HEARING MEMO FOR "HEALTH CARE REALIGNMENT AND REGULATION: THE DEMISE OF SMALL AND SOLO MEDICAL PRACTICES?"*

House Committee on Small Business

MEMORANDUM

To: Members, Small Business Subcommittee on Investigations, Oversight and Regulations
From: Committee staff
Date: July 16, 2012

On Thursday, July 19, 2012 at 10:00 a.m., the Small Business Subcommittee on Investigations, Oversight and Regulations will meet in Room 2360 of the Rayburn Building for the purpose of receiving testimony on small and solo physician practice consolidation.

---

* This is an edited, reformatted and augmented version of a Official Hearing Memo presented July 16, 2012 before the House Committee on Small Business, Subcommittee on Investigations, Oversight and Regulations.

I. INTRODUCTION

The practice of medicine has always been evolving due to research, but also for technological, societal and legal reasons.[1] For many years, medicine seemed to be a cottage industry, with physicians typically opening or joining a practice after medical school.[2] Over the past ten years, however, increasing numbers of physicians, particularly those in small and solo practices, have found independent practices to be economically unfeasible.[3] For a number of reasons, they are affiliating with larger medical practices or hospitals. The result may be a dramatic shift in the delivery of health care.

This hearing will provide an opportunity for Members to learn more about the reasons for these changes, and some assessments of what they mean.

II. THE CHANGING MEDICAL PRACTICE

In 2007-2008, there were about 741,000 physicians in the United States.[4] According to the American Medical Association (AMA), 78% of practicing primary care physicians[5] were in physician- owned offices, while 18% practiced in hospital or other institutional settings.[6] AMA counted 28% of physicians in physician-owned solo practices, 24% in practices of two to four physicians and 13% in practices of five to nine.[7]

According to the American Association of Orthopaedic Surgeons, the percentage of orthopaedic surgeons in small and solo practices has declined since 2004. In 2004, 76% reported practicing in small or solo practices; by 2010,the percentage was 64%.[8] In 2004,17% of orthopaedic surgeons reported practicing in large multi-specialty groups, academic centers or hospitals; by 2010,it was 30%.[9]

The nonpartisan Center for Studying Health System Change found that the trend of physicians joining larger practices and small practices merging has been going on for over ten years.[10] Its physician survey reflects both hospital purchases of physician practices and individual physicians (including those completing residencies) accepting positions with hospitals.[11]

In 2011,Accenture reported that physicians were continuing to sell their businesses and seek positions with health care systems and hospitals.[12] Accenture recent analysis of its survey data predicts that by 2013, less than one-third of physicians will be in private practices.[13] Similarly, an article in the

New England Journal of Medicine found that half of all practicing U.S. physicians are employed by hospitals or integrated delivery systems.[14]

A combination of factors has produced this apparent trend. Younger physicians want a stable income, a lifestyle free from being on call and the financial pressures of private practice, as well as financial assistance with medical school debt, malpractice insurance and health information technology.[15] Established physicians have found years of rising costs and meager increases in Medicare, Medicaid and private insurer reimbursement rates, changing regulations, an inability to recruit younger partners, and frustration with administrative tasks to be wearing on them.[16]

Some physicians also believe the share of patients from whom they cannot collect any money is increasing.[17] And they complain that Medicare reduced payments to doctors for certain tests or drugs by 10-40%, depending on the practice, but not hospitals.[18] For example, some physician offices that invested in diagnostic equipment, were subject to suspicion that they were sometimes ordering tests because they received a financial benefit. Once Medicare scaled back payments, some affected physicians could not make ends meet.[19] After Medicare's decision, the chief executive officer of the American College of Cardiology estimated that the number of cardiologists in private practice dropped by 50%.[20] Cardiologists who have a Medicare-heavy patient load, for example, may find that reimbursement cuts can destabilize their practices.[21] Oncologists were once permitted to profit from drug sales, purchasing quantities of drugs at wholesale prices and selling them to patients at higher prices, but Medicare later revised and lowered the reimbursement for those drugs. [22]

There have been reports of physicians facing bankruptcy.[23] Some say the economics of providing health care must change; that it's too expensive for them to practice, and they must turn away those who they can no longer subsidize.[24] Some are even taking on a second job.[25] Physicians have also cited the federal government's push for health information technology systems as a reason to sell or close their practice.[26]

At the same time, hospitals have seen lower levels of admissions as patients postpone non-essential (and sometimes essential) diagnostic tests and procedures due to the economic downturn. Hospital employment of physicians is seen as a way to increase referrals and admissions.[27] This increases a hospital's market share and may allow it to save on centralized and bulk purchasing of drugs and supplies.[28] In fact, some believe hospitals' employment of physicians is a kind of loss leader, with hospitals losing money on physician employment and recouping it on referrals to specialists who use their facilities.[29]

Hospitals must attract and employ the right combination of physicians from high-growth and revenue-producing specialties, such as cardiology, radiology and oncology, to bolster their patient volume.[30] Some hospitals have found financially-strapped physician practices to be good values and offered to purchase them, promising the physicians attractive salaries in part because hospitals can sometimes qualify for higher Medicare reimbursements.[31]

III. THE TREND'S EFFECT ON SMALL BUSINESSES

A. Small and Solo Medical Practices

The shift away from private practice to larger practices and hospitals means that physicians, depending on their resources and geographic location, may have more choices.

Physicians considering hospital or larger practice employment may find they need solid medical training and decision-making skills, as well as a team player attitude and knowledge of health information technology. Hospitals typically lose money when physician productivity falls, so some have replaced salaries with productivity- and quality-based [32] compensation.[33] Some physicians report feeling rushed with patients.

Hospitals often invite physicians employed there to take roles in management and governance to strengthen loyalty and improve clinical care.[34] The doctors who find this type of employment rewarding value its stability and feel relieved of private practice administrative burdens so they can concentrate on patient care.[35]

There are physicians who become hospital employees and regret their decision. Although they once felt burdened by administrative tasks, for example, as employees they may feel frustrated by the lack of control. Some private practice physicians who are feeling financial pressures don't want to become hospital employees or sell their practice.

They but want to keep practicing, but can't afford to, and sometimes can't even give away their solo practices.[36] The recession has made owning a small business more difficult, perhaps even more so for physicians, who have not trained to run a business.

Small and solo practices can be disadvantaged in negotiating with pharmaceutical companies and insurers. Large group practices can often negotiate higher fees from insurers and better prices from pharmaceutical companies because of their high patient volume.[37]

For a physician, the decision on what type of employment is best may be the model that provides the best trade-offs between autonomy and employment.[38]

Many physicians are considering leaving the practice of medicine at a time when the United States is experiencing a continuing physician shortage, especially of primary care physicians.[39] To meet the demand needed by an aging population and the expansion of health insurance provided by the health care law, we must enact policies that will encourage more students to study medicine.

B. Small Stakeholder Companies

Stakeholder small businesses include the medical device, health IT systems, pharmaceutical and office supply companies, for example, which call on physician offices as customers. These businesses, whose customers are physicians now employed by hospitals or larger practices, may find that they need different sales strategies.[40]

Instead of the physician who owns a small practice, or the physician's office manager, the stakeholder may now be dealing with a hospital or large practice's corporate purchasing officer.

That organization may already have a long-standing sales relationship with another company. These arrangements may have implications for negotiating, pricing and competition.[41]

IV. Issues for the Subcommittee

The Subcommittee Members may want to consider the following issues:

A. Are there real trends from small and solo practices to larger practices and hospitals?
B. What is the economic impact of fewer small and solo practices?
C. Will the health care law accelerate this trend? D. Can small and solo practices survive?

CONCLUSION

This hearing will provide an opportunity for Members to learn more about the current physician practice arrangements, the reasons for them, and their implications.

End Notes

[1] THE PHYSICIANS FOUNDATION, HEALTH REFORM AND THE DECLINE OF THE PHYSICIAN PRACTICE 4 (2010) [hereinafter Decline of Physicians] at http://www.physiciansfoundation.org/ uploaded Files/Health%20Reform%20and%20the% 20Decline%20of%20Physi cian%20Private%20Practice.pdf.

[2] 5. J. Swensen, M.D., M.M.M., G. 5. Meyer, M.D., E. C. Nelson, D.Sc., M.P.H., G.C. Hunt, M.D., M.B.A.,D. B. Pryor, M.D., J.l. Weissberg, M.D., G.S. Kaplan, M.D., J. Daley, M.D., G.R. Yates, M.D., M.R. Chassin, M.D., M.P.P., M.P.H., B. James,M.D., M.Stat., & D. Berwick, M.D.,M.P.P., From Cottage Industry to Postindustrial Care- the Revolution in Health Care Delivery, N. Engl. J. Med. (Feb. 4, 2010), at http://www.nejm.org/doi/fuii/ 10.1056/NEJMp0911199.

[3] See, e.g., Parija Kavilanz, Doctors Going Broke, CNN MONEY (Jan. 9, 2012), at http: //money.cnn.com/2012/01/05/smallbusiness/doctors broke/index.htm, and Gardiner Harris, More Doctors Giving Up Private Practices, N.Y. TIMES (Mar. 25, 2010),at http://www.nvtimes. com/2010/03/26/hea lth/policy/26docs.htmI?pagewa nted=alI.

[4] DONALD BARR,M.D.,PH.D., INTRODUCTION TO U.S. HEALTH POLICY: THE ORGANIZATION, FINANCING AND DELIVERY OF HEALTH CARE IN AMERICA (3'd ed. 2011).

[5] Primary care was defined in this AMA survey as encompassing family practice, general internal medicine and pediatrics. Some organizations also include geriatrics in the definition of primary care.

[6] American Medical Association Survey Data (2007-2008). Email from Aiken Hackett, Assistant Director, Congressional Affairs, American Medical Association, to Committee staff (May 30,2012) (on file with recipient).

[7] /d.

[8] Email from Graham Newsom, Associate Director, American Association of Orthopaedic Surgeons, to Committee staff (June 6,2012) (on file with recipient).

[9] /d.

[10] Email from Paul Ginsburg, Ph.D., President, Center for Studying Health System Change, to Committee staff (June 6, 2012) (on file with the recipient).

[11] /d.

[12] CLINICAL TRANSFORMATION: DRAMATIC CHANGES AS PHYSICIAN EMPLOYMENT GROWS,ACCENTURE (2011) at http://www.accenture.com/us-en/Pages/insight-clinical-transformation-physician-employmentgrows.aspx?utmsource=feedburner&utm medium= feed&utmcampaign=Feed: +AccentureHealth and Life Sciences Research+ (AccentureHealth and Life Sciences Research) [hereinafter Accenture survey].

[13] /d.

[14] R.Kocher, M.D. & N.Sanhi, Hospitals' Race to Employ Physicians- The Logic Behind a Money-Losing Proposition, N. ENGL. J. MED. (May 12, 2011),at http://www.nejm.org/doi/fuii/10.1056/NEJMp1101959.

[15] MGMA PLACEMENT REPORT at 1. See also email from Paul Ginsburg, Ph.D. President, Center for Studying Health Systems Change, to Committee staff (June 6, 2012) (on file with the recipient).

[16] ACCENTURE SURVEY at 2.

[17] Gardiner Harris, More Doctors Giving Up Private Practices, N.Y. TIMES (Mar. 25, 2010),at http://www.nytimes.com/2010/03/26/health/policv/ 26docs.html?pagewanted=all.

[18] Manoj Jain, Doctors in Private Practice Are Now Joining Hospital Staffs, WASHINGTON Post (March 12,2012) at http://www.washing tonpost. com/national/health-science/doctors-in-private-practices-are-now- joining-hospital-staffs/2012/02/14/giQAEFz07R story.html.

[19] /d.

[20] Gardiner Harris, More Doctors Giving Up Private Practices, N.Y. TIMES (Mar. 25, 2010),at http://www.nytimes.com/2010/03/26/health/policv/ 26docs.html?pagewanted=all.

[21] Parjs Kavilanz, Doctors Going Broke, CNN MONEY (January 6,2012),at http://money.cnn.com/2012/01/0S/smallbusiness/doctors broke/index.htm.

[22] /d.

[23] /d.

[24] /d.

[25] /d.

[26] See Gardiner Harris, More Doctors Giving Up Private Practices, N.Y. TIMES (Mar. 25, 2010),at http:Uwww.nytimes.com/2010/03/ 26/health /policy/26docs. html?pagewanted =all;Gardiner Harris, Family Physician Can't Give Away Solo Practice, N.Y. TIMES (Apr. 11,2011) at http: Uwww.nytimes. com/2011/04/23/health/ 23doctor.html?pagewanted= all;and The Family Physician's Practice Affiliation Guide 3,Florida Academy of Family Physicians, at http://www.fafp.org/pdf/aco/FL practice affiliation guide 2011.pdf.

[27] Ann S. O'Malley, Amelia M. Bond & Robert A. Berenson, Rising Hospital Employment of Physicians: Better Quality, Higher Costs? Center for Studying Health Systems Change, at http:Uwww.hschange.com/ CONTENT/1230/.

[28] Manoj Jain, Doctors in Private Practice Are Now Joining Hospital Staffs, WASHINGTON Post (March 12, 2012) at http:Uwww.washingtonpost. com/national/health-science/doctors-in-private-practices-are-now- joining-hospital- staffs/2012/02/14/giQAEFz07R story.html.

[29] R. Kocher, M.D. & N. Sanhi, Hospitals' Race to Employ Physicians- The Logic Behind a Money-Losing Proposition, N. ENGL. J. MED. (May 12, 2011),at http:ljwww.nejm.org/doi/fuii/10.1056/NEJMpl101959.

[30] ACCENTURE SURVEY at 2.

[31] Manoj Jain, Doctors in Private Practice Are Now Joining Hospital Staffs, WASHINGTON PosT (March 12,2012) at http:Uwww.washingtonpost. com/national/health-science/doctors-in-private-practices-are-now-joining-hospital-staffs/2012/02/14/giQAEFz07R story.html.

[32] NEW ENGLAND JOURNAL at 3.

[33] Ann S. O'Malley, Amelia M. Bond & Robert A. Berenson, Issue Brief No. 136: Rising Hospital Employment of Physicians: Better Quality, Higher Costs? Center for Studying Health Systems Change, at http:Uwww. hschange.com/CONTENT/1230/.

[34] /d.

[35] Morning Edition: Hospitals Lure Doctors Away from Private Practice (NPR radio broadcast, October 13, 2010) at http:ljwww.npr.org/ templates/story/story.php?storyld=l30237412.

[36] Gardiner Harris, Family Practice Physician Can't Give Away Solo Practice, N.Y. TIMES (April22, 2011) at http://www.nvtimes.com/2011/04/ 23/health/23doctor.html? pagewanted=all.

[37] ld.

[38] ACCENTURE SURVEY at 3.

[39] Suzanne Sataline and Shirley S. Wang, Medical Schools Can't Keep Up, WALL ST. J. (April12,2010) at http:ljonline.wsj.com/article/SB10001424052702304506904575180331528424238.html.

[40] ACCENTURE SURVEY at 2.

[41] Id. at 3.

In: Physician Practices
Editor: Isaak Angelidis

ISBN: 978-1-62618-184-7

Chapter 4

TESTIMONY OF MARK SMITH, PRESIDENT, MERRITT HAWKINS. HEARING ON "HEALTH CARE REALIGNMENT AND REGULATION: THE DEMISE OF SMALL AND SOLO MEDICAL PRACTICES?"*

INTRODUCTION

Mr. Chairman and Distinguished Members of the Subcommittee,

My name is Mark Smith and I am the President of Merritt Hawkins, the largest physician search and consulting firm in the United States and a company of AMN Healthcare, the nation's largest health care workforce solutions company. In the course of my 22 years with Merritt Hawkins I have consulted with hundreds of physician practices and health care facilities across the country, and my company has produced numerous white papers, surveys, presentations and books concerning physician practice patterns, physician supply and demand trends, physician compensation, physician morale and related topics.

I appreciate the opportunity to address the subcommittee today on the decline of solo and small physician practices.

---

* This is an edited, reformatted and augmented version of a Testimony Presented July 19, 2012 before the House Committee on Small Business, Subcommittee on Investigations, Oversight and Regulations.

The Arc of Physician Practice

Those who remember the 1970s television show "Marcus Welby, M.D." may still have an image in mind of physicians as small business owners running their own practices, perhaps with the assistance of a younger partner or associate. This classic model of independent, small physician practice still exists, but it is rapidly becoming an anachronism. Today, physicians are more likely to be hospital or medical group employees than they are to be medical practice owners. This is particularly true of medical residents completing their training. In a 2011 survey of final-year medical residents conducted by Merritt Hawkins, only 1 percent of respondents indicated they would prefer an independent solo practice.[1] By contrast, 60 percent indicated they would prefer to be employed by a hospital, medical group, outpatient clinic or academic facility. In the 12-month period from April 1, 2011 to March 31, 2012, Merritt Hawkins conducted over two thousand, seven hundred physician search assignments on behalf of hospitals, medical groups and small physician practices nationwide. In only 47 of these assignments – or two percent – were we tasked with finding a physician to start a solo practice or to join a solo practitioner as a partner. By contrast, in 2004, 42 percent of Merritt Hawkins' search assignments featured a solo setting or a small practice partnership.[2]

Furthermore, in the 12 month period alluded to above, 63 percent of Merritt Hawkins' physician search assignments featured hospital employment of the physician, up from 56 percent the previous year and only 11 percent in 2004. If this trend continues, we project that in two years, 75 percent of all newly hired physicians will be hospital employees.

In short, virtually no one wants to be Marcus Welby anymore.

A study by the national consulting firm Accenture further underlines this trend. It indicates that in 2000, independent physicians owning their own practices comprised 57 percent of all physicians. That number declined to 43 percent in 2009 and is projected to decline to 33% by 2013.[3]

This represents a fundamental transformation in the structure of physician practices, away from the classic private practice model and towards employment and an increasingly diverse number of other practice styles.

Five Reasons

There are five primary reasons why this transformation is taking place that I will address in order. They include:

- Flat or declining reimbursement
- Growing regulatory and administrative paperwork Malpractice insurance costs
- The implementation of information technology The effects of health reform

Reimbursement

In the days of Marcus Welby, both Medicare and private insurers typically paid physicians retrospectively for "usual, customary and reasonable charges." The physician used his or her judgment regarding patient treatment and generally was paid for services invoiced at an amount above the physicians' cost of doing business.

This system has been repeatedly modified since in an effort to reduce costs and manage care. Physician reimbursement in some cases has been cut or has not kept pace with inflation. The result is that many physicians now see little connection between their own labor and business costs and the amount for which they are reimbursed.

In a national survey of physicians Merritt Hawkins conducted on behalf of the non-profit group The Physicians Foundation, over 68 percent of physicians indicated that Medicaid pays them less than their cost of doing business, over 43 percent said some HMOs and PPOs pay them less than their costs, and over 36 percent said Medicare pays them less than their costs.[4] In some cases, physicians are not paid at all for their services. Over 53 percent of physicians surveyed said they provide $35,000 or more each year of uncompensated care.

This is a difficult business model to sustain. Many physicians have responded by seeing more patients (and consequently spending less time per patient) and by excluding certain types of patients from their practices. In the survey cited above, over 33 percent of physicians said they have closed their practices to Medicaid patients, over 30 percent have closed their practices to some HMO and PPO patients, and over 11 percent have closed their practices to Medicare patients. Nevertheless, some small private practices physicians are having trouble keeping their doors open. There have been reports in the media in recent months about a growing number of private practice physicians going out of business -- an unusual occurrence throughout most of my career.[5]

This trend may reach a culmination on January 1, 2013, when physicians are due for a 30 percent reduction of their Medicare reimbursement rates under Medicare's Sustainable Growth Rate (SGR) formula. Though these cuts have been deferred in the past, it is difficult for small private practices to operate in a climate of uncertainty in which their revenues could be reduced by a devastating margin.

By contrast, employment by a hospital, medical group or other entity provides physicians with the security of a salary and the freedom from the fear that their practices will go under.

Regulatory/Administrative Paperwork

Virtually all businesses in the United States are subject to regulatory compliance, and physician practices are no different. As small business owners, solo and small practice physicians must abide by equal opportunity employment laws, worker safety laws, local real estate ordnances and many other rules and regulations. On top of this, physicians work in one of the most highly regulated of all professions. It has been reported that the U.S. federal tax code runs to some 75,000 pages, whereas the Medicare regulatory code by which physicians must abide runs to 130,000 pages.

Physicians must spend a significant amount of time on paperwork to ensure that they are compliant with the laws regulating their profession. As third party payer reimbursement policies become more restrictive, physicians also must perform considerable documentation to ensure that they are paid.

In the physician survey referenced above, physicians reported that they spend an average of 15 hours per week on non-clinical paperwork duties, or about 26 percent of their total working hours. These administrative duties, and the general pressures of running a business, can be alien to the mindset and makeup of many physicians, who are essentially scientists by training and caregivers by inclination. Many physicians perceive that employment will reduce the amount of administrative and regulatory duties to which they are subject and allow them to focus on medicine.

Malpractice

Among the various costs of doing business, small private practitioners must pay for their own malpractice insurance. Malpractice insurance costs vary by region and by specialty and can be quite substantial. The annual cost for malpractice insurance for an obstetrician/gynecologist in Broward County, Florida, for example, is $158,157 per year.[6] As malpractice insurance rates remain high, employment becomes an attractive option to physicians because employers typically provide malpractice insurance as part of the employment contract.

Information Technology

For a variety of reasons, physicians are obliged to incorporate a growing level of information technology into their practices, particularly in the form of electronic medical records (EMR). Those who not do so face reductions in their Medicare reimbursement in coming years. While the federal government has provided funds for physicians to implement EMR, many still find it difficult to do so due to lack of time or available expertise. Sixty-nine percent of physicians in The Physicians Foundation survey referenced above indicated they have not implemented EMR due to lack of resources or expertise, 68 percent said they do not have the personnel to implement EMR, and 61 percent said they do not have the time. In addition, some physicians are doubtful that EMR will increase their efficiency and others have concerns about EMR and patient confidentiality.

The necessity of implementing information technology is a prominent example of how the resources, expertise and time of small medical practice owners is being taxed in today's increasingly complex and demanding medical practice environment.

A growing number of physicians are embracing employment as a potential refuge from these challenges and concerns.

Health Reform

Health reform is a driver of a number of health care trends, including the general decline of small, independent private practice. I include in the term "health reform" not just provisions of the Patient Protection and Affordable Care Act but also market forces taking place apart from the Act. So defined, health reform encourages the consolidation of physician practices and hospitals into larger entities. Larger organizations are required in the post reform era to achieve the economies of scale needed to expand access to care while reducing costs.

In addition, health reform encourages the formation of new delivery models such as Accountable Care Organizations (ACOs) which depend on both hospital/physician alignment and the use of advanced information technology. ACOs are risk bearing entities, and as such require a high level of administrative and business expertise. It is difficult for solo or small practice physicians to participate in these models, which more naturally lend themselves to hospital employment of physicians.

CONCLUSION

Combined, these factors and others have created conditions in which the small, private medical practice model is increasingly untenable. This model is only likely to persist in any numbers in smaller, rural areas where there are few physicians, and even here physicians will likely need to partner or affiliate with larger entities in some way. The solo, small practice model also may persist among those physicians willing and able to maintain "cash only" or so-called concierge practices in which physicians directly contract with patients and do not accept third-party payments. Whether the proliferation of this model in wide geographic areas is possible remains to be seen.

Otherwise, physicians are likely to be employed by multi-physician groups or by hospitals, as the era of Marcus Welby rapidly disappears in the rear view mirror.

Thank you for the opportunity to address the Subcommittee and for examining the challenges facing America's solo and small practice physicians.

End Notes

[1] Survey of Final-Year Medical Residents. Merritt Hawkins, 2011
[2] Review of Physician Recruiting Incentives. Merritt Hawkins, 2012
[3] Adopting to a New Model of Physician Employment. Accenture, August, 2011
[4] Survey: The Physicians Perspective. The Physicians Foundation, 2008
[5] Kavilanz, Parija. Doctors going broke. CNNMoney.com. Jan. 6, 2012
[6] www.mymedicalpracticeinsurance.com

In: Physician Practices
Editor: Isaak Angelidis

ISBN: 978-1-62618-184-7

Chapter 5

TESTIMONY OF DR. LOUIS MCINTYRE, WESTCHESTER ORTHOPEDIC ASSOCIATES. HEARING ON "HEALTH CARE REALIGNMENT AND REGULATION: THE DEMISE OF SMALL AND SOLO MEDICAL PRACTICES?"*

Mr. Chairman and members of the Committee, thank you very much for allowing me to participate in this hearing today.

I joined Westchester Orthopedic Associates in 1994. It was, and is, the oldest continuous orthopedic specialty practice in Westchester County, New York. When I joined the practice, it resided in a 3000 sq foot office and had 9 employees, including the four orthopedic surgeons that worked there. We wanted to grow our practice and improve the quality of the care we delivered to our patients. In 1995 we moved into a new 6000 sq foot office with better parking and access from all areas of our county with a central location close to interstate highways. We hired additional workers as the clerical demands of managed care insurance plans increased the need for insurance verification and pre-authorizations. We added an additional orthopedic surgeon to take care of patients with neck and back problems that year also. The build out for the new office space cost $500,000.

---

* This is an edited, reformatted and augmented version of a Testimony presented July 19, 2012 before the House Committee on Small Business, Subcommittee on Investigations, Oversight and Regulations.

The late 1990s brought two challenging trends: decreasing reimbursement and increasing costs of business secondary to the clerical demands of insurance companies and skyrocketing malpractice costs. Where in 1995 we had one employee to verify and authorize treatments for all our patients, we now needed one employee per doctor to satisfy these tasks and maintain quality service. The cost malpractice insurance, increased from $40,000 per year in 1994 to $110,000, for every doctor, in 2010. We attempted to negotiate increased rates of reimbursement with insurance companies to offset the increasing costs but were unsuccessful because of lack of market share. We formed a network of orthopedic surgeons to attempt to improve the economic power of private practices but were unable to affect reimbursement rates because of concerns over antitrust issues.

To address these issues, we embarked on an ambitious plan to increase our scope of practice by adding additional doctors and ancillary services to improve patient access to care, increase convenience, and improve our revenue stream. We hired doctors to manage pediatric orthopedic problems and pain management issues. In 2002 we added a Magnetic Resonance Imaging (MRI) machine with an additional 2000 sq feet of office and two employees. We implemented an Electronic Medical Record (EMR) to decrease costs and improve quality. We thus became very early adopters of a technology that is now mandated. Our total cost for the EMR implementation was about $500,000. This represents about $100,000 per doctor over the total span of implementation. Initially we saved about $15,000 per doctor per year starting 4 years after implementation in 2002. Additional costs related to upgrades for computerized physician order entry plus the hiring of EMR scribes to enter data negated this savings starting in 2009.

We also built an ambulatory surgery center adjacent to our office in an 11,000 sg foot building at a cost of $5,000,000. The surgery center employed 25 people and performed over 700 cases per month at its busiest in 2008. In 2005, we acquired an additional 5000 sq feet of office space in our building that had housed an MRI scanner. We updated the scanner and built a state of the art physical therapy (PT) center to standardize the quality of PT delivered to our patients. The build out for the MRI and PT cost $400,000.

When completely configured, we had just under 50 employees. All had health insurance and a generous profit sharing plan, as well as paid sick and vacation leave. Patients appreciated the convenience of being able to receive all of their musculoskeletal care needs from evaluation to imaging to physical therapy to surgery in a coordinated and contiguous setting. When I started we were a $2,000,000 business. We invested over $6,500,000 to grow and improve this business. The practice generated $5,400,000 in revenues at its height in 2007.

Unfortunately, the regulatory environment and insurance market worked against us. There was continued negative pressure on reimbursement from both Medicare and private payers. The American Academy of Orthopaedic Surgeons (AAOS) estimates that orthopedic surgeons' Medicare reimbursements revenue decreased 28% in the last decade. In addition, because reimbursement from insurers is based on the Medicare Resource Based Relative Value Scale (RBRVS), private insurers reimbursement had fallen in a similar fashion. Practice costs , however, have continued to rise, especially malpractice insurance rates as illustrated by an almost 300% rise in my rates from 1994 through 2010.

In 2009 and 2010, two laws passed by Congress further complicated the landscape for private practice. The American Recovery and Reinvestment Act (ARRA) mandated the adoption of EMR for all physicians serving Medicare patients. Even though we had implemented an EMR, the Meaningful Use Criteria accompanying the regulations still represented a significant burden for us in terms of data collection and quality reporting rules. Complying with the new rules would further increase our cost with no increase in reimbursement and the $44,000 per physician available from HITECH to offset the cost of purchasing an EMR would not even cover half our investment in the technology. The Patient Protection and Affordable Care Act (PPACA), enacted in 2010, represents another burden for private practices in terms of decreased reimbursement, mandated quality reporting, and the movement toward risk sharing reimbursement methodologies.

The combination of decreased reimbursement, increased reporting requirements, the need for huge outlays for technology improvements and uncertainty about future earning potential are driving private practice physicians to seek employed positions. Doctors know that they cannot meet the all demands placed upon them in an environment of shrinking revenues and increasing costs and take care of patients at the same time. Indeed, according to the AAOS , the employment of orthopedic surgeons by hospitals has increased 300% in the last 5 years. According to Merritt-Hawkins, a leading physician employment search firm, physician employment search assignments for hospital employed positions went from 11% in 2004 to 56% of all searches in 2011.

For all of the above cited reasons we decided to forgo private practice and become employees of White Plains Hospital last year. This year the other orthopedic group in our city also decided to become employees of the same hospital and will join our group in October. The hospital has embarked on an ambitious project to employ physicians in the ambulatory setting; the first time it has ever done so. The multispecialty practice next to us, WestMed, employs over 200 physicians. Clearly, the employed model is winning out over private practice in Westchester County.

There are advantages for both physicians and patients with the employed model. Doctors have more financial security knowing exactly what their income will be for a given timeframe. They no longer worry about losing money taking care of the uninsured and underinsured. They are freed from dealing with troublesome human resource issues and regulatory burdens, which become the purview of their employer. IT and the cost associated with it are also transferred to the employer.

Employment, however, significantly decreases physician autonomy in affecting the environment in which patient-care takes place. The management philosophy of hospital administrators is usually process driven while physicians are much more goal and outcome oriented. This does change how patients interface with a practice. Physicians are in the position to interact with patients on a daily basis and identify deficiencies in care delivery. Administrators are more removed and may not appreciate patient care issues that arise in the ambulatory setting. Hospitals are also more risk averse, and are less willing to examine new and untested practice projects.

As more physicians, especially those right out of training seek employed positions there will be a generation of physicians who will have never experienced private practice and the business aspect of medicine. They will be unaware of the costs and management issues of providing health care. There is concern that employed physicians will see less of a need to join and maintain membership in medical societies and specialty organizations that in the past have been oriented toward the private practice of medicine. How these concerns will affect the profession is unknown at this time.

Economically, there is concern that as the negative pressure on reimbursement continues, future contract negotiations between doctors and hospitals will become more contentious and will lead to dissatisfaction. Physicians may then band together and unionize to protect their economic rights. This would be a significant reversal of the profession toward physician, as opposed to patient, advocacy. Indeed, I believe this would herald the end of medicine as a profession and the start of medicine as a trade association.

Lastly, private practice is a significant economic engine employing vast numbers of people and paying taxes to support government services. A study conducted by the Medical Society for the State of New York in 2009 showed that the private practice of medicine was the fifth largest employer in Westchester County, second in business establishments, third 3rd in personal income taxes paid, and seventh in corporate sales taxes paid. Westchester Orthopedics paid significant federal and state corporate taxes plus sales taxes. Now it is part of a hospital and is tax exempt in all those categories. The loss of tax revenue resulting from private practice physicians migrating to hospital employment may be significant and worthy of further study.

There will not be employed positions for all of the doctors of Westchester County or the United States. There is, and will continue to be, and increased need for physicians with the implementation of PPACA starting in 2014. If private practice disappears, patient access to care, local employment and tax revenue will all suffer. We need to strengthen private practice as well as the other models of healthcare delivery to ensure patient access to quality care.

Thank for the opportunity to share my thoughts and experiences with your committee.

In: Physician Practices
Editor: Isaak Angelidis

ISBN: 978-1-62618-184-7

Chapter 6

Statement of Joseph M. Yasso, Jr., D.O., Heritage Physicians Group. Hearing on "Health Care Realignment and Regulation: The Demise of Small and Solo Medical Practices?"*

Chairman Coffman, Ranking Member Schrader, and Members of the Subcommittee, on behalf of the American Osteopathic Association (AOA), thank you for the opportunity to testify today on the impact health care realignments and regulation are having upon small and solo medical practices. My name is Joseph Yasso, I am a board certified osteopathic family physician in Independence, Missouri. I am currently the medical director of Heritage Physicians Group, a small physician practice, which is owned by the Hospital Corporation of America. My practice is comprised of three physicians, including myself and a family nurse practitioner. We provide the full array of family medicine services including pediatrics, adolescent health and women's health. We are located in a suburban area serving a large Medicaid population.

Currently, I sit on the Board of Trustees of the AOA. In my 35 years as an AOA member I have been able to interact and work with my colleagues as the practice of medicine has transformed. I directly witnessed this in my previous

* This is an edited, reformatted and augmented version of a statement presented July 19, 2012 before the House Committee on Small Business, Subcommittee on Investigations, Oversight and Regulations.

capacity as Chair of the AOA's Bureau of State Government Affairs and Bureau of Membership.

In over three decades treating patients after separating from the United States Army as a captain and flight surgeon, I have worked in various settings including small practices, hospitals and academic medicine at the Kansas City University of Medicine and Biosciences (KCUMB). Today, I am pleased to share with you my personal experience of how impactful health care realignment and regulations are upon decisions made by new and established physicians alike. After leaving the Army, I entered a small practice with two other physicians that we ultimately chose to sell in 1992 due to multiple financial and regulatory concerns, similar to those my colleagues in practice are facing today. I will speak to the challenges faced by small and solo practices, trends I see in my colleagues' practice types, and how opportunities exist in this evolution if incentives are appropriately aligned.

BACKGROUND ON THE OSTEOPATHIC PROFESSION

The osteopathic profession has a strong and distinguished history of educating, training and placing physicians in underserved communities. This commitment began in the late 1800's and continues today. Our academic and training model, while not unique to the osteopathic profession, places an emphasis on preparing osteopathic medical students for careers in general physician specialties such as primary care, obstetrics, general surgery and emergency medicine. Our academic curriculum, along with a community-based training model, is the primary reason that the profession has enjoyed great success in the production of primary care physicians and general surgeons. Today, 60.5 percent of all osteopathic physicians practice in a primary care specialty. Currently, one in five medical students in the United States is enrolled in a college of osteopathic medicine. We are one of the fastest growing fields in the health care sector.

Currently, there are 26 colleges of osteopathic medicine operating on 34 campuses. We estimate that 2 to 3 new colleges will open in the next few years. Many of our colleges are located in geographic regions with acute physician shortages, such as western Washington, Arizona, and the full span of Appalachia where we have four schools. This commitment to establishing colleges and training opportunities in areas of need is key to meeting the health care needs of underserved communities and is indicative of the profession's commitment to this cause. The nation's colleges of osteopathic medicine currently graduate more than 3,600 osteopathic physicians. In 2013 that number will grow to 4,700 and by 2015 over 5,000 osteopathic physicians will graduate each year. If current trends continue, by 2020 there will be over 100,000 practicing osteopathic physicians in the United States.

Challenges Faced by Small and Solo Practitioners

The health care delivery system is constantly evolving. Today, physician practices face new demands as required by statute and regulation. These include the adoption of electronic health records and electronic-prescribing systems, preparation for coding under ICD-10, implementation of quality measures, and adjusting to other changes in the health care delivery system. These additional policies and procedures are important and are primarily beneficial to efficiency as well as to providing improved patient care. However, each new requirement can be quite costly to a physician practice operating as a small business. The accumulated cost and subsequent time spent implementing new systems or procedures have an impact on revenue. For instance, making the decision to move forward with an electronic health record (EHR) system requires a considerable amount of time and financial investment for a physician practice. In a February 2012 survey conducted by the National eHealth Collaborative, stakeholders were asked "What are the biggest challenges to achieving widespread health information exchange?" The top response, funding and sustainability, garnered 61percent.

While physicians in all practice settings face unnecessary and costly administrative hassles, the burden on small practices is particularly disproportionate, detracting from the time available for patient care. A physicians' role in coordinating care and making needed referrals typically involves frequent interaction with managed care organizations and other third-party payers to obtain required approvals, services, and payment, resulting in paperwork and overhead expenses. For example, the new restriction that requires consumers who use their tax advantaged accounts to purchase over-the-counter (OTC) medications to obtain a prescription from their physician is counterintuitive to enhancing access to health care and promoting patient-centered care. This provision of the Affordable Care Act increases costs to the health care system and places a new administrative burden on already over-burdened physicians. The AOA was pleased to testify on this topic before the House Ways and Means Committee earlier this year.

The AOA has urged the Centers for Medicare and Medicaid Services (CMS) to re-evaluate penalty timelines associated with the value-based modifier, electronic prescribing, the Physician Quality Reporting System (PQRS), electronic health records and ICD-10. The "imminent storm" associated with implementation of these programs creates a burden faced by physicians in complying simultaneously. A March 28 letter sent to CMS by numerous physician organizations stated, "We urge CMS to re-evaluate the penalty timelines associated with these programs and examine the administrative and financial burdens and intersection of these various federal regulatory programs. We also urge CMS to use its discretionary authority provided by Congress under these programs to develop solutions for synchronizing these programs to minimize burdens to physician practices, and propose these solutions in the physician fee schedule proposed rule for calendar year 2013." The AOA appreciates CMS efforts to align its various programs; however more steps are needed to streamline the requirements, such as the various data submission deadlines involving such programs as PQRS, value-based payment modifier, the EHR incentive program, and e-Prescribing Incentive Program. These deadlines and other reporting requirements must be better aligned to eliminate the administrative burden and confusion caused by the current demands.

An additional overarching and overwhelming challenge faced by all physicians, one especially felt by those in small and solo practices, is the instability of the physician payment system stemming from the flawed sustainable growth rate (SGR) formula which threatens annual cuts to physician payments. This looming concern forces small practices with limited revenues and narrow margins to make difficult decisions about whether to lay off staff, reduce their Medicare patient population, defer investments or opt for early retirement. The AOA supports full repeal of the SGR and replacement with a payment model that appropriately compensates for the services they are providing patients.

Trends in Practice Types

Today's medical school graduates are faced with difficult decisions after completing their education and training. The average osteopathic medical school graduate has a debt nearing $200,000. As you can imagine, this makes the prospect of opening a small practice extremely daunting. To reach medical students early in the pipeline, Congress should examine options for targeted scholarship, loan deferment and loan forgiveness programs to encourage medical school graduates to invest in the small primary care practices so many communities are lacking.

In a recent environmental scan conducted by the AOA, a survey was sent to state associations and specialty colleges to collect information on issues and trends confronting the profession. The respondents were asked to report on the three most important medical practice trends. Overwhelmingly, a shift from private practice physicians to employed physicians was noted. In addition, the collective cost of increasing administrative, financial and licensing burdens on physicians was also a dominant trend.

This spring, the American College of Osteopathic Family Physicians (ACOFP) retained Avenue M Group, LLC to conduct a survey of its membership. The survey included questions and findings related to practice types and settings. The survey found that 60 percent of family physicians are "employees with no ownership stake in a practice." The most significant change in practice characteristics from a similar survey conducted in 2010 was the percentage of physicians who consider their primary employment setting to be a public non-profit hospital - 2 percent in 2010 increasing to 12 percent in 2012. Furthermore, new and established physicians are forced to consider and balance their personal financial debt, administrative and financial burdens resulting from rules and regulations, and their desire to practice in a specific type of setting. Often, the overwhelming collective burdens are cost prohibitive and outweigh desire for a practice setting akin to a small or solo practice. There are also physicians who wholeheartedly embrace the choice of becoming an employed physician. This option can provide physicians with greater security. Nonetheless, physicians should not be forced to enter an employed situation out of pure necessity, and should retain their option to choose their ideal practice type absent undue financial considerations and regulatory burdens.

Opportunities Through Aligned Incentives

The AOA believes opportunities exist in a patient-centered medical home model (PCMH) and within Accountable Care Organizations (ACOs) for physicians to continue managing patient care while still being able to operate as a small or solo practitioner. Neither model requires a physician to be employed by a hospital or large health system in order to be successful. Both PCMHs and ACOs allow for the sharing of resources such as equipment and facilities that a small or solo practitioner might not normally possess. In an effort to realize these opportunities, we have actively participated in the development of new payment models that support and advance the goals of care coordination and greater integration in delivery systems.

The PCMH provides opportunities for physicians to be paid for coordinating a patient's care, an activity that has not been valued traditionally. The AOA has actively engaged commercial insurers, business organizations, consumer groups and government health care programs on the development and implementation of patient-centered delivery models such as the PCMH. We have pursued this as a means of improving the delivery of health care, and also as a contributing solution to the escalating costs of health care. Numerous studies have demonstrated that greater coordination of health care services reduces overall spending on health care services. The spring 2012 survey found that 48 percent of family physicians currently identify their practice as a medical home or anticipate becoming a recognized medical home within 18 months.

ACOs also incentivize care coordination and allow physicians to benefit from shared savings stemming from a patient's improved health at a lower cost. Twenty-one percent of surveyed family physicians reported being part of an ACO, with 46 percent anticipating becoming a part of one in the next 18 months. In this regard, the AOA supports the efforts of the Center for Medicare and Medicaid Innovation (CMMI) in developing a shared-savings program that provides numerous options for providers. The Pioneer ACO program was designed for those providers already experienced in comprehensive coordinated care for their patients. In an effort to address initial cost concerns for new participants, the Advance Payment Model was created. This is a positive step toward ensuring all physicians can benefit from a shared-savings model without cost being a prohibitive factor. We believe that Congress should support the continued evolution of ACOs. We strongly support the concept of integrated delivery models as a means of improving the quality and efficiency of health care. We recommend that ACOs be better designed to allow for the virtual versus contractual alignment of physician practices as a means of achieving integration.

Appropriately aligned incentives can serve to foster success as a solo practice, a small practice, a group practice, or as an employed physician. Regulators should be cautious in creating additional financial burdens on physicians that would inhibit their ability to choose the practice setting that is most appropriate. Options should be retained for all practice settings that are not restricted in this regard.

CONCLUSION

In closing, the AOA believes that the transformation of the practice of medicine has undoubtedly impacted the ability of physicians to thrive in a small practice or as a solo practitioner. Physicians are faced with new financial and regulatory burdens that contribute to this conundrum. However, physicians are adapting to the changing practice of medicine by becoming patient-centered medical homes and participating in shared savings programs. As we work to improve the health care delivery system for patients, physicians must be provided appropriate payment and incentives to practice effectively in the setting of their choice. Patients deserve this level of access.

I would like to thank you and the members of the committee for affording me the opportunity to share my experiences and the AOA's perspective regarding this important topic affecting osteopathic physicians and our patients. The AOA appreciates the work that you do to promote policies that enable physicians to successfully operate as small businesses absent undue regulatory and financial burdens. We look forward to working with you in the weeks and months ahead to ensure that congressional action fosters, rather than impedes, the physician-patient relationship.

In: Physician Practices
Editor: Isaak Angelidis
ISBN: 978-1-62618-184-7

Chapter 7

STATEMENT OF SCOTT GOTTLIEB, M.D., RESIDENT FELLOW, AMERICAN ENTERPRISE INSTITUTE. HEARING ON "HEALTH CARE CONSOLIDATION AND COMPETITION AFTER PPACA"*

INTRODUCTION

Chairman Goodlatte, Ranking Member Watt, and Members of the Subcommittee, I appreciate the opportunity to testify here today.

By next year, about two-thirds of American physicians will be working as salaried employees of large groups and hospitals. This movement has been underway for years. Over the last decade, the number of independent physicians was falling by about 2% a year. But these trends are now accelerating. Many observers point to provisions in the recently enacted Patient Protection and Affordability Act (PPACA) as a primary driver. Starting in 2013, the number of independent physicians will start declining by 5% a year according to a recent report by Accenture Health.[1]

The largest proportion of these newly salaried physicians are being directly employed by hospitals or hospital owned medical practices.[2] Hospital physician employment rose 32% from 2000 to roughly 212,000 physicians in

* This is an edited, reformatted and augmented version of a statement presented May 18, 2012 before the House Judiciary Committee, Subcommittee on Intellectual Property, Competition and the Internet.

2010. That means that hospitals directly employ about a quarter of all U.S. physicians.[3,4]

These realities are reflected in multiple surveys. Another report found 70% of national hospital and health systems plan to hire more physicians in the next three years. Meanwhile, two-thirds of hospitals reported that they are seeing more requests from independent physician groups seeking direct employment or collaboration with hospitals.[5] This is confirmed by a recent review of the open job searches held by one of the country's largest physician-recruiting firms. It shows that nearly 50% are for jobs in hospitals, up from about 25% five years ago.[6]

According to the Medical Group Management Association, almost two-thirds of the doctors who signed employment contracts in 2009 entered into arrangements with hospitals. This includes half of all doctors' leaving residency training.[7] Surveys of physicians demonstrate that an increasing number of newly minted doctors prefer the salaried arrangements to the traditional private practice models. Recent survey data also shows that physicians believe the current employed trend will continue and be a preferred option for them.[8]

It's not only hospitals that are acquiring doctors. Health plans are also dipping their toes in the water, looking to purchase healthcare delivery organizations to gain more control over practices, utilization rates, and in turn costs. Toward the end of 2011, United Health Group purchased Monarch, the largest physician group in Orange County California with 2300 members. As another example, Pennsylvania-based insurer Highmark is teaming up with West Penn Allegheny Health System to compete with UPMC, the large, well-known medical center in Pittsburgh.[9]

Investment bankers who work on mergers and acquisitions in the healthcare services industry privately concede that there is a lot of activity among health plans looking to acquire physician networks. So far, the large health plans have not been able to buy as many assets as the hospitals. For their part, the doctors seem to prefer to sell their practices to hospitals rather than the health plans.

These trends aren't a consequence of natural market forces. It's the outgrowth of a deliberate industrial policy set in motion by changes in the way healthcare is being organized and reimbursed. These new arrangements have been hastened by PPACA. The law relies on layers of provisions designed to shift financial risk onto providers in a bid to move away from the fee-for-service reimbursement model that's blamed for excessive, and some argue inappropriate use of healthcare services.[10] PPACA contains deliberate constructs to industrialize healthcare by moving physicians into capitated arrangements and larger groups where reimbursement, utilization, and quality measures can be more tightly controlled. These arrangements have many champions, but also carry significant uncertainty.

As I will discuss at the close of my testimony, the only sure way that we're going to bend the cost curve is by coming up with fundamentally new ways to deliver healthcare services that improve efficiencies and enable us to get more medical care for each dollar we spend. These ideas are going to come forward the same way better ideas have always arisen – from start-ups backed by entrepreneurs, supported by investment capital, coming together in search of profits. Yet PPACA contains provisions that I fear tilt against these kinds of innovations. The legislation relies instead on arrangements that could serve to entrench existing players.

Principal among these new arrangements is the creation of Accountable Care Organizations (ACOs). This concept envisions that providers will consolidate into networks that will, in turn, take charge for the medical care of defined populations of patients. An ACO will be able to share in some of the savings that they achieve by reducing utilization and improving outcomes for the patients assigned to it. Along with other forms of capitated payment arrangements (such as bundled payments and medical homes) the combined effect of the legislation's payment reforms is to shift financial risk to providers. In the face of these changes, doctors are choosing to sell their medical practices rather than take on added uncertainty.

Many industry experts are asking whether the current trend to employ physicians is sustainable or just a revisiting of what occurred in the 1990s, when hospitals were employing physicians in response to managed care, growing competition, and pressure to aggregate market share. The 1990s mergers were mostly defensive gestures aimed at thwarting competition from expanding, for-profit hospital chains.

This time things may be different, and in many ways the same.

This time, there may be no turning back from these arrangements. Doctors who enter into these new salaried appointments may find themselves hard pressed to unwind these relationships, even should the terms change and these affiliations no longer appear financially attractive or personally rewarding.

The current consolidation is being hailed in some quarters as a needed industrialization of the practice of medicine - a way to make the delivery of medical care more efficient and scalable. There is a premise that once doctors become employed by larger groups and health systems, it will be easier to put in place measures to manage doctors' use of medical services in ways that can improve efficiencies and lower costs. There's also a perhaps excessive faith that larger, consolidated networks of providers will have the incentive, capital, and wherewithal to pursue management and technology improvements that lead to better coordination of care. There is plenty of reason to be skeptical of these assumptions.

Impact of Consolidation on Clinical Productivity

First, there's evidence that as doctors transition into becoming salaried employees of hospitals and health systems, their individual productivity (in terms of metrics such as volume and intensity of care delivered) generally declines outright, or is unfavorably impacted by these arrangements in other, more subtle ways.[11,12,13,14,15]

It's important to note that studies that have examined this question contain many limitations. This is because of the inherent difficulty in studying the impacts of different payment systems.[16] It's hard to look at controlled experiments that address questions of how doctors respond to different payment systems.

It's also true that data shows some offsetting economic impacts to these drops in productivity. For example, physicians' use of services such as diagnostic tests and procedures also shows corresponding decline when doctors move into salaried arrangements. The totality of the data suggests, however, that the reduction in costs generated by the salaried schemes (typically as a result of the delivery of fewer tests and treatments) may be partially, if not completely offset by the lower intensity of work (productivity) that physicians achieve under these arrangements.[17]

While it's generally hard to isolate the impact of payment structure on productivity, a number of studies have attempted to assess these impacts. In one study researchers used a resident continuity clinic to compare prospectively the impact of salary versus fee-for-service reimbursement on physician practice behavior. This model allowed randomization of physicians into salary and fee-for-service groups and separation of the effects of reimbursement from patient behavior.[18]

The authors found that physicians reimbursed by fee-for-services (FFS) scheduled more visits per patient than salaried physicians (3.69 visits versus 2.83 visits, $P < .01$) and saw their patients more often (2.70 visits versus 2.21

visits, P < .05) during the 9-month study. Fee-for-service physicians also provided better continuity of care than salaried physicians by attending a larger percentage of all visits made by their patients (86.6% of visits versus 78.3% of visits, P < .05), and by encouraging fewer emergency visits per enrolled patient (0.12 visits versus 0.22 visits, P < .01).[19]

Another review article surveyed the available literature examining how salaried arrangements impact physician productivity. It drew similar conclusions. The article found that salary payment reduces activity compared with fee for service. Capitation appeared to have a similar but more subdued effect. The authors concluded that "if cost containment is a key policy aim of government then salaried payment systems are more likely to achieve this compared with FFS and possibly more effective than capitation systems. However, cost containment by itself may be inefficient if it results in the provision of sub-optimal care."[20]

This data raises a fundamental choice: If the goal is reduce spending by driving down utilization then the salaried arrangements might provide a more direct means of imposing top-down controls. If the goal is to reduce costs by increasing productivity then the salaried arrangements might thwart these types of outcomes.

CONSOLIDATION CAN DRIVE UP HEALTHCARE COSTS

Concerns have also been raised about the potential for consolidation to drive up costs. If constructs such as ACOs end up fostering more market concentration among providers, they have they could merely shift costs to payors. "Must-have"[21] hospitals and physician groups can exert considerable market power to demand higher rates from insurers. There is plenty of empiric evidence demonstrating that these arrangements can add to costs. Studies of pricing have shown that some providers, particularly hospitals, can gain significant market power to negotiate higher-than-competitive prices as they gain this sort of local market share.[22]

While a full discussion of these economic issues is beyond the scope of my testimony today, we need to carefully consider the potential impact from the arrangements that are being encouraged under PPACA. It has been observed that exclusive relationships, particularly those involving highly sought after or high-quality specialist physicians and hospitals, could give a consolidated network such as an ACO undue leverage.[23] Exclusivity may also promote increased internal referrals within the network, which could magnify the effects of increased market power.[24] In the past, antitrust policy has generally proved ineffective in curbing provider strategies that capitalize on gains in market power to win higher payments.[25] For these reasons, we should be especially mindful of the potential risks of encouraging a rapid evolution toward these consolidated relationships.

While observers are pointing to other entities that might form ACOs (large multispecialty medical groups, venture capital backed services companies) the bottom line remains that hospitals are likely to dominate the formation of these new arrangements. There are two principal reasons. First, the largest avoidable costs are related to hospitalizations. Second, in many communities, the hospital is the only organized delivery system able to access capital and execute on the model.[26]

The hospitals also have an ulterior motive. It's still unclear if ACOs will be profitable, successful enterprises. But for a hospital to succeed with the model, it need not succeed in lowering costs. If the process of forming an ACO lets a hospital consolidate local providers, the hospital will wins even if the ACO fails to succeed.

Physicians, for their part, are being driven to these arrangements by changes in the landscape that sees their practice costs rising, their reimbursement falling, while the financial risk they need to bear under PPACA increases through more capitated arrangements. Seeing costs rise amidst shrinking revenue, doctors are finding the prospect of trading in their businesses for a salaried position at a hospital attractive.

The concern that ACOs and other consolidated networks could serve to increase healthcare costs have already been raised among a diverse group of observers, including employers,[27] the Federal Trade Commission (FTC)[28], as well as policymakers. For example, it has been suggested that the schemes may exacerbate cost shifting to commercially insured patients by ACOs looking to qualify for the Medicare cost-reduction bonuses.[29] This cost shifting may be enabled by the ACOs new market power. One study showed that this is what happened in California as independent practice associations flourished there.[30]

For their part, some hospitals and other dominant providers in local markets have long sought to concentrate their power. They have been checked in these efforts by legal uncertainty and anti-trust concerns. We need to be careful that the urge toward creation of ACOs and other entities capable of bearing risk not be used to provide a guise to enable consolidation that is fundamentally unattractive. The widespread political appeal of ACOs should not be allowed to influence how the FTC and Justice Department interpret their responsibilities in these areas.[31]

Otherwise, we could end up with the worst of both outcomes: consolidated providers that reduce efficiencies and raise costs, without any offsetting benefits from the (still largely untested) ACO model.[32] In part, the nod toward hospitals to be the consolidators and the entities that stand up ACOs should heighten these concerns. Hospitals are an industry with some unique attributes, but it's been said that nothing about the specifics of the health care industry suggests that the unregulated use of market power in this industry is socially beneficial. [33]

PPACA LEAVES CONSIDERABLE UNCERTAINTY AMONG PROVIDERS

Finally, the consolidation is leaving a great deal of uncertainty among providers about what is permissible and appropriate and, as a business matter, what physicians should be doing. This is distorting the kinds of business decisions that get made. Many of the mergers are being driven merely out of a desire to gain market share rather than pursue efficiencies because providers don't trust that the business arrangements will be legally or financially sustainable in the long run.

In part, this uncertainty is heightened by the fact that when it comes to concepts like ACOs, that much of these basic ideas have been tried before, without success.

Among the sweeping changes of the Balanced Budget Act (BBA) of 1997 was a provision enabling providers to contract directly with Medicare through the formation of a provider-sponsored organization (PSO). This provision was part of a package that created a new Medicare Part C, giving beneficiaries the choice to elect to receive benefits through the traditional fee-for-service Medicare or through enrollment in a "Medicare Choice" plan that took financial risk, and was eligible to offer health insurance or health benefits coverage.

A PSO was widely defined as a managed care contracting and delivery organization that accepted full risk for beneficiary lives. The PSO received a fixed monthly payment to provide care for Medicare beneficiaries. PSOs could be developed as for-profit or not-for-profit entities of which at least 51% must be owned and governed by health care providers (physicians, hospitals or allied health professionals).[34] As a practical matter, these PSOs were structured similarly to how the ACOs are being conceptualized. The two concepts also aimed at achieving some of the same goals in terms of giving providers an incentive to better coordinate care, and to introduce other efficiencies and controls to reduce the use of services deemed wasteful.[35]

Yet the Provider Sponsored Organizations failed badly. The reasons that these entities couldn't succeed seem to mirror some potential shortcomings in the ACO model. This history only heightens the uncertainty in the provider community around not only whether the consolidated entities now being created will be legally permissible, but also whether they are sustainable and whether the government will continue to partner with these new organizations once the current fashion fades.

Most of the PSOs had inadequate resources to finance their risk and weak management. They lacked the capacity to introduce cost-saving innovations in how they coordinated and delivered care, and manage the use of services. A few of these ventures survived, evolved, and went on to have success, most failed badly.[36] Some of the successful ventures include the Geisinger Health System in Pennsylvania and Intermountain Health Care in Utah. But most of these PSO ventures failed.

The very changes to the Medicare reimbursement schedule that's driving doctors toward consolidation, only serve to underscore how uncertain the entire landscape is and, at times, how variable, if not predictable, Medicare can be when it comes to entering into business relationships with providers and provider-let entities.

As the Part B reimbursement schedule is dramatically reduced for many procedures such as cardiology and radiology, doctors and hospitals see an advantage to moving these services under the Part A billing scheme, which has remained comparatively intact. The magnitude of the cuts to certain Part B procedures is adding to provider concerns that they cannot rely on their Medicare-based revenue models.

The resulting effort to link up with hospitals, and move from the Part B to Part A billing scheme, is a temporary arbitrage, to be sure. It's another reason why the consolidation that looks attractive now to the hospitals may be unwieldy and unsustainable once the Medicare payment schedule catches up with these new realities. It's another reason why the consolidation that is taking place in the provider community may fall far short of its hoped for effects of improving efficiencies, driving greater coordination of care, and ultimately lowering costs. And it's another reason why there is so much uncertainty about the long-term structures.

For their part, the hospitals are experiencing economic loses as they acquire medical practices – another reason providers are engaging in these relationships on shaky ground. The losses stem in part because reimbursement levels don't leave much room for operating profits. It is also a function of the fact that the hospitals have been focused on acquiring specialty practices like cardiology and surgical specialties, which require the payment of larger, longer-term employment contracts. The losses that hospitals experience in acquiring practices are likely to exceed the potential gain sharing that they stand to earn under PPACA for operating under new shared savings arrangements created by PPACA.[37] This, of course, begs the question as to whether hospitals will merely shift the costs onto payors once they gain sufficient local market concentration. There is ample evidence, from past experience, to demonstrate this can be precisely what happens. [38,39,40]

Finally, providers also need to face the prospect that whatever relationships they enter into now may be hard to unwind should the legal or reimbursement environment change with respect to concepts like ACOs and the consolidation taking place today around hospitals. In the late 1990s, when physicians sold their practices to practice management companies (such as Medpartners and PhyCor) many of these companies eventually failed. Once these outfits folded, doctors were able to unwind the relationships that they had with these firms and go back to the individual practices. Today's current round of consolidation may not end as well.

Hospitals will realize that these relationships are not financially sustainable owing to declining hospital reimbursement, an inevitable equalization between the Part A and Part B payment schemes, and the high cost of owning and managing physicians. Physicians will have a hard time going back to their old arrangements. In many cases, they simply won't have the capital to regain their prior medical practices.

A 2011 survey by the American Medical Group Association, looking at the operating margins of large, often multi-specialty medical groups, would suggest that running a large group of physicians (whether they are employed by an independent multi-specialty group or a hospital) isn't profitable in today's payment environment. This financial analysis only serves to underscore these points, and the reason to be uncertain about the new arrangements that are taking shape in today's market.

The cost of practicing medicine continues to rise while reimbursement rates remain largely flat, or decline slightly over time. As a result, the survey of operating margins of large medical groups shows that most groups are operating at a loss. The northeast has some of the worst performing groups.

According to the survey, groups in this region are operating at an average loss of around $10,000 per physician.[41]

There is a possibility that, through pursuit of policy constructs that aim to consolidate providers into larger networks, we end up with the worst of both worlds: A Medicare policy failure that drives private-sector costs higher.[42]

Does Consolidation Leave a Role for Entrepreneurship?

In the end, PPACA's most significant challenge to organizational change in how providers are structured and services delivered is the legislation's relationship to innovation and entrepreneurship in this space. In my opinion, the modest rewards offered to accountable care organizations, through gain sharing, may not be enough to incentivize these groups to make meaningful investments in costly new systems and infrastructure that lead to genuine improvements in the coordination of care.

As a result, the entities taking advantage of the opportunity set may be those who have other motives. They will be the existing market participants who stand to gain through the ability to consolidate providers and gain local market power.

Historically, innovations in the delivery of healthcare -- from the advent of the first HMO to creation of long term care hospitals and home infusion (to name just several) - arose as the result of start-up outfits, often backed by venture capital, and headed by entrepreneurs who were in search of above market returns on invested capital. Under the existing rules, this often meant that new arrangements sought to earn profits by moving patients from higher cost settings of care to lower cost settings and capturing some of the money they saved the system in that process.[43]

But PPACA contains deliberate provisions aimed at regulating returns on invested capital; discouraging different forms of entrepreneurship. These provisions are, in many cases, the expression of a political philosophy that guides a number of provisions in PPACA. That philosophy views profits earned on the provision of care as money that should have been channeled instead into direct patient care.

The result is that entrepreneurs are not pursuing new health services ventures. Capital flowing to these endeavors has fallen sharply. The lack of incentive for entrepreneurs further entrenches existing players, meaning that tools that could help better coordinate care (for example, healthcare information technology) is only adopted through outright subsidies to existing providers, rather than through the creation of new approaches to replace an existing way of delivering care.

I work with investors who support entrepreneurs creating some of these new ideas. I have also served as a consultant to, and board member, of firms working on entrepreneurial healthcare services start-ups. I worry that PPACA advances a number of provisions that tilt too much against these entrepreneurs. The combined effect of these policies will serve to potentially freeze out disruptive new models.

There are other legacy practices that create impediments to innovation, entrepreneurship, and genuine change in the delivery of healthcare services. For example, existing laws restrict innovative ways to provide primary care (PPACA merely restricts how we pay for it). We could develop entities that make better use of skilled nurses and other non-physicians providers to reach into homes, workplaces and communities to provide early care more efficiently and cheaply.

This would cause "prevention" to rise rather than having PPACA make "prevention" free without addressing the fact that people often don't see doctors because it's inconvenient. Such efforts would require changes in laws that empower certain providers over others and create barriers to more flexible approaches to delivering care. In the past, physicians have been resistant to extending more responsibility to non-physician providers. I expect this resistance to diminish as the incentives change under new payment schemes. Under capitated schemes, there's more incentive to move patients from costly hospitals and offices and (where appropriate) into lower costs settings and providers. Under these arrangements, doctors may be keener to share increasing responsibilities with other providers.

CONCLUSION

In a well functioning market that creates proper incentives for innovation in delivery of healthcare, consumers would have a closer relationship to the insurance product that they carry and their purchase of routine healthcare. In a well functioning market, the insurance product would be portable across employers and states, and would enable multi-year contracts, guaranteed-renewable products, and other elements similar to the way consumers buy life insurance today.

Such a market would provide cash vouchers to individuals priced out of the system because of their economic or medical circumstances. Under the current scheme, where health insurance products are tightly regulated, where government agencies and not consumers choose what is covered, and where profits are punished, it leaves little room for entrepreneurship in how healthcare services are delivered.

Yet the only way we're going to bend the healthcare cost curve is by introducing genuine innovations in how we provide medical care – new approaches that lower costs while providing more healthcare for each dollar that we spend. These innovations won't arise as a result of the critical mass created through carefully orchestrated mergers. These ideas won't be incubated inside CMS.

Nor are these concepts likely to arise from new twists on old concepts like capitation and PSOs. Instead, genuine innovation in the delivery of healthcare is going to come about the way it always has – from entrepreneurs who raise capital in search of profitable new ways to re-engineer old systems, appealing to consumers by bringing them a better service at a more affordable price. PPACA tries to engineer its own new constructs, while pursuing provisions that could crowd out entrepreneurs from developing their own ideas. We could end up with neither.

End Notes

[1] Clinical Transformation: Dramatic Changes as Physician Employment Grows, Accenture Health, 2011

[2] Anne Mutti and Jeff Stensland. Provider consolidation and prices. Presentation before the Medicare Payment Advisory Committee. October 9, 2009

[3] 2012 Edition of the American Hospital Association Statistics

[4] Haydn Bush. Hospital Statistics Chart Rise in Physician Employment. Hospital and Health Networks Daily, January 06, 2012

[5] Karen M. Cheung. 70% hospitals, health systems plan more physician employment. Fierce Healthcare, October 12, 2011

[6] Scott Gottlieb. No, You Can't Keep Your Health Plan. The Wall Street Journal, May 18, 2010

[7] Medical Group Management Association. Physician Placement Starting Salary Survey: 2010 Report Based on 2009 Data. June 4, 2010

[8] Survey by McKesson Practice Consulting and Modern Medicine, 2011

[9] Rita Numerof. Massive Healthcare Consolidation in the PPACA Era, April 13, 2012

[10] Atul Gawande. The Cost Conundrum, What a Texas town can teach us about health care. The New Yorker, June 1, 2009

[11] Lawton Robert Burns and Ralph W. Muller. Hospital-Physician Collaboration: Landscape of Economic Integration and Impact on Clinical Integration. Milbank Quarterly 2008;86:375–434

[12] Christopher D. Ittnera, David F. Larckerb, Mina Pizzinic. Performance-based compensation in member-owned firms: An examination of medical group practices, May 2007

[13] Wolinsky F, Marder W. Spending time with patients, the impact of organisational structure on medical practice. Medical Care 1982; 20(10):1051–9

[14] I S Kristiansen, K Holtedahl. Effect of the remuneration system on the general practitioner's choice between surgery consultations and home visits. Journal of Epidemiology and Community Health 1993;47:481-484 doi:10.1136/jech.47.6.481 http://jech.bmj.com /content/47/6/481.abstract?ijkey=286b3bd9c25afb8bb73203854199b0c2b49 d86e0&keytype2=tf_ipsecsha

[15] Gosden T, Forland F, Kristiansen IS, Sutton M, Leese B, Giuffrida A, Sergison M, Pedersen L. Impact of payment method on behavior of primary care physicians: a systematic review. Journal of Health Service Research Policy 2001 Jan;6(1):44-55

[16] Gosden T, Forland F, Kristiansen IS, Sutton M, Leese B, Giuffrida A, Sergison M, Pedersen L. Capitation, salary, fee-for-service and mixed systems of payment: effects on the behavior of primary care physicians. Cochrane Database Systematic Reviews 2000;(3):CD002215.

[17] T. Gosden, L. Pedersen and D. Torgerson. How should we pay doctors? A systematic review of salary payments and their effect on doctor behavior. QJM 1999;92:47-55

[18] Gerald B. Hickson, William A. Altemeier, James M. Perrin. Physician Reimbursement by Salary or Fee-for-Service: Effect on Physician Practice Behavior in a Randomized Prospective Study. Pediatrics 1987;80:344-350

[19] Gerald B. Hickson, William A. Altemeier, James M. Perrin. Physician Reimbursement by Salary or Fee-for-Service: Effect on Physician Practice Behavior in a Randomized Prospective Study. Pediatrics 1987;80:344-350

[20] T. Gosden, L. Pedersen and D. Torgerson. How should we pay doctors? A systematic review of salary payments and their effect on doctor behavior. QJM 1999;92:47-55

[21] These must have groups are generally providers that health plans need to include in networks to be attractive to employers and consumers in a local market.

[22] Ginsburg PB. Wide variation in hospital and physician payment rates evidence of provider market power. Res Briefs 2010 Nov;(16):1-11

[23] Berenson RA, Ginsburg PB, Christianson JB, Yee T. The growing power of some providers to win steep payment increases from insurers suggests policy remedies may be needed. Health Affairs 2012 May;31(5):973-81

[24] Richard M. Scheffler, Stephen M. Shortell, Gail R. Wilensky. Accountable Care Organizations and Antitrust Restructuring the Health Care Market. Journal of the American Medical Association 2012;307(14):1493-1494. doi:10.1001/jama.2012.451.__http://eresources.library.mssm.edu:11635/article.aspx?doi=10.1001/jama.2012.451

[25] Berenson RA, Ginsburg PB, Kemper N. Unchecked provider clout in California foreshadows challenges to health reform. Health Affairs 2010 Apr;29(4):699-705

[26] Jeff Goldsmith. Accountable Care Organizations: The Case for Flexible Partnerships Between health Plans and Providers. Health Affairs, January 2011 vol. 30 no. 1 32-40

[27] Employers express anti-trust and cost-shifting concerns on ACOs. America's Health Insurance Plans Coverage. June 3, 2011. http://www.ahipcoverage.com/2011/06/03/employers-express-antitrust-and-cost-shifting-concerns-on-acos. Accessed October 2012

[28] Federal Trade Commission, Department of Justice. Statement of antitrust enforcement policy regarding accountable care organizations participating in the Medicare shared savings program. Federal Register 2011;76(209):67026-67032

[29] Remarks of J. Thomas Rosch. Accountable Care Organizations: What Exactly Are We Getting? Commissioner, Federal Trade Commission, before the ABA Section of Antitrust Law Fall Forum, Washington, DC. November 17, 2011. http://www.ftc.gov/speeches/rosch/111117fallforumspeech.pdf

[30] Robert A Breneson, Paul B. Ginsbur, Nicole Kemper. Unchecked provider clout in California foreshadows challenges to health reform. Health Affairs 2010;29:699

[31] Federal Trade Commission, Department of Justice, Antitrust Division. Proposed Statement of Antitrust Enforcement Policy Regarding Accountable Care Organizations Participating in the Medicare Shared Savings Program. Federal Register Vol. 76, No. 75. Tuesday, April 19, 2011

[32] Remarks of J. Thomas Rosch. Accountable Care Organizations: What Exactly Are We Getting? Commissioner, Federal Trade Commission, before the ABA Section of Antitrust Law Fall Forum, Washington, DC. November 17, 2011. http://www.ftc.gov/speeches/rosch/111117fallforumspeech.pdf

[33] Gaynor M. Why don't courts treat hospitals like tanks for liquefied gases? Some reflections on health care antitrust enforcement. Journal of Health, Politics, Policy and the Law 2006 Jun;31(3):497- 510

[34] Stephen C. Gleason, Jacque J. Sokolov, and Christine Henshaw. Provider Sponsored Organizations: A Golden Opportunity in Medicare Managed Care Physicians and other providers will soon have a chance to bypass the middleman and compete in managed Medicare. Family Practice Management 1998 Mar;5(3):34-45

[35] Judith R. Peres. PSOs offering new partnership potential; provider service organizations: a possible gateway to 21st-century long-term care - Forecast '98. February 1998

[36] Jeff Goldsmith. Accountable Care Organizations: The Case for Flexible Partnerships Between health Plans and Providers. Health Affairs, January 2011 vol. 30 no. 1 32-40

[37] Jeff Goldsmith. Accountable Care Organizations: The Case for Flexible Partnerships Between health Plans and Providers. Health Affairs, January 2011 vol. 30 no. 1 32-40

[38] Vogt WB, Town R. How has hospital consolidation affected the price and quality of hospital services. Princeton (NJ): Robert Wood Johnson Foundation; 2006. Research Synthesis Report No. 9

[39] Berenson RA, Ginsburg PB, Kemper N. Unchecked provider clout in California foreshadows challenges to health reform. Health Affairs. 2010;29(4):699–705

[40] Anne Mutti and Jeff Stensland. Provider consolidation and prices. Presentation before the Medicare Payment Advisory Committee. October 9, 2009

[41] American Medical Group Association. 2011 Medical Group Compensation and Financial Survey Finds Continued Financial Losses in Most Regions, Average Increase in Physician Compensation at 2.4%. August 16, 2011

[42] Jeff Goldsmith. Accountable Care Organizations: The Case for Flexible Partnerships Between health Plans and Providers. Health Affairs, January 2011 vol. 30 no. 1 32-40

[43] Chris van Gorder and Eric Topol. Embracing the Future. Modern healthcare, May 14, 2012. 24

In: Physician Practices
Editor: Isaak Angelidis
ISBN: 978-1-62618-184-7

Chapter 8

TESTIMONY OF EDMUND F. HAISLMAIER, SENIOR RESEARCH FELLOW, CENTER FOR HEALTH POLICY STUDIES, THE HERITAGE FOUNDATION. HEARING ON "HEALTH CARE CONSOLIDATION AND COMPETITION AFTER PPACA"*

Mr. Chairman and members of the Committee, thank you for inviting me to testify on the subject of "Health Care Consolidation and Competition after PPACA."

My name is Edmund F. Haislmaier. I am Senior Research Fellow in Health Policy at The Heritage Foundation. The views I express in this testimony are my own, and should not be construed as representing any official position of The Heritage Foundation.

My testimony today focuses on how I expect competition and consolidation to play out in the health insurance sector under the new rules and regulations established in the Patient Protection and Affordable Care Act (PPACA).

The PPACA significantly expands, both in scope and in detail, the federal regulation of commercial health insurers. A number of its provisions are likely, over time, to reduce competition in that sector. The reduction in

* This is an edited, reformatted and augmented version of a testimony presented May 18, 2012 before the House Judiciary Committee, Subcommittee on Intellectual Property, Competition and the Internet.

competition will result from provisions in the PPACA that standardize coverage, increase premiums, raise barriers to market entry, and encourage industry consolidation.

STANDARDIZING COVERAGE

The first set of relevant provisions are those that have the effect of standardizing health insurance coverage. When government imposes regulations that standardize a product, producers of the item are, obviously, less able to compete on the basis of product differentiation. The product becomes more of a commodity and competition among suppliers becomes focused mainly on price. Other factors, such as convenience or brand identity, may enable some producers to charge marginally higher prices, but even that pricing power is fairly limited in a commoditized market.

At least five provisions of the PPACA will intentionally standardize health insurance to varying degrees:

1) Section 1302 instructs the Department of Health and Human Services (HHS) to set, and periodically update, an "essential health benefits package" of minimum health insurance coverage requirements.
2) Section 1302 also limits deductibles for employer plans in the small-group market and limits total enrollee cost-sharing for all health plans to the levels specified in the tax code for qualified High Deductible Health Savings Account plans.
3) Section 1201(4) requires all individual and small group health insurance policies to provide coverage for the essential health benefits package.
4) Section 1001(5) requires health insurers and employer plans to cover numerous preventive services with no enrollee cost-sharing.
5) Section 1001(5) prohibits health insurers and employer plans from setting annual or lifetime coverage limits "on the dollar value of benefits."

In a commodity market where competition is focused principally on price, firms that are able to reduce their costs through economies of scale can generally offer better prices and thus gain market share at the expense of their competitors. As a result, markets for commodities tend to be dominated by a few, large firms. Those firms achieve their dominant size by either underpricing smaller rivals or acquiring competitors. The provisions of the PPACA that standardize and commoditize coverage are likely to drive a similar dynamic in the health insurance market. Furthermore, because these are new, federal standards, the effects will be national in scope. Even carriers that have long been dominant in a particular state or region will find it harder to maintain their position and keep larger, national players at bay.

INCREASING COVERAGE COSTS

The above provisions will not only standardize coverage, but in many cases will increase coverage costs as well. For example:

- The Administration conducted an economic analysis of the effects of their regulations implementing the PPACA's preventive services coverage requirement. They concluded that, "The Departments estimate that premiums will increase by approximately 1.5 percent on average for enrollees in non-grandfathered plans. This estimate assumes that any changes in insurance benefits will be directly passed on to the consumer in the form of changes in premiums."[1]
- In its regulations implementing the PPACA's provision that prohibits plans imposing annual limits on the dollar value of benefits after 2014, and sets minimum annual limits for prior years, HHS established a waiver process for years before 2014, "if compliance with these interim final regulations would result in a significant decrease in access to benefits or a significant increase in premiums."[2] HHS has granted temporary waivers of the annual limits provision to plans with a total of over 4 million enrollees.[3] Thus, when the complete prohibition on annual limits takes effect in 2014, at least 4 million individuals will be priced out of their current coverage, and it is likely that this provision will increase premiums for millions more.
- Congress instructed HHS to define and periodically update an "essential health benefits package." HHS has not yet proposed regulations specifying the initial design of the essential health benefits package and has only issued “bulletins” outlining the approaches that it is considering. Given that the statute requires coverage for some categories of benefits not typically included in most current health

plans -- such as "habilitative" services -- it is likely that the eventual package of required benefits will increase premiums.

The significance of these increased costs is that they generate a dynamic for further plan standardization. The more expensive the required coverage becomes the more insurers will look to keep premiums in check by limiting or cutting benefits that are not required. Indeed, State governments have behaved exactly this way in managing their Medicaid programs. As the cost to states of paying for mandatory Medicaid benefits has increased, states have responded by limiting or discontinuing optional Medicaid benefits.

Similarly, it was fear of this same dynamic occurring that led Congress to amend the PPACA provision requiring coverage of preventive services so as to overrule the US Preventive Services Task Force's recommendation on breast cancer screening. At that time the USPSTF had just revised its recommendation on breast cancer screening from starting at age 40 to starting at age 50. Breast cancer groups were concerned that making coverage mandatory at age 50 would induce plans to no longer pay for screening for women between the ages of 40 and 50. Congress responded by amending the PPACA to require coverage of breast cancer screening using the prior recommendation of age 40.[4]

The foregoing example also illustrates another effect of the benefit mandates in the PPACA. Over time there is likely to be ever more detailed standardization of health insurance coverage as provider and patient groups lobby HHS and Congress to expand coverage requirements, while insurers and employers, looking to control rising plan costs, seek greater regulatory certainty with respect to the limits they may impose on required benefits.

Thus, by giving HHS authority that is both broad and discretionary to define what constitutes "essential benefits," Congress set in motion a dynamic that will result in increasing standardization of health insurance coverage. That increasing standardization shrinks the scope for competition among insurers and is likely to result in industry consolidation, as the regulated product becomes more of an undifferentiated commodity.

THE "MINIMUM LOSS RATIO" REGULATION

Another provision of the PPACA that will likely have a major effect in reducing insurer competition and driving consolidation within the health insurance industry is the so-called "minimum loss ratio" (MLR) regulation. [5]

This provision established, effective January 1, 2011, new federal rules governing how health insurers spend premium dollars. These rules are commonly referred to as "minimum loss ratio" regulations—meaning that they specify the minimum share of premium income that an insurer must spend on claims costs and "activities that improve health care quality."

The minimum levels are set in the PPACA at 85 percent for large group plans and 80 percent for small group and individual plans. The PPACA further stipulates that if an insurer spends less than the required minimum in a given year, then the insurer must refund the difference to policyholders. Thus, for example, if an insurer is required to spend 80 percent of premium income on claims costs for a particular product but only spends 75 percent, the insurer is required to rebate five percent of the premium collected to policyholders.

New Barrier to Market Entry

One of the effects of the minimum loss ratio regulations is that they create a barrier to market entry for new carriers. As with many start-up companies, a substantial initial capital investment is required to create a new insurer. That investment is needed to fund initial marketing and sales efforts to attract paying customers, and to build-out the operational and administrative infrastructure for billing customers, paying claims, etc. Similar to other new businesses, a new insurer initially operates at a loss until it achieves enough "scale" - that is, it acquires enough customers - that revenues exceed expenses, and it become profitable.

The MLR regulations effectively constrain the amount, and delay the timing, of any excess premium revenues that a start-up health insurer could plan to either reinvest in growing its business (say, through additional marketing) or repaying its initial investors. Thus, the MLR regulations push further into the future a new company's projected "break-even" point, and may also necessitate additional start-up capital beyond what was previously projected.

Of course, it is uncertain whether a particular start-up insurer would succeed, even without having to deal with the constraints imposed by the MLR regulations. However, what is certain is that imposing the new MLR regulations raises the bar for an "in-process" start-up, and increases the risk and initial capital requirements for an "in-planning" start-up venture.

In at least one reported case investors decided to terminate an "in-process" start-up health insurer, at least in part, due to the effects of the new MLR regulations on its business plan.6 What is unknowable are how many attempts to create new health insurers that were still in the planning stage were simply abandoned once investors determined that the added burden of complying with the new minimum loss ratio regulations make it too expensive or too risky to go forward.

MARKET CONSOLIDATION

A number of established companies that currently provide health insurance can also be expected to exit the market over the next several years. The ones most likely to leave are those with multiple lines of coverage, for which offering health insurance is just part of their larger business. In general, the minimum loss ratio regulations will make offering health insurance less profitable while, as previously noted, the benefit requirements will also make it more of a commodity business. Companies offering multiple lines of insurance will be inclined to discontinue, or sell to competitors, their health plans and focus instead on the other lines of insurance that they offer -- such as life, auto, property, or liability coverage - or on non-insurance business opportunities. The smaller the company, or the smaller the share of a company's total business represented by health insurance, the more likely it is that the company will exit the postPPACA health insurance market.

For example, on September 30, 2010, Principal Financial Group, Inc. announced that it was exiting the major medical health insurance market and transferring its existing book of business to UnitedHealth Group.[7] Principal will instead focus on its other lines of business, which include managing retirement and investment plans, and offering life, disability, dental and vision insurance products (none of which are subject to the PPACA's new federal insurance regulations). To be sure, such business decisions are often the product of multiple considerations, but the MLR provisions in the PPACA will certainly discourage companies with other options from continuing to offer health plans.

FAVORING FOR-PROFIT INSURERS

Still another unintended consequence of the minimum loss ratio regulations is that they will increase the competitive advantage of for-profit insurers over their non-profit rivals. Because the MLR requirement constrains the share of premium income that an insurer can "retain," it limits an insurer's ability to accumulate the capital needed to expand, either through increased marketing and sales efforts or by purchasing business from other carriers. Non-profit insurers have no other source of investment capital beyond whatever excess premium income they can accumulate after paying claims costs and administrative expenses. However, for-profit insurers can finance their capital needs by issuing equity shares. Since the proceeds of a share offering are not premium income, the MLR restrictions do not apply.

Thus, the minimum loss ratio regulation is likely to not only spur increased consolidation in the health insurance industry, but to also drive that consolidation toward a market dominated by a few, very large, for-profit, insurers. It is easy to envision large, for profit health insurers applying the same "roll-up" strategy of raising capital through equity offerings and then using the proceeds to buy smaller competitors that has been successfully applied in other sectors. Such an outcome is probably not something that the authors of the PPACA either intended or envisioned.

MULTI-STATE PLANS

Another provision in the PPACA that favors large, national health insurers over smaller or regional ones is the requirement in Section 1334 that the Office of Personnel Management directly contract with a select number of insurers to offer "multi-state" plans. Section 1334 sets a four year schedule for offering multi-state plans in all the states, and specifies that multi-state plans are "deemed to be certified by an Exchange" as qualified plans. That deeming provision gives the multi-state plans a guarantee of access to the subsidized coverage market that is not guaranteed to their competitors.

RATE REVIEW

The insurer rate review provisions of the PPACA offer yet another incentive for smaller carriers to exit the health insurance market and big carriers to get bigger. While Congress did not give HHS authority to deny insurer rate increases, HHS has shown that it is willing to use its new rate review powers to "name and shame" insurers if they significantly increase premiums. Secretary Sebelius has also threatened to deny uncooperative insurers access to the federally subsidized exchange markets that are scheduled to open in 2014.[8]

The logical business strategy for surviving in that kind of a market is for a carrier to become big enough that it can retain some level of pricing power in the face of persistent government attempts to impose price regulations. Becoming "too big" or "too important" to fail will be the best strategy for a company seeking to protect itself against the threat that government price regulation could make its business unprofitable.

Combined Effects

Collectively, these regulations mean that the PPACA has unleashed a market dynamic that will drive toward greater consolidation in the health insurance industry, eventually resulting in fewer and larger carriers dominating the market - with a consequent reduction in choice and competition for consumers. How this new market dynamic will likely play out can be seen from past experience in other sectors where "consolidators" - such as Staples and Office Depot - built market-dominating firms through a strategy of raising investment capital and then deploying it to acquire small and mid-sized competitors.

Indeed, a prominent supporter of the PPACA explicitly, and correctly, wrote that the legislation "fundamentally transforms health insurance" into "a regulated industry ... that, in its restructured form, will therefore take on certain characteristics of a public utility."[9]

What was left unsaid is that the characteristics of public utility economics are markets dominated by a few large firms, with low rates of return and captive customers, in which the firms' pricing power is constrained by government regulation, but government's exercise of regulatory power is constrained by the need to keep the remaining firms profitable to avoid the widespread social and economic dislocation that would occur should they be driven out of existence. In essence, this is a prescription for achieving market equilibrium through an economic "mutually assured destruction" stand off - with little or no remaining consumer choice or product innovation.

Mr. Chairman, this concludes my prepared testimony. I thank you and the rest of the Committee for inviting me to testify before you on this issue. I will be happy to answer any questions that you or members of the Committee may have.

End Notes

[1] Federal Register, Vol. 75, No. 137, July 19, 2010, p. 41738

[2] Federal Register, Vol. 75, No. 123, June 28, 2010, p. 37191.

[3] Total enrollment in plans granted waivers is 4,039,774. Lists of those waiver recipients, with enrollment figures, can be found at Annual Limits Policy: Protecting Consumers, Maintaining Options, and Building a Bridge to 2014, U.S. Department of Health and Human Services, at http://cciio.cms.gov/resources/files/approved_applications_for_ waiver. html.

[4] New Section 2713(a)(5) of the Public Health Service Act (42 U.S. Code § 300gg-13(a)(5)) as added by PL 111–148 § 1001(5).

[5] New § 2718 of the Public Health Service Act (42 U.S. Code § 300gg–18) as added by PL 111-148 § 1001(5) and then amended by §10101(f).

[6] Michael Schwartz, "Startup health insurer shutting," Richmond BizSense, June 4, 2010, at: http://www.richmondbizsense.com/2010/06/04/startup-health-insurer-shutting and Michael Schwartz, "With healthcare reform looming, nHealth was losing millions," Richmond BizSense, June 11, 2010, at: http://www.richmondbizsense.com/2010/06/11/with-healthcare-reform-looming-nhealth-was-losingmillions/

[7] Principal Financial Group, "The Principal Financial Group to Exit Medical Insurance Business," press release, September 30, 2010, at: http://phx.corporate-ir.net/phoenix. zhtml?c=125598&p=irolnewsArticle&ID=1477633&highlight=

[8] Letter of Health and Human Services Secretary Kathleen Sebelius to Karen Ignagni, President and CEO of America's Health Insurance Plans, September 9, 2010.

[9] Sara Rosenbaum, J.D., A "Broader Regulatory Scheme" — The Constitutionality of Health Care Reform, New England Journal of Medicine, 10.1056/NEJMp1010850, October 27, 2010, at NEJM.org.

In: Physician Practices
Editor: Isaak Angelidis
ISBN: 978-1-62618-184-7

Chapter 9

STATEMENT OF THOMAS L. GREANEY, CO-DIRECTOR, CENTER FOR HEALTH LAW STUDIES, SAINT LOUIS UNIVERSITY SCHOOL OF LAW. HEARING ON "HEALTH CARE CONSOLIDATION AND COMPETITION AFTER PPACA"*

Chairman Goodlatte, Ranking Member Watt, Committee Ranking Member Conyers and Members of the Subcommittee, I much appreciate the opportunity to testify on the important issue of health care consolidation and competition policy in the context of health reform. By way of introduction, I am the Chester A. Myers Professor of Law and Director of the Center for Health Law Studies at Saint Louis University School of Law. I have devoted most of my 24-year academic career to studying issues related to competition and regulation in the health care sector, writing numerous articles on the subject and co-authoring the leading casebook in health law. Before that I served as Assistant Chief in the Antitrust Division of the United States Department of Justice, litigating and supervising cases involving health care. My professional affiliations include membership in the American Health Lawyers Associations and I serve on the Advisory Board of the American Antitrust Institute.

---

* This is an edited, reformatted and augmented version of a statement presented May 18, 2012 before the House Judiciary Committee, Subcommittee on Intellectual Property, Competition and the Internet.

Let me summarize the key points of my analysis of the market concentration problem:

- The Affordable Care Act depends on and promotes competition in provider and payor markets.
- Hospital market concentration is the result of various "merger waves" over the last twenty years facilitated by erroneous court decisions and lax antitrust enforcement, and exacerbated by government policies limiting entry and competition.
- Problematic concentration is largely caused by horizontal combinations— mergers and joint ventures among rivals. By contrast, vertical integration, such as combinations of hospitals with physicians, is generally procompetitive, because reducing fragmentation improves both the quality of care and the capacity of providers to eliminate wasteful services.
- The Affordable Care Act encourages procompetitive consolidations through payment reforms and incentives to form efficient delivery systems such as accountable care organizations.
- It would be erroneous to claim that the Affordable Care Act is somehow responsible for anticompetitive consolidation when in fact such mergers and joint ventures are efforts to *avoid* the procompetitive aspects of the Act.
- The recent resurgence in antitrust law enforcement should limit future increases in concentration and curb the exercise of market power, but will not unwind most prior consolidations.

The provider monopoly problem calls for countermeasures such as encouraging development of accountable care organizations organized in competitive structures and reducing barriers to entry.

Competition Policy and the Affordable Care Act

I'd like to begin with an important proposition that is sometimes lost in the rhetoric about health reform. The Affordable Care Act both depends on and promotes competition in provider and insurance markets. A key point is that the new law does not regulate prices for commercial health insurance or prices in the hospital, physician, pharmaceutical, or medical device markets.

Instead the law relies on (1) competitive bargaining between payers and providers and (2) rivalry within each sector to drive price and quality to levels that best serve the public.

Why do we need government intervention to make health care markets perform more efficiently? The answer lies in a witches' broth of history, provider dominance, ill-conceived government payment and regulatory policies, and perhaps most importantly, market imperfections that are endemic to delivery of services, insurance, and third party payment. Justification for regulation to promote competition can be found in virtually every economic analysis of health care. Markets for providing and financing care are beset with myriad market imperfections: inadequate information, agency, moral hazard, monopoly and selection in insurance markets that greatly distort markets. Add to that governmental failures— payment systems that reward intensity and volume but not accountability for resources or outcomes; restrictions on referrals that impede efficient cooperation among providers; and entry impediments in the form of licensure and CON, to name a few. Finally, toss in a strain of professional norms that are highly resistant to marketplace incentives-- and you have the root causes of our broken system.

Looking at the result in health care markets, we find the worst of two worlds: both fragmentation and concentration. As I'll discuss in a minute, hospital and specialty provider markets are highly concentrated while most primary care physicians remain in "silos" of solo or small practice groups. In most places, there is scant "vertical integration" among providers of different services—a phenomenon that impedes effective bargaining to reduce costs and prevent overutilization of services, and also has adverse effects on the quality of health services patients receive because it inhibits coordination of care.

The Affordable Care Act tackles these problems on many fronts. My article, The Affordable Care Act and Competition Policy: Antidote or Placebo?,[1] describes these measures in some detail, but I will focus on a few of the most important. Although it may be counterintuitive to those who dichotomize between competition and regulation, law can foster competition by imposing rules and standards, and even by mandating purchasing or creating competition-enabling institutions. As I have argued since the early days of the "competitive revolution" in health care, this kind of regulation is a condition precedent for effective markets.[2]

To briefly recap some of the ACA's competition-improving steps:

First, a centerpiece of reform is the Health Insurance Exchange. At bottom, exchanges are really just efficient markets for offering and purchasing health insurance analogous to farmers markets or travel websites. The ACA adopts regulations that are necessary to make insurance products comparable and understandable, that require basic minimums of coverage, and that protect against the insurance industry's long-standing practice of chasing down only good risks-- all textbook efforts to make competition work efficiently in the insurance market.

Second, Medicare payment and delivery reform plays a critical—and generally unappreciated—role in promoting competitive markets both private and public. Underlying the myriad changes in payment policy and the ACA's pilot programs and other innovations, such as value based purchasing, accountable care organizations and reforms to bidding in the Medicare Advantage program, is the understanding that Medicare policy strongly influences the private sector. Private payors often follow Medicare's lead on payment methods and depend on the program to set quality standards. Moreover, the incentives it creates in the way medicine is delivered has unquestioned spillover effects on commercial health plans. Most notable in this regard are the prodigious efforts undertaken by the ACA to redirect federal payment *away* from fee-for-service payment.

Third, the ACA seeks to create incentives for providers to develop innovative organizational structures that can respond to payment mechanisms that rely on competition to drive cost containment and quality improvement. The watchword here is *integration*. Congress recognized that it was essential to stimulate formation of organizations that could receive and distribute reimbursement and be responsible for the quality of care under the new payment arrangements contained in the ACA and developing in the private sector such as bundled payments and global reimbursements. Given the badly fragmented structure of health delivery, a critical innovation is the Medicare Shared Savings Program which fosters development of Accountable Care Organizations to serve *both* Medicare beneficiaries and private payers and employers.

Finally, the new law deals with a very significant public goods market failure—the underproduction of research and the inadequate dissemination of information concerning the effectiveness and quality of health care services and procedures. The Act does so by subsidizing research and creating new entities to support such research and to disseminate information about outcome and medically-effective treatments. Numerous other provisions attempt to correct flaws in Medicare and Medicaid reimbursement methodologies and add incentives to improve quality by using "evidence based medicine."

The important take-away is that much of the extensive regulation contained in the new law is explicitly designed to promote competition. It aims to encourage the redesign of payment and delivery systems so that private payers and providers can interact in the marketplace to provide the best mix of cost and quality in health care. As I'll discuss in a moment, however, there are obstacles to realizing the potential benefits of the competitive strategy for health care reform.

CONCENTRATION AND ANTITRUST ENFORCEMENT

So, what could possibly go wrong? Many observers, including myself, have pointed to the extensive concentration that pervades health care markets and constitute a serious impediment to effective competition. It is important however to put this phenomenon into context-- both as to how it came about and what can be done about it.

First it should be understood that although we have experienced a "merger wave" in recent years, it is not the first, nor is it responsible for the widespread concentration we see in many markets today. Hospital consolidation has proceeded in spurts several times over the past twenty years, with the biggest wave occurring in the mid-1990s. The Robert Woods Johnson Synthesis Project analysis summarized this phenomenon.

In 1990, the typical person living in a metropolitan statistical area (MSA) faced a concentrated hospital market with an HHI [the index of concentration used in antitrust cases] of 1,576. By 2003, however, the typical MSA resident faced a hospital market with an HHI of 2,323. This change is equivalent to a reduction from six to four competing local hospital systems.[3]

Notably, the largest number of hospital mergers was undertaken *after* the defeat of the Clinton Health Reform proposal and during a time when managed care was at its zenith. While academics disagree on what caused the sharp increase in mergers, recent studies suggest that hospitals' anticipation of increased cost pressures from managed care led them to consolidate. Moreover, one thing is clear: a series of unsuccessful antitrust challenges to hospital mergers in federal court gave a green light to consolidation. And, as the government antitrust agencies themselves admit, these decisions caused federal and state enforcers to back away from challenging hospital mergers for almost seven years.[4] Adding to this tale of misfortune is the widely-held opinion that the courts got it wrong: the majority of judicial decisions allowing hospital mergers found unrealistically large geographic markets that did not conform with sound economic analysis.[5]

The result of this spike in hospital concentration was disastrous for the American public. A large body of literature documents the existence, scope and effects of market concentration. One well-regarded compilation of the numerous studies of this issue spells out the link between hospital market concentration and escalating costs of health insurance: hospital consolidation in the 1990s raised overall inpatient prices by at least 5%, and by 40% or more when merging hospitals were located close to one another.[6] Another important study, undertaken by the Massachusetts Attorney General, documents the effects of "provider leverage" on health care costs and insurance premiums, notably finding prices for health services are uncorrelated with quality, complexity, proportion of government patients, or academic status but instead are positively correlated with provider market power. [7] A leading economist summarized the impetus to merge with rivals in the face of pressure from payers to compete:

> I have asked many providers why they wanted to merge. Although publicly they all invoked the synergies mantra, virtually everyone stated privately that the main reason for merging was to avoid competition and/or obtain market power.[8]

Provider concentration has a double effect-- one in commercial markets the second on government payers, especially Medicare. The most obvious effect as described above is to increase dominant providers' ability to command higher prices and resist efforts to limit unnecessary procedures. A second effect, often overlooked, is the cost-elevating impact of provider market concentration upon government payers. Examining the effect of hospital concentration on Medicare payments, the Medicare Payment Advisory Commission (MedPAC) has found that high hospital margins on private-payer patients tend to induce more construction and higher hospital costs and that, "when non-Medicare margins are high, hospitals face less pressure to constrain costs, [and] costs rise."[9] These factors, MedPAC observes, explain the counterintuitive phenomenon that hospital Medicare margins tend to be low in markets in which concentration is highest, while margins are higher in more competitively structured markets.

The key point to be derived from the past twenty years of experience with hospital consolidation is that, if not checked by vigilant antitrust enforcement, it can undermine the benefits that competition offers. Further, mergers that concentrate local markets have largely been driven by a desire to gain bargaining leverage. (It is important to note of course that not all consolidation is harmful:

many hospital mergers do not affect local markets as they substitute a stronger, more efficient owner not currently competing in the market or they involve relatively small competitors in the same market.) In sum, it would be highly misleading to suggest that the Affordable Care Act is somehow responsible for a new wave of attempted anticompetitive provider mergers, when in fact those mergers are an effort to *avoid* the very pro-competitive policies the new law puts in place.

Turning to the payer side, health insurance markets have a long history of consolidation and increasing concentration in the individual and small group market, where, according to some data, two firms have greater than fifty percent of the market in twenty-two states, and one firm has more than fifty percent in seventeen states.[10]

The results in these markets appear to confirm what economic theory predicts: higher premiums for consumers and high profits for the insurance industry. Summarizing studies indicating that private insurance revenue increased even faster than medical costs, economists at the Urban Institute concluded that "the market power of insurers meant that they were not only able to pass on health care costs to purchasers but to increase profitability at the same time."[11] While some studies question the extent of insurers' exercise of market power, bilateral market power is unlikely to serve consumer interests. Finally, experience suggests that entry into concentrated insurance markets is far from easy and may be unlikely to occur in markets with few insurers.

A recent study by the Antitrust Division of the Department of Justice found that entry in such insurance markets was impeded by the difficulty of securing provider contracts.[12] Congress addressed the problem in several ways: encouraging formation of new competition via nonprofit insurance cooperatives and multi-state health plans. Although the proposal to include a public option plan in every market was rejected, by improving insurance markets, reducing risks of adverse selection, and establishing health insurance exchanges, the ACA took steps designed to induce de novo entry into concentrated insurance markets.

THE RESURGENCE OF ANTITRUST ENFORCEMENT

In recent years the Federal Trade Commission, the Antitrust Division, and a number of State Attorneys General have stepped up antitrust enforcement. The federal antitrust agencies' cases, along with competition advocacy in the legislative and regulatory arenas, have focused on (1) stopping anticompetitive mergers, (2) challenging the exercise of market power by dominant providers and insurers, (3) urging legislators to reject or remove barriers to competition or legislative exemptions from the antitrust laws, and (4) attacking competitor collusion, most notably between manufacturers of branded pharmaceuticals and generic entrants and provider collusion in managed care negotiations. In addition, state attorneys general and private litigants have brought a number of important antitrust cases principally in the merger area.[13] (A description of the leading antitrust cases of the last two years, prepared for the biannual Antitrust in the Health Care Conference sponsored by the American Bar Association and the American Health Lawyers Association, is submitted as an appendix to this testimony).

These cases and legislative comments constitute a significant and necessary step toward protecting the competitive policies that undergird the Affordable Care Act. In the merger area, for example, the FTC succeeded in obtaining a federal court injunction blocking a hospital merger in Rockford, Illinois[14] and stopped another highly concentrative merger of hospitals in Toledo, Ohio via an administrative proceeding.[15] The Department of Justice challenged, and settled by consent decree requiring divestitures, a merger of health insurers that would reduce competition in Medicare Advantage contracting[16] and forced another health plan to abandon its plan to acquire its leading rival.[17]

Together these cases should send a strong signal that consolidations will be closely scrutinized. However, the FTC suffered a notable setback in a challenge to a merger to monopoly between two hospitals in Albany Georgia in which the Court of Appeals allowed the merger to go forward based on a controversial application of the State Action Doctrine.[18]

A second series of cases involve challenges to the actions of dominant providers or dominant payers. These cases represent a marked departure from the posture of the agencies over the last two decades in which the government agencies have rarely taken on cases of monopolization or abuse of dominant position.

The conduct at issue involves a variety of "exclusionary" actions: vertical arrangements that foreclose rivals without significant efficiency justifications. For example, the Antitrust Division challenged a dominant insurer's insistence on "most favored nations" clauses from contracting hospitals that severely disadvantaged rival insurers. [19] In another case, settled by consent decree, the Division challenged a near-monopoly hospital's demands for exclusionary discounts from insurers.[20]

PRESERVING THE POTENTIALLY PRO-COMPETITIVE EFFECTS OF ACCOUNTABLE CARE ORGANIZATIONS

Of the many important innovations contained in the Affordable Care Act, the Medicare Shared Savings Program (MSSP), which promotes the development of accountable care organizations, has undoubtedly garnered the most attention. The ACO strategy takes direct aim at the twin problems of the health care system: fragmented delivery and payments that reward volume rather than performance. Because they will be accountable for the full range of care needed by beneficiaries, ACOs need to establish integrated networks of providers that can monitor quality and provide seamless, cost-effective care. The Affordable Care Act explicitly encourages Medicare ACOs to also serve the commercially-insured sector and self-funded employers.

From the standpoint of competition policy, ACOs offer an important opportunity for providers to align in entities capable of delivering care that consumers (employers, insurers and individuals) can compare and negotiate with to get the best bargain in price and quality. Thus *both* provider integration and rivalry are key to the success of the concept. CMS, the FTC and the Department of Justice have worked closely together to establish guidelines[21] that will help providers assess the antitrust boundaries when forming ACOs. CMS has approved 27 ACOs and is reviewing another 150 applicants under the MSSP program. Together with 32 ACOs previously approved under the Pioneer ACO program (designed for integrated systems), over 1 million Medicare beneficiaries will be served by ACOs. In addition, many private insurers have inaugurated ACO programs.

Several procompetitive aspects of the agencies' regulations and policy statements should be noted. First, the MSSP allows ACOs considerable flexibility in the way they organize themselves. ACOs may be formed by joint ventures among providers and exclusive contracting is permitted only to the extent it does not impair competition. Exceptions are established for rural providers that recognize the special competitive circumstances they face. Dominant providers are constrained to some extent and cautioned about specific practices that interfere with payers' ability to engage in competitive contracting. Finally, CMS will gather data and monitor carefully the performance of participating ACOs.

There are, to be sure, legitimate concerns that ACOs may form in a manner that allows providers to aggregate market power that can be exercised over private health plans and employers. At the same time, ACOs offer a distinct opportunity to increase the competitiveness (and hence the quality and cost-effectiveness) of the delivery system. The antitrust agencies and CMS appear to have set out a framework capable of monitoring the competitive implications of ACOs as they develop.

ADDRESSING THE CONCENTRATION PROBLEM

While the antitrust agencies' efforts to promote and protect competition in health care markets is commendable, it is also the case that antitrust law has little to say about monopolies lawfully acquired, or in the case of consummated mergers, entities that are impractical to successfully unwind. Given the high level of concentration in many hospital markets and a growing number of physician specialty markets, it is particularly important to encourage other measures that promote competition.

Although there is no single "silver bullet" to solve the problem posed by extant provider concentration, there are a number of steps that reduce the market power exercised in such markets. To begin with, hospital concentration may be lowered by reduction of government-imposed barriers to entry such as Certificate of Need laws and excessive restrictions on physician-controlled specialty hospitals. In addition allowing middle-level professionals, such as nurse practitioners and physician assistants to practice within the full scope of their professional license under state law may increase the number and viability of new organizational arrangements such as medical homes and accountable care organizations that may be able to exert pressure on dominant providers. Further, federal and state legislatures should stoutly resist pleas for immunity or special protections from competition laws; there is a strong consensus, based on the nation's experience, that such exemptions harm consumer welfare.[22]

A second means of dealing with provider concentration is to use the full measure of authority under the antitrust laws to challenge the abuse of market power by dominant hospitals, physician groups and pharmaceutical companies. Among the important issues on the antitrust agenda are resisting claims of "State action" where the state legislation does not follow the Supreme Court's requirement that the defense is available only where state law truly endorses anticompetitive conduct and the state actively supervises the effects on consumers. Other steps might include retrospective challenges to recent mergers where divestiture is feasible. Further, following some path breaking scholarship by Professors Havighurst and Richman, antitrust law may be deployed to charge dominant hospitals with illegal tying or bundling, so as to force them to compete on the services that they do not monopolize.[23]

Finally, it may be possible to strengthen private market participants' to negotiate with dominant providers. For example, state health insurance exchanges or state regulators might require unbundling of hospital services as Havighurst and Richman suggest. For its part, CMS should carefully review the performance of ACOs, and where appropriate, decline renewal of contracts if market power has been exercised over private payers. Likewise, regulations and payment policies that favor ACOs controlled by primary care providers rather than dominant hospitals could serve to reduce the impact of the latter's market power.

CONCLUSION

A core concern of the Affordable Care Act is promoting competition in health care. Responses to the law such as anticompetitive mergers and cartel activity should be understood as efforts to avoid the discipline the new market realities will impose. Vigorous enforcement of the antitrust laws is essential to dealing with those problems, but at the same time the law is of limited help in dealing with extant market power. Legislators and regulators should be alert to opportunities to improve the prospects for entry and increased competitive opportunities where monopoly power is present.

End Notes

[1] Thomas L. Greaney, The Affordable Care Act and Competition Policy: Antidote or Placebo?, 89 Or. L. Rev. 811 (2011).

[2] See Thomas L. Greaney, Competitive Reform in Health Care: The Vulnerable Revolution, 5 Yale. J. on Reg. 179 (1988)(predicting that competition in health care would not succeed if regulation and infrastructure do not support it).

[3] Robert Vogt & Robert Town, How Has Hospital Consolidation Affected the Price and Quality of Hospital Care? (2006) http://www.rwjf.org/files/research/no9researchreport.pdf.

[4] An Assistant Director of the FTC's Bureau of Competition acknowledged, "Both the FTC and the DOJ left the hospital merger business and determined that these cases were unwinnable in federal district court." Victoria Stagg Elliot, FTC, in Turnabout, Takes a Closer Look at Hospital Mergers, AmericanMedicalNews (April 9, 2012).

[5] See e.g., Cory S. Capps, The Silent Majority Fallacy of the Elzinga Hogarty Criteria: A Critique and New Approach to Analyzing Hospital Mergers (2001), available at http:// www.nber.org/papers/w8216.

[6] Vogt & Town supra note 3.

[7] Massachusetts Attorney General, Examination of Health Care Cost Trends and Cost Drivers Pursuant to G.L. c. 118G, § 61/2(b) (March 16, 2010), available at: http://www.mass. Gov /Cago/docs/healthcare/final report w cover appendices glossary.pdf

[8] David Dranove, THE ECONOMIC EVOLUTION OF AMERICAN HEALTH CARE: FROM MARCUS WELBY TO MANAGED CARE 122 (2000).

[9] MEDICARE PAYMENT ADVISORY COMM'N, REPORT TO THE CONGRESS: IMPROVING INCENTIVES IN THE MEDICARE PROGRAM xiv (2009) available at http://www.medpac.gov/documents/mar09_entirereport.pdf.

[10] Karen Davenport & Sonia Sekhar, Interactive Map: Insurance Market Concentration Creates Fewer Choices, CTR. FOR AM. PROGRESS (Nov. 5, 2009), http://www.american progress.org/issues/2009/11/insurance_market.html.

[11] John Holahan & Linda Blumberg, Urban Inst., Health Policy Ctr., CAN A PUBLIC INSURANCE PLAN INCREASE COMPETITION AND LOWER THE COSTS OF HEALTH CARE REFORM? 3 (2008), available at http://www.urban. org/health_policy/ url.cfm?ID =411762.

[12] The Department of Justice's study concluded: [T]he biggest obstacle to an insurer's entry or expansion in the small- or mid-sized-employer market is scale. New insurers cannot compete with incumbents for enrollees without provider discounts, but they cannot negotiate for discounts without a large number of enrollees. This circularity problem makes entry risky and difficult, helping to secure the position of eXisting incumbents. Christine A. Varney, Assistant Att'y Gen., Antitrust Div., U.S. Dep't of Justice, Remarks as Prepared for the American Bar Association/American Health Lawyers Association Antitrust and Healthcare Conference (May 24, 2009), available at http://www.justice.gov /atr/public/ speeches/258898.pdf.

[13] Because my testimony today focuses on provider and payor competition, I am omitting what is undoubtedly the most significant antitrust enforcement effort in health care, the challenge to pay-for-delay agreements in the pharmaceutical sector. These cases, currently tangled in a series of conflicting decisions from federal appellate costs, are estimated to involve potential costs of $3.5 billion per year.

[14] In the Matter of OSF Healthcare System and Rockford Health System, FTC Docket No. 9349 (Nov. 17, 2011) available at www.ftc.gov/os/adjpro/d9349/111118rockfordcmpt.pdf

[15] In the Matter of ProMedica Health System, Inc., FTC Docket No. 9346 (March 28, 2012) available at www.ftc.gov/os/adjpro/d9346/120328promedicabrillopinion.pdf

[16] United States v. Humana Inc. and Arcadian Management Services, (D.D.C. March 28, 2012) available at www.justice.gov/atr/cases/humana.html.

[17] Press Release, U.S. Dep't of Justice, Blue Cross Blue Shield of Michigan and Physicians Health Plan of Mid-Michigan Abandon Merger Plans (Mar. 8, 2010), available at http://www.justice.gov/atr/public/press_releases/2010/256259.pdf.

[18] Federal Trade Commission v. Phoebe Putney Health System, Inc., 663 F.3d 1369 (11th Cir. Aug. 9, 2011). The Solicitor General has filed a petition for certiorari in this case.

[19] United States v. Blue Cross Blue Shield of Michigan, No, 2:10-14155-DPH-MKM (filed Oct. 18, 2010) available at http://www.justice.gov/atr/public/press releases/2010/263227.htm.

[20] United States v. United Regional Health Care System, Case No.: 7:11-cv-00030-O (September 29, 2012) available at http://www.justice.gov/atr/cases/unitedregional.html.

[21] Federal Trade Commission and U.S. Department of Justice, Statement of Antitrust Enforcement Policy Regarding Accountable Care Organizations Participating in the Medicare Shared Savings Program (October 28, 2011) available at www.ftc.gov/os/fedreg/ 2011/10/111020aco.pdf.

[22] As the nonpartisan Antitrust Modernization Commission has explained, antitrust exemptions "should be recognized as a decision to sacrifice competition and consumer welfare" that benefits small, concentrated interest groups while imposing costs broadly upon consumers at large. Antitrust Modernization Comm'n, Report and Recommendations 350 (2007), available at http://govinfo.library.unt.edu/amc/report_recommendation/amc_ final_report. pdf.

[23] Clark C. Havighurst & Barak D. Richman, The Provider Monopoly Problem in Health Care, 89 Or. L. Rev. 847 (2011).

In: Physician Practices
Editor: Isaak Angelidis

ISBN: 978-1-62618-184-7

Chapter 10

STATEMENT OF MARTIN GAYNOR, PROFESSOR, CARNEGIE MELLON UNIVERSITY. HEARING ON "HEALTH CARE INDUSTRY CONSOLIDATION"*

1. INTRODUCTION

Health care is a very large and important industry. Hospital and physician services are a large part of the U.S. economy. In 2009, hospital care alone accounted for 5.4% of GDP roughly twice the size of automobile manufacturing, agriculture, or mining, and larger than all manufacturing sectors except food and beverage and tobacco products, which is approximately the same size. Physician services comprise 3.6% of GDP (Martin et al., 2011). The net cost of health insurance - current year premiums minus current year medical benefits paid was 1% of GDP in 2009. The share of the economy accounted for by these sectors has risen dramatically over the last 30 years. In 1980, hospitals and physicians accounted for 3.6% and 1.7% of U.S. GDP, respectively, while the net cost of health insurance in 1980 was 0.34% (Martin et al., 2011).

Of course, health care is important not only because of its size. Health care services can save lives or dramatically affect the quality of life, thereby substantially improving wellbeing and productivity.

---

* This is an edited, reformatted and augmented version of Statement given on September 9, 2011 before the House Committee on Ways and Means, Subcommittee on Health.

As a consequence, the functioning of the health care sector is vitally important. A well functioning health care sector is an asset to the economy and improves quality of life for the citizenry. By the same token, problems in the health care sector act as a drag on the economy and impose a burden on individuals.

As documented below, there has been a tremendous amount of consolidation among health care providers. Consolidation has also been occuring among health insurers. Consolidation can bring efficiencies -- it can reduce inefficient duplication of services, allow firms to combine to achieve efficient size, or facilitate investment in quality or efficiency improvements. On the other hand, consolidation can enhance the market power and lead to increased prices or reduced quality.

The research evidence shows that providers in more concentrated markets charge higher prices to private payers, without accompanying gains in efficiency or quality. Further, the burden of higher provider prices falls on individuals, not insurers or employers. Even though individuals with private, employer provided health insurance pay a small portion of provider fees directly out of their own pockets, then end up paying for increased prices in the end. Insurers facing higher provider prices increase their premiums to employers. Employers then pass those increased premiums on to their workers, either in the form of lower wages (or smaller wage increases) or reduced benefits (greater premium sharing or less extensive coverage, including the loss of coverage). There is less research evidence on the impacts of consolidation in health insurance markets, but that evidence shows insurers in more concentrated markets charge higher premiums to large employers, and pay lower prices to providers.

This represents a real, and serious problem. The U.S. health care system depends on private markets to deliver health care and for a large part of the financing of care. If these markets are not functioning well due to the exercise of market power this creates problems for the entire system.

2. CONSOLIDATION

While not a new phenomenon, there has been substantial consolidation in the health care industry in recent years. There was a large amount of consolidation in hospital markets in the 1990s. Consolidation activity slowed down starting around 2002, but has turned up in the past couple of years.

Figure 1 presents information on hospital merger and acquisition activity from 1998 through the first two quarters of 2011. As can be seen, there were a large number of mergers and acquisitions in the 1990s, with the pace slowing down in the early 2000s, and some pick up in activity in the past couple of years.

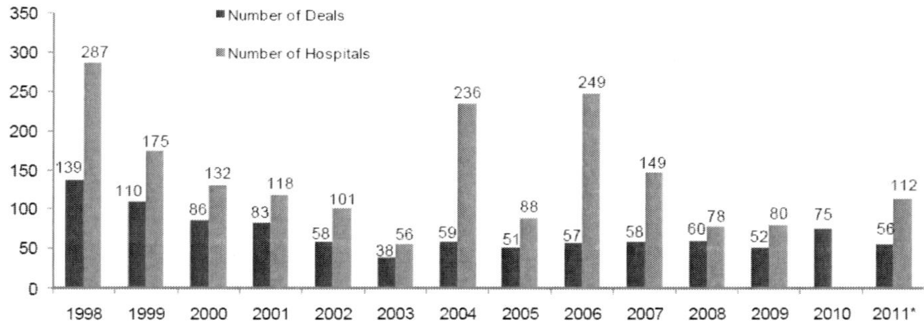

Figure 1. Hospital Mergers and Acquisitions, 1998-2010. Source: Irving Levin Associates, Inc., The Health Care Acquisition Report, Sixteenth Edition, 2010.

Some additional information is contained in Figure 2, which charts the number of hospitals that are members of systems from 2000 to 2009. Members of hospital systems are often jointly owned and operated, so can be considered to be one firm. As can be seen, membership has been increasing substantially over time, thereby diminishing the number of independent hospitals.

The Herfindahl-Hirschmann Index (HHI) is a measure of how concentrated shares are within a market, and is widely employed as a measure of market structure. The HHI is the sum of squared market shares in the market. It increases as market shares are more concentrated among a small number of firms. It reaches its maximum value of 10,000 for a monopoly (the square of the monopolist's market share of 100 percent), and reaches a minimum value when the market is equally divided.

Table 1 presents numbers for the population-weighted, Herfindahl-Hirschmann Index for hospitals for selected years from 1987 to 2006.[1] Two things are clear from this table. U.S. hospital markets are highly concentrated and have become even more concentrated over time. From the table it is easily seen that hospital markets have become significantly more concentrated. In 1987, the mean HHI was 2,340 and by 2006 the HHI is was 3,161 – an increase of over 900 points. In 1992, the mean hospital concentration levels (2,440) were (barely) below the recently updated Federal merger guidelines'

(Federal Trade Commission and Department of Justice, 1992) cut-off point for classifying a market as "Highly Concentrated" (HHI ≥ 2,500), but by 2006 the mean concentration level (3,261) rose to well above this threshold. Town et al. (2006) note that mergers and acquisitions are the primary reason for the increase in hospital concentration over this period.

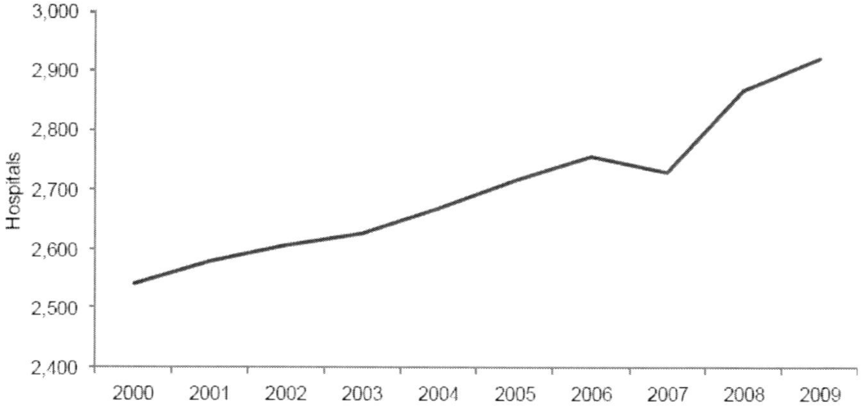

Figure 2. Number of Hospitals in Health Systems, 2000-2009. Source: American Hospital Association.

Table 1. Hospital Market Concentration, U.S., 1987-2006[a]

Year	Mean HHI[b]	Change[c]
1987	2,340	—
1992	2,440	100
1997	2,983	543
2002	3,236	253
2006	3,261	25

[a] Source: American Hospital Association. Data are for U.S. Metropolitan Statistical Areas with population < 3 million.

[b] Herfindahl-Hirschmann Index. Means weighted by MSA population.

[c] Total change from the previous year in the table.

To provide some context for these numbers, a market with 5 equally sized firms would have a HHI of 2,000, 4 equally sized firms would have an HHI of 2,500 and a market with 3 equally sized firms would have an HHI of 3,333. That is, the increase in the HHI over the last 20 years is the equivalent of moving from approximately 5 equally sized firms to a market with between 3 equally sized firms.

While hospital markets are highly concentrated on average, there is also wide variation in concentration. Figure 3 shows a scatterplot of the MSA level market concentration in 1990 and in 2006. This figure displays two phenomena. First, it shows the distribution of HHIs across MSAs. Most MSAs are "Highly Concentrated." In 2006, of the 332 MSAs in the U.S., 250 had HHIs greater than 2,500. Second, it is clear from Figure 3 that the increase in hospital concentration was a broad phenomenon – the vast majority of MSAs became more concentrated over this period. Particularly striking is the number of moderately concentrated MSAs in 1990 that by 2006 had become highly concentrated.

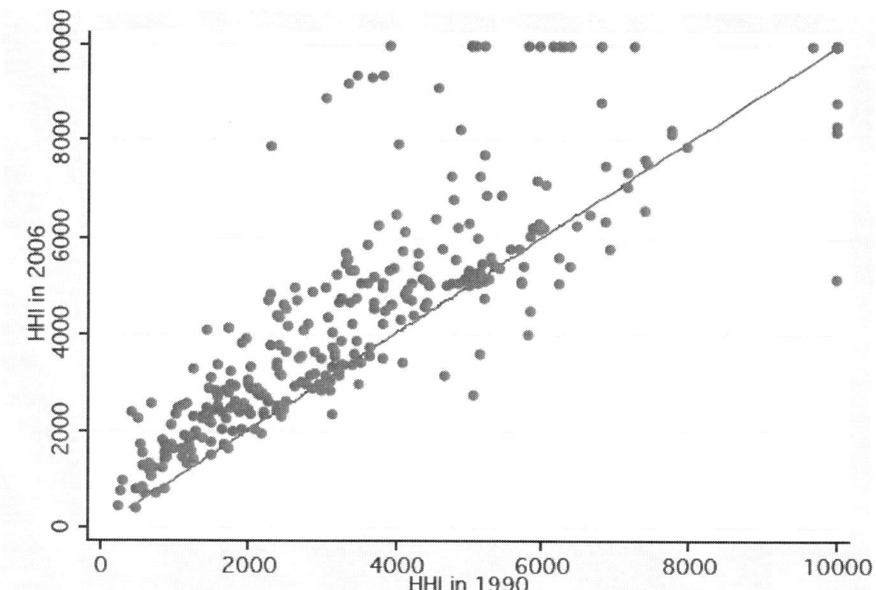

Figure 3. Scatterplot of MSA HHI in 1990 and HHI in 2006.

An obvious question is why this wave of hospital consolidation occurred. Fuchs (2007) and others point to the rise of managed care as the principal factor driving this massive consolidation. A cursory glance at Figure 4 suggests this causal explanation. The idea is that the rise of HMOs introduced aggressive price negotiations between hospitals and health plans, thereby giving hospitals a strong incentive to acquire bargaining power through consolidation. The rise of HMOs during the 1990s is widely credited with significantly reducing health care cost growth, primarily through tough price negotiations (see, e.g., Cutler et al., 2000).

Early suggestive evidence is provided by Chernew (1995), who finds that in the 1980s there is a relationship between HMO penetration and the number of hospitals operating in the market. Dranove et al. (2002) examine data from the 1981 to 1994 and find a correlation between metropolitan area HMO penetration in 1994 and the change in market structure. However, Town et al. (2007) examine the change in hospital market structure and the change in HMO penetration and find little correlation. Some have suggested that it wasn't the realization of the rise of managed care, but the anticipation (which in some cases may have been in error) that led hospitals to consolidate. Work in progress by Town and Park (2011) provides support for this hypothesis. They find that HMO exit, a measure of the exuberance of expectations regarding the demand for managed care in a location, is correlated with hospital consolidation.

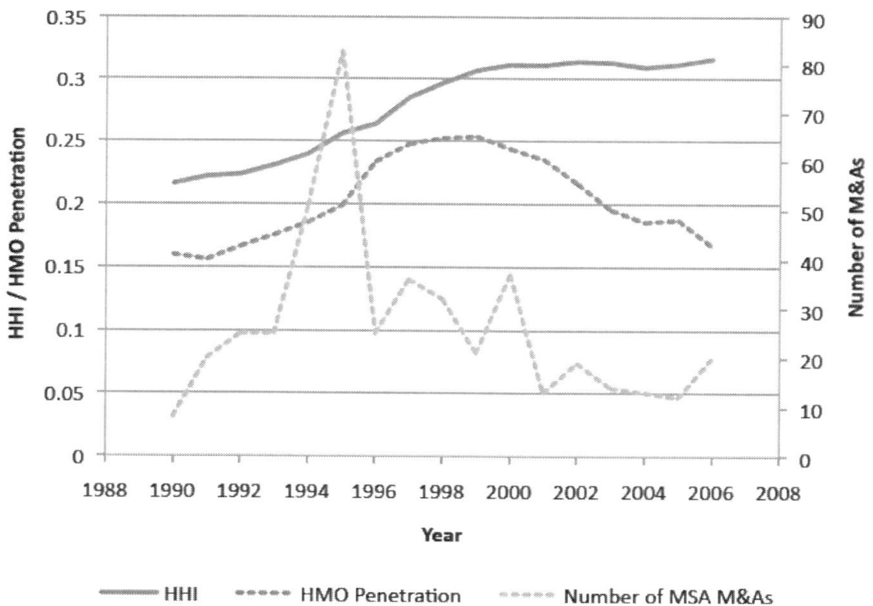

Figure 4. Trends in Hospital Concentration, M&A Activity and HMO Penetration: 1990-2006.

There have also been substantial changes in market structure in U.S. physician markets. Liebhaber and Grossman (2007) report that the percent of physicians in solo or 2 person practices declined from 40.7 percent in 1996-97 to 32.5 percent in 2004-05. Further, the proportion in practices of 3-5 physicians fell over the same period. The proportion of physicians practicing in groups of 6 or more grew from 15.9 percent to 21.8 percent. The number of physicians in other practice settings (primarily employed by others) grew from 31.2 to 36.0 percent over this period. Since the number of physicians per 1,000 persons has not really changed (~2.5) since 1997 (National Center for Health Statistics, 2011), this represents an increase in concentration.

There is no good systematic information on the structure of local physician markets. Those markets, especially for specialized services, may be very concentrated, but there is no information generally available at the national level. Schneider et al. (2008) constructed HHIs for physician organizations in California at the county level for 2001.

They find the average county HHI for physician organizations was 4,430, implying a high degree of concentration on average. They found that 17 percent of California counties had a physician organization HHI below 1,800, 33 percent had an HHI between 1,800 and 3,600, and 50 percent had an HHI above 3,600.

Tables 2, 3, and 4 provide information about health insurance market structures for the U.S. This information shows consistently high levels of concentration in health insurance markets.

Table 2. Insurance Market Concentration, U.S., 2004-2008[a,b]

Year	Median HHI	Change	Mean HHI	Change
2004	3,544	—	3,939	—
2005	3,748	204	4,077	138
2006	2,986	-762	3,440	-637
2007	3,558	572	3,944	504
2008	3,276	-282	3,727	-217

[a] Source: See American Medical Association (2010) for more information on the data and calculations. American Medical Association (AMA) calculations for the combined HMO+PPO markets using January 1st enrollment data from HealthLeaders-InterStudy's (HLIS) Managed Market Surveyors c HealthLeaders-Inter-Study.

[b] MSA-level HHIs for HMO+PPO markets.

Table 2 contains measures of HHI for HMO plus PPO markets in the U.S. from reports from the American Medical Association (AMA). They show high levels of concentration (although lower than for hospitals). The numbers show insurance market concentration declining somewhat over time (although not consistently). However, there are some concerns about the accuracy of these numbers (see Capps, 2009; Dafny et al., 2011a).

Dafny (2010) and Dafny et al. (2011b), using data on the large employer segment of the insurance market, also show increasing concentration in health insurance markets. Dafny (2010, Figure 5) documents an increase in the percentage of markets with 1-4, 5-6, or 7-9 insurance carriers in the U.S. from 1998-2005, and a decrease in the percentage of markets with 9-10 or more than 10 carriers. Dafny et al. (2011b) state that the mean HHI in their sample increased from 2,286 to 2,984 from 1998-2006, the median four firm concentration ratio increased from 79 to 90 percent, and the mean number of carriers per market fell from 18.9 to 9.6. They show (Figure 1 in their paper) that 78 percent of the markets they study had increases in the HHI of 100 points or more from 2002 to 2006, and 53 percent experienced increases of 500 points or more. Table 3 has mean HHIs by year from the data used in those papers. These numbers indicate that the large employer segment of the health insurance market is concentrated and has grown more so over time. These numbers are roughly similar in magnitude to those calculated by the AMA. However they show concentration increasing over time (by about 400 points from 2004-2008), while the AMA numbers exhibit a slight decrease over time.

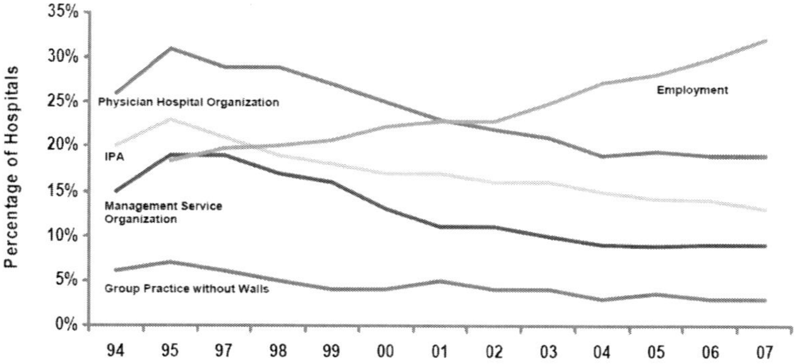

Figure 5. Physician-Hospital Trends, 1994-2007. Source: American Hospital Association.

Table 3. Large Employer Insurance Market Concentration, U.S., 1998-2009[a]

Year	Self + Fully Insured Mean HHI[b]	Change	Fully Insured Only Mean HHI[b]	Change
1998	2,172	—	2,984	—
1999	1,997	-175	2,835	
2000	2,175	178	3,092	
2001	2,093	-82	3,006	
2002	2,280	187	3,158	
2003	2,343	63	3,432	
2004	2,519	176	3,706	
2005	2,609	90	3,951	
2006	2,740	131	4,072	
2007	2,873	133	4,056	
2008	2,916	43	4,201	
2009	2,956	40	4,126	

[a] Source: These #s were graciously provided by Leemore Dafny. The data are for large multisite employers and do not represent the totality of the insurance market. For more information on the data source, see Dafny (2010).

[b] Weighted by # of enrollees.

A recent report by the U.S. Government Accountability Office (Government Accountability Office, 2009) compiled information on the market structure of the small group health insurance market in the U.S. Table 4 reproduces numbers from that report. As can be seen, those markets appear to be fairly heavily concentrated, and increasing in concentration. A recent paper by Schneider et al. (2008) utilizes a unique data source for California to construct HHIs for insurance plans at the county level for 2001. They find an average insurance HHI for California counties of 2,592. They report that 21 percent of counties have HHIs below 1,800[2], 55 percent had HHIs between 1,800 and 3,600 and 24 percent had HHIs above 3,600. The information from these various data sources seem broadly consistent.

Table 4. Small Group Insurance Market Structure, U.S., 2000-2003[a]

Year	Median Market Share, Largest Carrier	# of States with 5 _rm concentration ratio ≥ 75%
2002	33%	19 (of 34; 56%)
2005	43%	26 (of 34; 77%)
2008	47%	34 (of 39; 87%)

[a] Source: Government Accountability O_ce (2009).

It is worth noting that, based on the data in Table 3 the increase in concentration in health insurance markets appears to occur much later than the increase in concentration in hospital markets. The major increase in hospital market concentration occurred in the mid to late 1990s. Insurance market concentration, at least for large employers, starts increasing in 2002.

In addition to "horizontal" consolidation between firms in the same industry (hospitals and hospitals, physician practices and physician practices), there has been some "vertical" consolidation between hospitals and physician practices. 5 shows the trends in the proportions of hospitals with various kinds of integration with physicians. As can be seen, various forms of integration between physicians and hospitals grew and peaked during the 1990s, and have declined since then, with the exception of physician employment by hospitals, which has increased substantially over this time period.

In addition to information on market structure, there is some information on trends in prices and the contribution of health care prices to overall health care cost growth. Akosa Antwi et al. (2009) document a 100% increase in hospital prices in California from 1999-2006, although they do not find market concentration to be a contributor to the increase. Martin et al. (2011) decompose U.S. health spending growth into growth due to prices versus growth due to nonprice factors (e.g., population, intensity of care). They find that prices account for 60% of the increase in overall spending from 2008 to 2009. The proportion of health spending growth due to prices varies over time (see Exhibit 6 in Martin et al., 2011), but has been growing steadily since 2001.

Some recent reports from state governments document growth or variation in health care prices. A report from the Massachusetts Attorney General's office (Massachusetts Attorney General, 2010) finds that price increases caused most of the increases in health care spending in the state in recent years. The report also finds significant variation in prices and that the variation is uncorrelated with quality of care, but is correlated with market leverage. A report on Pennsylvania hospitals found substantial variation in prices for heart surgery, but no correlation of prices with quality (Pennsylvania Health Care Cost Containment Council, 2007).

Overall, the statistics presented here paint a picture of health care markets that are concentrated and becoming more so over time. There is also some evidence that prices are rising faster than quantities, and that price variation isn't related to quality but may be due to market power.

3. EVIDENCE ON THE IMPACTS OF CONSOLIDATION

Most of the evidence on the impacts of consolidation come from hospital markets. Unfortunately there are very few studies of competition in physician markets, mainly due to lack of data.

3.1. Hospitals

3.1.1. Price

There has been a lot of research on the impact of hospital market consolidation on prices paid by private payers. The overwhelming finding in the literature is that consolidation leads to higher prices (see Dranove and Satterthwaite, 2000; Gaynor and Vogt, 2000; Vogt and Town, 2006; Gaynor and Town, 2012, for reviews of the evidence).

Examining the distribution of realized hospital prices (for the privately insured) alone is informative about the functioning of hospital markets. Ginsburg (2010) uses administrative claims data for 8 geographic areas from four large private insurers to construct inpatient hospital prices. He finds that there is significant variation both within and across regions in hospital prices. For example, San Francisco has the highest average hospital prices in 2008, with prices equal to 210% of the Medicare reimbursement rate. The lowest rate is Miami-South Florida with mean prices that are 147% of Medicare rates – the mean price in San Francisco is 43% higher than Miami. Within San Francisco, the interquartile range is 116 percent of the Medicare price. Of course, there are a number of possible reasons for this variation. Cost, quality and demand differences will generally imply price differences. However, it seems unlikely that there is enough variation across those factors to generate such wide variation in price.

There are a number of different methods that have been used to estimate the impact of hospital consolidation on prices. The most direct approach compares price increases at merging hospitals with those at similar hospitals which did not merge (see Capps and Dranove, 2004; Dafny, 2009; Haas-Wilson and Garmon, 2011; Krishnan, 2001; Spang et al., 2001; Sacher and Vita, 2001; Tenn, 2011; Thompson, 2011). The vast majority of these studies find price increases of at least 10 percent due to merger, with some estimates of price increases due to merger of 40 percent or greater.

For example, Haas-Wilson and Garmon (2011) evaluate the Evanston Northwestern and Highland Park hospitals in the northern suburbs of Chicago.

They find a price increase of 20 percent due to that merger. Tenn (2011) examines the merger of two hospitals in California: Summit and Alta Bates. He finds that prices at Summit hospital increased between 28 and 44 percent after the merger.

Another source of information on the impacts of hospital consolidation comes from studies which examine the impact of hospital market concentration (measured as the HHI) on price. These studies don't examine the effects of mergers directly, but allow one to calculate the expected impact of a merger based on its impact on market concentration. Vogt and Town (2006) calculate the average estimated impact of a merger of two equal sized hospitals in a five hospital market (a "5 to 4" merger).[3] They find that such a merger is estimated to increase prices by 5 percent.

Last, a few research papers have estimated the impacts of hospital mergers using simulation. These papers estimate models of hospital competition, then use the estimated parameters of those models to simulate the impacts of mergers (Town and Vistnes, 2001; Capps et al., 2003; Gaynor and Vogt, 2003; Brand et al., 2011). These papers find estimated impacts of mergers ranging from 5 to 53 percent increases in price. Town and Vistnes (2001) examine mergers among hospitals in Los Angeles and Orange Counties, California, where there are more than 120 hospitals between the two counties. They find that many of the mergers they examine would result in price increases of 5 percent or greater, in spite of the large number of hospitals in these counties. Capps et al. (2003) examine a 3 hospital merger in the southern suburbs of San Diego County, California, and find a price increase due to the merger of over 10 percent. Gaynor and Vogt (2003) find that a three-to-two hospital merger in San Luis Obispo, California (which was attempted, but blocked by the FTC) would have raised prices by over 50 percent. Brand et al. (2011) consider the recent proposed acquisition of Prince William hospital in Manassas, Virginia by Inova health system in Northern Virginia. They estimate that the acquisition would have led to price increases at Prince William hospital of anywhere from 19 to 33 percent.

Overall, these studies consistently show that hospital consolidation raises prices, and by nontrivial amounts. Consolidated hospitals that are able to charge higher prices due to enhanced market power are able to do so on an ongoing basis, making this a permanent rather than a transitory problem.

3.1.2. Not-for-Profit Firm Behavior

The hospital sector is characterized by the fact that there is a mixture of firms with different ownership types. Not-for-profits are the most common, but there are substantial numbers of for-profit hospitals and public hospitals. One question that is relevant in this setting is whether not-for-profit hospitals behave any differently with regard to their pricing behavior.

A number of studies (e.g., Keeler et al., 1999; Simpson and Shin, 1997; Dranove and Ludwick, 1999; Capps et al., 2003; Gaynor and Vogt, 2003) have addressed the issue of not-for-profit/for-profit differences in competitive conduct. Those studies do not find any significant differences in pricing behavior. In particular, the effects of consolidation on pricing do not appear to differ depending on whether a hospital is not-for-profit.

A recent study by Capps et al. (2010) examines whether not-for-profit hospitals are more likely than for-profit hospitals to offer more charity care or unprofitable services in response to an increase in market power. The implication is, that if there were such a difference, not-for-profits would be spending their profits from market power on socially beneficial activities. Capps et al. examine 7 years of data on California hospitals and find no evidence of any such differences – not-for-profits do not engage in any more socially beneficial activities than do for-profits when they possess market power.

3.1.3. Costs

It is clear that mergers can result in efficiencies because of economies of scale, increased purchasing power, the ability to consolidate services, or the the transfer of managerial techniques and skill to the acquired hospital. However, mergers also have the potential to increase costs. Larger systems imply larger bureaucracies. In addition, hospital costs are not necessarily exogenous to market structure. Hospitals that are able to bargain for higher prices may have the incentive to use the resulting profits for the benefit of physicians and hospital executives (e.g., through capital expenditures that benefit physicians or increases in executive compensation or perks). This is particularly likely if there is no residual claimant (as is the case for not-for-profit organizations) or monitoring by the residual claimant is costly. Thus, the analysis of cost impacts is central to understanding the impact of hospital mergers. The evidence presented above suggests that, on average, hospital mergers result in increases in price. Consequently if there are significant cost reductions associated with mergers they are not passed onto the purchasers of hospital services in the form of lower prices.

A few studies do directly examine the impact of hospital mergers on costs. Dranove and Lindrooth (2003) examine mergers of previously independent hospitals that consolidate financial reporting and operate under a single license post-merger. They find that, on average, these hospitals experience post-merger cost decreases of 14 percent. System mergers in which the hospitals were not as fully integrated (as measured by the use of multiple licenses) did not realize cost savings. These findings suggest that integration of merging hospitals is necessary to achieve meaningful efficiencies. A recent study by Harrison (2010) finds that immediately following a merger costs declined, but eventually rose to pre-merger levels. This finding that is difficult to reconcile with the view that mergers require significant upfront costs but have benefits accrue in later years. The circumstances in which mergers are most likely to result in meaningful cost decreases are those in which the merging facilities operate as a more fully integrated entity. To be clear, however, the presence of any cost savings does not mean that they are necessarily passed on to consumers.

3.1.4. Quality

A number of research studies have examined the impacts of hospital consolidation on various measures of quality, although the most commonly used measure of quality is mortality (adjusted for patient severity of illness). The results in this literature are mixed, although the results are strongest for markets with regulated prices (see Gaynor, 2006; Vogt and Town, 2006; Gaynor and Town, 2012, for surveys).

A number of studies have examined the impact of market concentration on patient mortality for Medicare patients. There are a variety of findings, but the strongest studies find that market concentration significantly increases mortality (Kessler and McClellan, 2000; Kessler and Geppert, 2005).

Kessler and McClellan find that risk-adjusted one year mortality for Medicare heart attack (acute myocardial infarction, or AMI) patients is significantly higher in more concentrated markets. In particular, patients in the most concentrated markets had mortality probabilities 1.46 points higher than those in the least concentrated markets (this constitutes a 4.4 percent difference) as of 1991. This is an extremely large difference – it amounts to over 2,000 fewer (statistical) deaths in the least concentrated vs. most concentrated markets.

The English National Health Service (NHS) adopted a set of reforms in 2006 that were intended to increase patient choice and hospital competition, and introduced regulated prices for hospitals based on patient diagnoses (analogous to the Medicare Prospective Payment System). Two recent studies examine the impacts of this reform (Cooper et al., 2010; Gaynor et al., 2010) and find that, following the reform, risk-adjusted mortality from heart attacks fell more at hospitals in less concentrated markets than at hospitals in more concentrated markets. Gaynor et al. (2010) also look at mortality from all causes and find that patients fared worse at hospitals in more consolidated markets.

The results of studies which examine impacts of competition for privately insured patients are more mixed. A number of studies find that quality is positively affected by competition, a number find that it is negatively affected by competition, and some find no effect. As a consequence, there is no clear impact of the impact of hospital consolidation on quality for privately insured patients that can be ascertained from the current research literature.

A recent study by Cutler et al. (2010) examines not only the impacts of competition on quality, but also impacts on costs. Cutler et al. use the repeal of entry restricting regulation (hospital certificate of need regulation; CON) in Pennsylvania to examine the effect of entry of hospitals into the CABG surgery market. They find that entry led to increased quality, but that the gains from reduced mortality due to entry are approximately offset by the additional costs incurred by entering firms.

A recent paper by Romano and Balan (2011) attempts to directly assess the impacts of hospital mergers on quality. Romano and Balan study the impact on quality of care of a consummated merger between two hospitals in the Chicago suburbs (Evanston Northwestern Hospital and Highland Park Hospital). This merger was the subject of an antitrust suit by the Federal Trade Commission, and the authors provided evidence on the case. They find no significant impact of the merger on many quality measures, but there is a significant negative impact on some and a few with positive impacts. They estimate that the merger led to heart attack, pneumonia, and stroke mortality going up at Evanston Northwestern Hospital, although not at Highland Park. There was some improvement in quality for some nursing-sensitive quality measures: the incidence of decubitis ulcers (bedsores) fell at both merged entities, as did infections at Evanston Northwestern. Conversely, the incidence of hip fractures rose at Evanston Northwestern. Last, they found increases in some measures of obstetric outcomes (birth trauma to the newborn, obstetric trauma to the mother), and decreases in some other measures. They conclude that overall there is no reason to infer that the merger had salutary effects on quality.

Overall, the research evidence suggests that hospital consolidation can have a negative impact on quality in markets with regulated prices, like Medicare. However, the current research evidence where prices are market determined (the privately insured) does not indicate a clear impact of consolidation on quality in those markets in general.

3.2. Physicians

As stated previously, there is relatively little research on competition in physician services markets, mainly due to lack of available data. There are some studies, however, which shed some light on this topic.

Economics suggests that there is a minimum population necessary for a given area to support a physician of a particular specialty. Further, the smaller the total number of physicians in a given specialty, the larger the population necessary to support a physician.

If the total number of physicians expands, then competition will lead to lower incomes for physicians in larger communities, and physicians will diffuse out to smaller areas, so the minimum population necessary to support a physician will fall. Rosenthal et al. (2005) test this hypothesis by examining communities in states in which the total number of physicians doubled from 1970 to 1999. They find that communities of all sizes gained physicians over this period, but that the impact was larger for smaller communities, implying that competition among physicians did increase due to the increased number of doctors.

Some recent work by Schneider et al. (2008) examines the impact of physician and insurer market concentration on physician prices. They find that physician market concentration is associated with significantly higher prices. A 1 percent increase in the physician HHI leads to 1-4 percent higher physician prices. Conversely, they find that the health insurer HHI has no statistically significant impact on physician prices.

3.3. Insurers

Until recently there has been very little research on competition by health insurance firms. Part of the reason for this has been the paucity of sufficient data for given markets to construct measures of prices or market shares in the U.S. and internationally. For the U.S., there are detailed household level data (the Medical Expenditure Panel Survey, http://www.meps.ahrq.gov/mepsweb/) on health insurance decisions and prices, but these data are from surveys of approximately 4,000 households selected to be nationally representative. As a consequence, they don't fully describe the choices in a given market, or catalog the prices of alternatives, let alone the market shares of sellers. Other data (National Association of Insurance Commissioners, http://www.naic.org) do capture market shares, but at the level of a state. Since the vast majority of health insurance restricts enrollees' choices to a network of providers, most of whom are local, the geographic market for health insurance is often local, and smaller than a state. In addition, there are no comprehensive data on health plans' networks of providers. The most comprehensive data on health insurance markets has been for private insurance associated with the Medicare program (Medigap coverage, Medicare+Choice/Medicare Advantage).

Dafny (2010) is one of the first of some new studies on insurance market competition. Dafny uses data from a benefits consulting firm on the plans purchased and premiums paid by a large number (776) of large employers over the period 1998-2005. While these data are not necessarily complete by market or nationally representative, they do represent the most extensive and comprehensive data set with prices and quantities for the insurance market.

She examines the effect of shocks to employer profitability on the changes in the insurance premiums they pay. The idea is that if insurers possess no market power then the premiums they charge will not vary with employer profitability. Only if insurers have market power will they be able to price discriminate based on employer profitability. Dafny finds evidence that premiums increase with the buyer's profitability. She also finds that the effect of employer profitability on insurance premiums falls with the number of firms in the market. More precisely, what Dafny finds is that the effect of increased profitability for an employer is to increase premiums in markets with few insurers by more than in markets with a large number of insurers, for the *same* employer.

It is notable that there are significant effects of employer profitability in insurance premiums even for markets with 9-10 insurers (the effect is insignificant for markets with 10 or more insurers). It seems surprising that insurers would possess market power in markets with 8-9 rivals (9-10 firms total). This empirical result does raise some doubts, but research by Dranove et al. (2003) found patterns in 1997 suggesting there may be market power in HMO markets with up to 6 firms. In any event, Dafny is a contribution that opens a line of empirical research on competition in health insurance markets.

Dafny et al. (2011b) employ the same dataset as in Dafny (2010), but examine how the growth rate of an employer's health insurance premiums is affected by health insurance market concentration (HHI). Initial estimates reveal no significant effect of insurer market concentration on premium growth. Of course, market concentration may be codetermined with premium growth, making it difficult to tease out a clear effect. In order to deal with that problem Dafny et al. examine changes in local market concentration due to a large merger in 1999 between two national health insurers: Aetna and Prudential Healthcare. Using this, they find a significant impact of the predicted change in HHI due to the merger on the change in premiums. They find that the cumulative effect of insurer market consolidation on premiums is approximately 7 percent.

Dafny et al. also recognize that insurers may have bargaining power (market power in a posted price world) with regard to providers. They therefore examine the effect of insurer concentration on changes in earnings and employment for physicians and for nurses as a way of testing for the presence of insurer monopsony power. They find that the merger reduced physician earnings growth on average by 3 percent, while nurses' earnings rose by approximately 6-10ths of one percent. There is no significant effect on physician employment, while nurse employment grows as a result of the merger induced increase in concentration. This doesn't seem to be evidence of monopsony power, but it is consistent with plan concentration leading to downward pressure on physician earnings and ultimately to substitution of nurses for physicians.[4] Overall, while the estimation results depend crucially on the use of the Aetna-Prudential merger as a driver of changes in local insurance market concentration, they show evidence of a significant relationship between changes in insurer market concentration and changes in premiums, implying a link between market structure and the exercise of market power.

Maestas et al. (2009) document substantial price variation in Medigap insurance markets, even though plans are standardized. They find that insurers have substantial differences in costs, and hence loading fees, which contribute to the observed variation in prices. This conclude that price dispersion is caused by substantial search costs – Maestas et al. estimate an average search cost for consumers in the market of $72 and a maximum of $144.

Starc (2010) also examines the Medigap market for insurance, using a model that allows for both adverse selection and market power. She documents that the market is highly concentrated – the national 4 firm concentration ratio is 83 percent (compared to 44 percent for private passenger automobile insurance or 34 percent for life insurance), and two firms (UnitedHealth, 46 percent and Mutual of Omaha, 24 percent) account for almost all of that. Starc documents substantial price dispersion for Medigap policies, confirming Maestas et al., and documents a positive relationship between premiums and market concentration, the same qualitative result as in Dafny et al. (2011b), albeit for a very different market. A one percent increase in the two-firm concentration ratio is associated with a 0.26 percent increase in premiums.

Starc then uses the estimates from her model to find the impacts of adverse selection and market power in the Medigap market. She finds that adverse selection increases premiums by 9 percent and reduces the size of the market (lowers insurance coverage) by 18 percent. Starc goes on to calculate the impact of market power by calculating what premiums would be if they were set equal to costs. This is estimated to lead to large reductions in prices – 44 and 45 percent, respectively. These results emphasize the substantial market power exercised in this market.

Lustig (2010) examines the market for Medicare+Choice plans in 2000-2003. Medicare+Choice are private managed care plans that Medicare beneficiaries may choose as an alternative to traditional Medicare (the current version of this program is called Medicare Advantage). Lustig allows for both adverse selection and market power in his model. He finds that consumers' health risk has no significant impact on insurers' costs. Lustig then goes on to use the model estimates to simulate the gains to consumers and producers when adverse selection is eliminated and compare that to what he actually observes. The gain from eliminating adverse selection is simulated for markets with increasing numbers of insurers to generate effects of competition. Lustig finds that the gains to eliminating adverse selection increase steadily in the number of insurance firms. For example, in one of his simulations Lustig finds that removing adverse selection eliminates 17 percent of the difference in consumer and producer benefits between the observed and socially optimal outcomes where there's a monopoly, while it eliminates 35 percent of the difference in a duopoly, and 50 percent where there are 6 or more firms. This implies that when there is market power most of the welfare loss is due to the exercise of market power as opposed to adverse selection.

A paper by Town and Liu (2003) estimates a model of the Medicare+Choice market, the predecessor of Medicare Advantage, i.e., the market for private Medicare plans. They use their estimates to calculate the impacts of the program and of competition. They find that the creation of the M+C program resulted in approximately $15.6 billion in consumer surplus and $52 billion in profits from 1993 to 2000 (in 2000 dollars), i.e., $67.6 billion in value to consumers and producers. They also find evidence of competitive effects. Consumer benefit increases with the number of plans in a county, and most of the increase is due to increased premium competition. Comparing monopoly markets versus markets with four firms, they find that 81 percent of the difference in consumer benefit (higher in quadropoly markets) is due to increased premium competition. Of the remainder, 3 percent is from increased product variety and 8 percent from prescription drug coverage.

3.4. Vertical Integration

Vertical integration between hospitals and physicians or insurers and providers can in principle provide efficiencies by aligning incentives, allowing for better coordination of care and joint investments which enhance efficiency or the quality of care. At the same time, integration can potentially harm competition by foreclosing rivals from access to key inputs. An integrated system which has locked up all the orthopedists in town, for example, may make it difficult to impossible for another hospital to offer orthopedic services or for a freestanding ambulatory surgery center to enter the market and compete on orthopedic services. Separately, integration may eliminate competition among previously independent providers. For example, physicians who had previously been in competition all become members of the same firm once they integrate with a hospital system (or an insurer).

There is very little evidence at present on the impact of vertical integration on market power. In part, that is because vertical integration has not been that common in health care. It was quite rare until the mid-1990s, and then declined rapidly thereafter. Integration between hospitals and physician practices peaked in 1996 at approximately 40 percent of all hospitals, and declined thereafter (Burns and Pauly, 2002; Ciliberto, 2005). This pattern was repeated with vertical integration of hospitals into the insurance market, although the extent of vertical integration was never as great as between hospitals and physicians (Burns and Pauly, 2002). This growth coincided with the growth of managed care, and in particular with the perceived growth in managed care organizations' negotiating power with hospitals. Burns et al. (2000) find that hospital-physician alliances increase with the number of HMOs in the market. They infer that providers may be integrating in order to achieve or enhance market power. More recently, Berenson et al. (2010) conducted 300 interviews with health care market participants, and report that increased bargaining power through joint negotiations listed as one of several reasons for hospital-physician alliances.

Certain types of vertical relations in health care have been the subject of significant antitrust scrutiny — exclusive dealing between physician practices and hospitals (usually for a specialized service, e.g., radiology, anesthesiology, or pathology), and most-favorednations clauses between insurers and providers, which require the provider to give the insurer a rate as low as it gives to any buyer (see Gaynor and Haas-Wilson, 1998; Haas-Wilson, 2003, for reviews of vertical issues in health care).[5]

In spite of the interest in this topic, there is relatively little evidence on the effects of vertical restraints in health care. Ciliberto and Dranove (2005) and Cuellar and Gertler (2005) are the only two papers (of which I am aware) which examine the competitive impacts of vertical integration in health care. Both papers look at the effects of hospital-physician practice integration on hospital prices. The two studies find opposite results – Cuellar and Gertler find evidence consistent with anticompetitive effects of physician-hospital integration, while Ciliberto and Dranove find no such evidence.

Research on efficiencies from integration does not find much evidence of positive gains from integration. Burns and Muller (2008) review the empirical evidence on hospital-physician relationships. They find little evidence of an impact of integration on costs, quality, access or clinical integration. Madison (2004) investigates the relationship between hospital-physician affiliations and patient treatments, expenditures, and outcomes using data on Medicare heart attack patients. She finds little evidence of any impacts of hospital-physician relationships.

4. Who Pays for Higher Provider Prices?

As mentioned previously, when consolidation leads to providers obtaining higher prices from providers the impact ultimately falls on consumers, not insurers or employers. Research evidence consistently shows that higher health insurance costs for employers are passed on to employees in the form of lower wages (or lower wage increases) (see Gruber, 1994; Jensen and Morrisey, 2001; Bhattacharya and Bundorf, 2005; Baicker and Chandra, 2006; Adams, 2007; Emanuel and Fuchs, 2008). In addition, there is recent evidence that hospital mergers have increased the number of the uninsured. Town et al. (2006) find that private insurance rolls declined by approximately .3 percentage points or approximately 695,000 lives in 2003 due to the effects of hospital mergers, with the vast majority of those who lost private insurance joining the ranks of the uninsured.

As a consequence, even though privately insured consumers typically pay a very small share of provider fees directly, they bear the brunt of the impact of higher fees by ultimately receiving reduced total compensation from their employers.

5. Policy

There are a number of policy levers that can be considered to deal with consolidation in the health care industry. They include antitrust enforcement, enhancing supply by facilitating the entry of new providers (including new forms of providers), policies designed to enhance the responsiveness of demand, and rate regulation. These policies need not be pursued in isolation. For example, vigorous antitrust enforcement is likely to be most effective paired with policies that facilitate entry. Even under rate regulation providers compete for patients via quality or other means. Taking steps to maintain or enhance that competitive environment can substantially improve performance even if prices are regulated. Policies that enhance the entry of new providers can ultimately reduce the need for intensive antitrust enforcement or rate regulation.

5.1. Antitrust

The standard approach to the injurious effects of market consolidation is vigorous antitrust enforcement. Antitrust enforcement must be applied judiciously. Consolidation or integration can be efficiency enhancing, and those cases should be allowed and encouraged. However, the evidence does not support efficiency enhancing consolidation in general, at least in hospital markets.

While there is some evidence that prices are higher in more concentrated physician and insurance markets, we do not have direct research evidence on the impacts of consolidation on efficiencies or quality in those markets.[6]

Antitrust enforcers should carefully examine proposed mergers and block those they find anticompetitive. This policy can be successfully pursued, but it should be recognized that many markets (especially for hospitals) are already highly concentrated.

Another policy is to prosecute cases against consummated mergers, where the merged entities have exercised market power and not realized any substantial efficiencies. In addition, enforcers can pursue anticompetitive behavior intended to harm competition (for example, attempting to prevent entry or force exit of competitors). The enforcement agencies' resources are limited, so there are only so many cases of this sort they can pursue. It is possible, however, that vigorous enforcement against egregious offenders may have a chilling effect on the exercise of market power by others, who fear the possibility of detection and prosecution.

Another aspect of antitrust enforcement is providing safe harbors for integration that is considered to be efficiency enhancing. While efficient forms of organization should be allowed to emerge and flourish, care must also be taken to avoid allowing integration that is only a sham with regard to efficiency and is truly for the purpose of enhancing market power.

This is true in general, but is currently salient with regard to the Accountable Care Organizations (ACOs) which are part of the health reform law. As indicated previously, integration among hospitals and doctors has the potential to be efficiency enhancing, but can also cause harm to competition, and can potentially make it more difficult for innovative organizations to enter markets. This is a factor which must be given serious consideration.

Last, it is sometimes proposed that allowing firms on one side of a market to acquire market power is an appropriate response if firms on the other side of the market already possess it (e.g., allowing providers to acquire market power if insurers have substantial market power). This is sometimes called countervailing power.

The notion is that having a sort of balance of market power on both sides of the market is better than only having market power on one side. This is not necessarily the case.

First, it must be true that one side of the market does indeed have market power and it is causing harm. Hard bargaining over price (or other matters) is not in and of itself of harmful market power.

Second, the best response is to deal directly with the problem, and try to eliminate or reduce the extant market power. Antitrust enforcement is the most likely tool for this. This is certainly better than creating a situation with more market power.

Third, if it is not possible for some reason to deal directly with the extant market power on one side of the market, having market power on both sides does not necessarily improve matters. It can do so, but it can also make things worse. If the only way firms have to increase their bargaining power is by restricting the quantity they sell, then countervailing power will make things worse than market power on only one side of the market.

5.2. Supply Side Policies

Another policy lever are policies that facilitate the entry of new providers, and in particular allow for innovation. It may be that markets (again, hospital markets in particular) have become so concentrated that the effectiveness of antitrust enforcement is limited. That may leave inefficiencies in place in the short run. However, in the long run, as the technology of medicine changes, new types of providers will likely emerge and compete with current organizational forms. We have already seen some of this via the entry of free standing ambulatory surgery centers, retail clinics, and specialty hospitals. In the case of insurance, a key factor governing entry is the ability to field an attractive network of providers. Making sure that providers, particularly those that are perceived as "must-have" providers, are available to potential entrants is a critical factor. Regulation can play a role as well. Relatively few states have retained certificate of need regulation for health care facilities, but such regulation can raise the costs of entry. Insurers have to deal with differing sets of regulations in every state, and are not allowed to pool risk across states. Such factors may also raise the costs of entry.

Facilitating the entry of new firms, and in particular innovative new forms, can ameliorate or eliminate the effects of current consolidation in the long run. As stated previously, however, care still must be taken to ensure that such entry is possible, and not foreclosed by integration, so antitrust enforcement also plays a key role here. Obviously, such a process will take time, although change can sometimes occur very rapidly.

5.3. Demand Side Policies

Competition can only occur if demand by payers or consumers is sufficiently responsive to price or quality differences across providers, and if there's sufficient choice of providers. Selective contracting by private payers is a mechanism which helps to create an environment where competition among providers is possible. If payers contract with every provider in a market, then they have very little bargaining power. Policies that enhance the ability of payers to selectively contract with providers are important, but they will only be effective if there is sufficient choice among providers.

Transparency, providing information about prices or quality to the public, is a policy that has received substantial attention, and has been implemented by some states. In principle, it seems as more information should be better.

However, this is not necessarily the case. Making pricing information public can make it easier for firms to collude. In addition, it's not clear that heavily insured consumers have sufficient incentive to pay attention to price differences. Even consumers who have policies with a lot of cost sharing will not face much of the impacts of price differences if they obtain an expensive treatment. Expensive treatments put most consumers well beyond their deductibles and copays so that they bear little to none of any price differences across providers.[7] Of course, expensive treatments account for the majority of medical spending.

Providing clear and understandable information about products (providers' and insurers') so consumers can understand what they are obtaining can facilitate competition (again, conditional on sufficient alternatives). If consumers have little information or don't understand the information they have, they tend to rely on reputations, brand names, etc. This tends to decrease the responsiveness of demand to prices or other factors and enhances firms' market power.

5.4. Rate Regulation

A possible response to highly concentrated markets is rate regulation. If markets are highly concentrated and there appears little hope of competition, then price regulation is an economic policy that can be employed. However, moving to a regulated price environment for the privately insured would be a nontrivial undertaking, with all of the issues associated with regulation and bureaucracy. Evidence from state hospital rate regulation programs in the 1970s and 1980s indicates a mixed pattern of success. The setup and administration of the program played a large role in whether they were effective. Nonetheless, there is evidence that finds that mandatory rate regulation program in a number of states did reduce the rate of growth of hospital expenses (by a little more than 1 percent) (Dranove and Cone, 1985; Sloan, 1983).

References

Akosa Antwi, Y. O. D., Gaynor, M., and Vogt, W. B. (2009). A bargain at twice the price? California hospital prices in the new millennium. Forum for Health Economics and Policy, 12(1):Article 3. http://www.bepress.com/fhep/12/1/3.

American Medical Association (2010). Competition in health insurance: A comprehensive study of U.S. markets. Technical report, American Medical Association, Chicago, IL. 2006-2010 editions.

Berenson, R., Ginsburg, P., and Kemper, N. (2010). Unchecked provider clout in California foreshadows challenges to health reform. *Health Affairs,* 29(4):699.

Brand, K., Garmon, C., Gowrisankaran, G., Nevo, A., and Town, R. (2011). Estimating the price impact of hospital mergers: Inova's proposed acquisition of Prince William hospital. unpublished manuscript, Federal Trade Commission, University of Arizona, Northwestern University, University of Minnesota.

Burns, L., Bazzoli, G., Dynan, L., and Wholey, D. (2000). Impact of HMO market structure physician-hospital strategic alliances. *Health Services Research,* 35(1):101– 132.

Burns, L. and Muller, R. (2008). Hospital-physician collaboration: Landscape of economic integration and impact on clinical integration. *Milbank Quarterly,* 86(3):375– 434.

Burns, L. R. and Pauly, M. V. (2002). Integrated delivery networks: A detour on the road to integrated health care? *Health Affairs,* 21(4):128–143.

Capps, C., Carlton, D., and David, G. (2010). Antitrust treatment of nonprofits: Should hospitals receive special care? unpublished manuscript, Bates White LLC, University of Chicago, University of Pennsylvania.

Capps, C. and Dranove, D. (2004). Hospital consolidation and negotiated PPO prices. *Health Affairs,* 23(2):175–181.

Capps, C., Dranove, D., and Satterthwaite, M. (2003). Competition and market power in option demand markets. *RAND Journal of Economics,* 34(4):737–63.

Capps, C. S. (2009). Federal health plan merger enforcement is consistent and robust. *White Paper,* Bates White LLC.

Chernew, M. (1995). The impact of non-IPA HMOs on the number of hospitals and hospital capacity. *Inquiry,* 32(2):143–154.

Ciliberto, F. (2005). Does organizational form affect investment decisions? unpublished manuscript, University of Virginia.

Ciliberto, F. and Dranove, D. (2005). The effect of physician-hospital affiliations on hospital prices in California. *Journal of Health Economics,* 25(1):29–38.

Cooper, Z., Gibbons, S., Jones, S., and McGuire, A. (2010). Does hospital competition save lives? Evidence from the English NHS patient choice reforms. unpublished manuscript, London School of Economics.

Cuellar, A. E. and Gertler, P. J. (2005). Strategic integration of hospitals and physicians. *Journal of Health Economics,* 25(1):1–28.

Cutler, D., McClellan, M., and Newhouse, J. (2000). How does managed care do it? *RAND Journal of Economics,* 31(3):526–548.

Cutler, D. M., Huckman, R. S., and Kolstad, J. T. (2010). Input constraints and the efficiency of entry: Lessons from cardiac surgery. American Economic *Journal: Economic Policy,* 2(1):51–76.

Dafny, L. (2009). Estimation and identification of merger effects: An application to hospital mergers. *Journal of Law and Economics,* 52(3):pp. 523–550.

Dafny, L. (2010). Are health insurance markets competitive? *American Economic Review,* 100:1399–1431.

Dafny, L., Dranove, D., Limbrock, F., and Scott Morton, F. (2011a). Data impediments to empirical work in health insurance markets. unpublished manuscript, Northwestern University, Yale University.

Dafny, L., Duggan, M., and Ramanarayanan, S. (2011b). Paying a premium on your premium? Consolidation in the U.S. health insurance industry. American Economic Review, forthcoming.

Dranove, D., Gron, A., and Mazzeo, M. (2003). Differentiation and competition in HMO markets. *Journal of Industrial Economics,* 51(4):433–454.

Dranove, D. and Lindrooth, R. (2003). Hospital consolidation and costs: Another look at the evidence. Journal of Health Economics, 22:983–997.

Dranove, D. and Ludwick, R. (1999). Competition and pricing by nonprofit hospitals: a reassesment of Lynk's analysis. *Journal of Health Economics,* 18:87–98.

Dranove, D., Simon, C., and White, W. (2002). Is managed care leading to consolidation in health-care markets? *Health Services Research,* 37(3):573–594.

Dranove, D. D. and Satterthwaite, M. A. (2000). The industrial organization of health care markets. In Culyer, A. and Newhouse, J., editors, Handbook of Health Economics, chapter 20, pages 1094–1139. *Elsevier Science,* North-Holland, New York and Oxford.

Federal Trade Commission and Department of Justice (1992). Horizontal merger guidelines. Issued April 2, 1992, Revised September, 2010.

Fuchs, V. (2007). Managed care and merger mania. *Journal of the American Medical Association,* 277(11):920–921.

Gaynor, M. (2006). What do we know about competition and quality in health care markets? Foundations and Trends in Microeconomics, 2(6). http://www.nowpublishers.com/product.aspx?product=MIC&doi=0700000024.

Gaynor, M. and Haas-Wilson, D. (1998). Vertical relations in health care markets. In Morrisey, M. A., editor, Managed Care and Changing Health Care Markets, chapter 7, pages 140–163. AEI Press, Washington, DC.

Gaynor, M., Moreno-Serra, R., and Propper, C. (2010). Death by market power: Reform, competition and patient outcomes in the British National Health Service. unpublished manuscript, Carnegie Mellon University, Imperial College.

Gaynor, M. and Town, R. J. (2012). Competition in health care markets. In McGuire, T. G., Pauly, M. V., and Pita Barros, P., editors, Handbook of Health Economics, volume 2, chapter 9. Elsevier North-Holland, Amsterdam and London. forthcoming.

Gaynor, M. and Vogt, W. B. (2000). Antitrust and competition in health care markets. In Culyer, A. and Newhouse, J., editors, Handbook of Health Economics, chapter 27, pages 1405–1487. *Elsevier Science,* North-Holland, New York and Oxford.

Gaynor, M. and Vogt, W. B. (2003). Competition among hospitals. *Rand Journal of Economics,* 34(4):764–785.

Government Accountability Office (2009). State small group health insurance markets. Technical report, U.S. Government Accountability Office, Washington, DC. GAO-09- 363R.

Haas-Wilson, D. (2003). Managed Care and Monopoly Power: The Antitrust Challenge. Harvard University Press, Cambridge, MA.

Haas-Wilson, D. and Garmon, C. (2011). Hospital mergers and competitive effects: Two retrospective analyses,. *International Journal of the Economics of Business,* 18(1):17– 32.

Harrison, T. (2010). Do mergers really reduce costs? evidence from hospitals. *Economic Inquiry,* 49:1–16.

Keeler, E., Melnick, G., and Zwanziger, J. (1999). The changing effects of competition on non-profit and for-profit hospital pricing behavior. *Journal of Health Economics,* 18:69–86.

Kessler, D. and McClellan, M. (2000). Is hospital competition socially wasteful? *Quarterly Journal of Economics,* 115(2):577–615.

Kessler, D. P. and Geppert, J. J. (2005). The effects of competition on variation in the quality and cost of medical care. *Journal of Economics and Management Strategy,* 14(3):575–589.

Krishnan, R. (2001). Market restructuring and pricing in the hospital industry. *Journal of Health Economics,* 20:213–237.

Liebhaber, A. and Grossman, J. M. (2007). Physicians moving to mid-sized, single-specialty practices. Technical report, Center for Studying Health System Change, Washington, DC. Tracking Report No. 18.

Lustig, J. (2010). Measuring welfare losses from adverse selection and imperfect competition in privatized Medicare. unpublished manuscript, Boston University.

Madison, K. (2004). Hospital–physician affiliations and patient treatments, expenditures, and outcomes. *Health services research,* 39(2):257–278.

Maestas, N., Schroeder, M., and Goldman, D. (2009). Price variation in markets with homogeneous goods: The case of Medigap. Working Paper No. 14679, National Bureau of Economic Research.

Martin, A., Lassman, D., Whittle, L., and Catlin, A. (2011). Recession contributes to slowest annual rate of increase in health spending in five decades. *Health Affairs,* 30:111–122.

Massachusetts Attorney General (2010). Investigation of health care cost trends and cost drivers, pursuant to G.L. c.118G, § 6 1/2(b). Preliminary report, Office of Attorney General Martha Coakley, Boston, MA. January 29.

Moriya, A. S., Vogt, W. B., and Gaynor, M. (2010). Hospital prices and market structure in the hospital and insurance industries. *Health Economics, Policy and Law,* 5:459–479.

National Center for Health Statistics (2011). Health, United States, 2010. Technical report, National Center for Health Statistics, Center for Disease Control, Hyattsville, MD.

Pennsylvania Health Care Cost Containment Council (2007). Cardiac surgery in Pennsylvania 2005. Report, Pennsylvania Health Care Cost Containment Council, Harrisburg, PA. June.

Romano, P. and Balan, D. (2011). A retrospective analysis of the clinical quality effects of the acquisition of Highland Park hospital by Evanston Northwestern healthcare. *International Journal of the Economics of Business,* 18(1):45–64.

Rosenthal, M. B., Zaslavsky, A., and Newhouse, J. P. (2005). The geographic distribution of physicians revisited. *Health Services Research,* 40(6, Part 1):1931–1952.

Sacher, S. and Vita, M. (2001). The competitive effects of a not-for-profit hospital merger: a case study. *Journal of Industrial Economics,* 49(1):63–84.

Schneider, J., Li, P., Klepser, D., Peterson, N., Brown, T., and Scheffler, R. (2008). The effect of physician and health plan market concentration on prices in commercial health insurance markets. *International Journal of Health Care Finance and Economics,* 8:13–26.

Shen, Y., Wu, V., and Melnick, G. (2010). Trends in hospital cost and revenue, 1994-2005: How are they related to HMO penetration, concentration, and for-profit ownership? *Health Services Research,* 45(1):42–61.

Simpson, J. and Shin, R. (1997). Do non-profit hospitals exercise market power? unpublished manuscript, Federal Trade Commission.

Sorensen, A. T. (2003). Insurer-hospital bargaining: Negotiated discounts in post-deregulation Connecticut. *Journal of Industrial Economics,* 51(4):469–490.

Spang, H., Bazzoli, G., and Arnould, R. (2001). Hospital mergers and savings for consumers: Exploring new evidence. Health Affairs, 20(4):150–158.

Starc, A. (2010). Insurer pricing and consumer welfare: Evidence from Medigap. unpublished manuscript, Harvard University.

Tenn, S. (2011). The price effects of hospital mergers: A case study of the sutter-summit transaction. *International Journal of the Economics of Business,* 18(1):65–82.

Thompson, E. (2011). The effect of hospital mergers on inpatient prices: A case study of the New Hanover-Cape Fear transaction,. *International Journal of the Economics of Business,* 18(1):91–101.

Town, R. and Vistnes, G. (2001). Hospital competition in HMO networks. *Journal of Health Economics,* 20(5):733–752.

Town, R., Wholey, D., Feldman, R., and Burns, L. (2006). The welfare consequences of hospital mergers. *Working Paper* No. 12244, National Bureau of Economic Research.

Town, R., Wholey, D., Feldman, R., and Burns, L. (2007). Revisiting the relationship between managed care and hospital consolidation. *Health Services Research,* 42(1):219–238.

Town, R. J. and Liu, S. (2003). The welfare impact of Medicare HMOs. *RAND Journal of Economics,* 34:719–736.

Town, R. J. and Park, M. (2011). Market structure beliefs and hospital merger waves. unpublished manuscript, University of Minnesota.

Vogt, W. B. and Town, R. J. (2006). How has hospital consolidation affected the price and quality of hospital care? Research Synthesis Report 9, Robert Wood Johnson Foundation, Princeton, NJ.

Wu, V. (2009). Managed care's price bargaining with hospitals. *Journal of Health Economics,* 28:350–360.

End Notes

[1] The table contains population weighted, averages for all but the largest Metropolitan Statistical Areas (MSA)(based on admissions). The sample is limited to those MSAs with a population less than 3 million in 1990 because it is likely there are multiple hospital markets in MSAs larger than 3 million population.

[2] The old Federal merger guidelines cutoff for considering a market highly concentrated (Federal Trade Commission and Department of Justice, 1992).

[3] This results in an 800 point increase in the HHI, from 2000 to 2,800. As reported in 1, the average HHI rose by about this amount from 1997 to 2002, albeit from a higher base.

[4] Sorensen (2003) and Wu (2009) find that health plans who are better able to channel patients can extract greater discounts from hospitals. Shen et al. (2010) and Moriya et al. (2010) find health insurer concentration reduces hospital prices, while Schneider et al. (2008) find no effect of insurer concentration on physician prices.

[5] Complaints about exclusive contracts between hospitals and physician practices are the most numerous type of antitrust case brought in health care. One of these cases was decided by the Supreme Court (Jefferson Parish Hosp. Dist. No. 2 v. Hyde, 466 U.S. 2(1984)), and represents an important legal precedent on exclusive dealing and tying. There have also been a number of cases on most-favorednations clauses, e.g., Ocean State Physicians Health Plan v. Blue Cross & Blue Shield, 883 F.2d 1101 (1st Cir. 1989), cert. denied, 494 U.S. 1027 (1990) and Blue Cross & Blue Shield v. Marshfield Clinic, 65 F.3d 1406 (7th Cir. 1995), cert. denied, 116 S. Ct. 1288 (1996).

[6] Nonetheless, if prices are higher in more concentrated markets, that is evidence that any efficiencies that consolidated firms may realize are not being passed on to consumers in the form of lower prices.

[7] This doesn't mean that being insured against large losses is bad – it isn't. Consumers should be insured against large risks. It just means that it's not realistic to expect them to pay attention to prices in such a situation.

In: Physician Practices
Editor: Isaak Angelidis
ISBN: 978-1-62618-184-7

Chapter 11

STATEMENT OF PAUL B. GINSBURG, PRESIDENT, CENTER FOR STUDYING HEALTH SYSTEM CHANGE. HEARING ON "HEALTH CARE INDUSTRY CONSOLIDATION"*

Chairman Herger, Congressman Stark and members of the Subcommittee, thank you for the invitation to testify on health care industry consolidation. My name is Paul Ginsburg, president of the Center for Studying Health System Change (HSC) and research director of National Institute for Health Care Reform (NIHCR).

Founded in 1995, HSC is an independent, nonpartisan health policy research organization affiliated with Mathematica Policy Research. HSC also has served since 2008 as the research arm of the nonpartisan, nonprofit National Institute for Health Care Reform, a 501(c) (3) organization established by the International Union, UAW; Chrysler Group LLC; Ford Motor Company; and General Motors to conduct health policy research and analysis to improve the organization, financing and delivery of health care in the United States—www.NIHCR.org.

Our goal at HSC is to inform policy makers with objective and timely research on developments in the health care system and their impact on people. We do not make specific policy recommendations. Our various

* This is an edited, reformatted and augmented version of a Statement Presented September 9, 2011 before the House Committee on Ways and Means, Subcommittee on Health.

research and communication activities may be found on our Web site at www.hschange.org.

I and colleagues at HSC have conducted and published research on the issue of leverage between health care providers and private insurers for some time. Much has been based on the Community Tracking Study site visits, a project that has followed 12 nationally representative metropolitan communities since 1996,[1] and a similar project conducted in six California metropolitan areas in 2008-09.

THE SHIFTING BALANCE OF NEGOTIATING POWER

In the early 1990s, health plans pressured hospitals and physicians to cut costs, accept lower payment rates and assume financial risk for patients' care. This phenomenon occurred across the country, albeit to varying degrees in different markets. What prompted health plans to suddenly act so aggressively in their local markets? Ultimately, the broader economic climate emboldened them, as employers got serious about controlling costs during a severe recession, shifting employees into managed care products that had restrictive provider networks and tight utilization management. At the same time, hospitals began a wave of mergers and acquisitions to address excess capacity and to strengthen their clout with insurers.

Just a few years later, perhaps abetted by the economic boom of the late-1990s, a significant backlash against managed care developed, ultimately shifting the balance of power in favor of providers, particularly hospitals. More concerned with recruiting and retaining employees than with controlling health care costs, employers embraced health insurance products with broad provider networks. Without a credible threat of excluding a provider from their networks, health plans lost an important bargaining chip. It's important to note that many physicians, except for large multispecialty and single-specialty practices, did not experience the same gains in negotiating leverage, but that may be changing as physicians form larger groups or seek employment by hospitals.

When the economy slowed again, employers did not limit provider choice, but instead began to pass responsibility for containing costs to their employees through higher patient cost sharing in the form of larger deductibles, coinsurance and copayments. Provider demands for higher payment rates and other favorable contract terms led to a spate of plan-provider contract showdowns in the early 2000s, when many providers threatened and some actually dropped out of health plan provider networks.[2]

HIGHER PRICES AND SPENDING GROWTH

As insurers abandoned tightly managed care practices and moved to create broad provider networks, health care spending for employer-sponsored insurance began accelerating in the late-1990s with increased volume initially playing a larger role in more rapid spending growth than higher prices. In the wake of highly publicized and sometimes disruptive contract disputes in the early 2000s, health plans and providers in many markets reached a —separate peace,|| with plans—and employers tacitly—agreeing to go along with higher payment rates to get along.

Despite the 2001 recession, employers stayed the course on maintaining broad provider choice, and health care spending continued to escalate. As the adjustment in volume to the looser managed care environment was completed, a larger portion of health care spending growth was attributable to higher prices, particularly for hospitals. At the same time, many hospitals shifted their competitive strategies from a wholesale approach—vying for managed care contracts—to a retail approach—marketing directly to patients and physicians on the basis of the latest technology and amenities. Many hospitals also pursued aggressive specialty-service-line expansion for profitable services, such as cancer, cardiac and orthopedic care.

While health care spending growth has slowed in recent years, it still continues to outpace growth in the economy and wages by 1 to 2 percentage points. Despite the great recession of 2007-09, employers remain reluctant to restrict provider choice and continue to increase patient cost sharing at the point of service and, most recently, by asking workers to pay a larger share of premiums.[3]

PROVIDER LEVERAGE

During HSC's recently completed 2010 site visits, insurers consistently cited higher payment rates to obtain hospital and large physician group participation in health plan networks as a major factor driving higher insurance premiums. Hospitals often acknowledged that private insurance payment rates were rising more rapidly than their costs but attributed the spread to increasingly constrained Medicare and Medicaid payment rates. However, there is evidence that many hospitals have grown lax about controlling costs and have the market power to demand higher payment rates from private insurers to stay profitable regardless of Medicare rates.[4] Likewise, previous HSC research examining six California metropolitan areas documented considerable increases in provider leverage over time, resulting in striking differences in payment rates to providers with strong leverage vs. those with little leverage.[5]

Turning to quantitative evidence, American Hospital Association data indicate that the ratio of private payer rates to hospital costs increased from 116 percent in 2000 to 134 percent in 2009.[6] A recent HSC study found wide variation in private insurer payment rates to hospitals and physicians across and within local markets.[7] Looking across eight health care markets Cleveland, Indianapolis, Los Angeles, Miami, Milwaukee, Richmond, San Francisco and rural Wisconsin - average inpatient hospital payment rates of four large national insurers ranged from 147 percent of Medicare in Miami to 210 percent in San Francisco. In extreme cases, some hospitals commanded almost five times what Medicare paid for inpatient services and more than seven times what Medicare paid for outpatient care.

Variation within markets was just as dramatic. For example, the hospital with prices at the 25th percentile of Los Angeles hospitals received 84 percent of Medicare rates for inpatient care, while the hospital with prices at the 75th percentile received 184 percent of Medicare rates. The highest-priced Los Angeles hospital with substantial inpatient claims volume received 418 percent of Medicare. While not as pronounced, significant variation in physician payment rates also exists across and within markets and by specialty. Those specialties covered in the study received higher rates in relation to Medicare than primary care physicians. Few would characterize the variation in hospital and physician payment rates found in this study to be consistent with a highly competitive market.

FACTORS CONTRIBUTING TO PROVIDER LEVERAGE

Provider consolidation is clearly a factor behind provider leverage. Consolidation has increased both through mergers and through attrition of weaker providers, especially hospitals. Mergers and acquisitions are subject to antitrust review, while increased consolidation from competitors leaving the market is not. Although recent studies by economists have reported clear results that hospital mergers increase prices,8earlier notions that hospital mergers could lower prices through increased efficiency led to many Federal Trade Commission (FTC) setbacks in blocking hospital mergers that might harm the public.

A recent study by James Robinson provided additional empirical evidence that faced with shortfalls between Medicare payments and projected costs, hospitals in concentrated markets focus on raising prices to private insurers, while hospitals in competitive markets focus on cutting costs.[9] This is consistent with earlier Medicare Payment Advisory Commission (MedPAC) findings that hospitals with substantial negotiating leverage do not have to be as efficient and can allow unit costs to increase, which will result in lower or negative Medicare margins, because the hospitals can obtain higher private insurance rates to offset their high costs.[10]

But provider consolidation is not the only factor driving provider leverage. Hospitals can achieve must-have status—meaning health plans must include them in their networks to offer insurance products attractive to employers and consumers—in a variety of ways. Hospital reputation for perceived quality—not to be confused with measured clinical quality—is a particularly powerful factor. Some independent hospitals that do not have large market shares have substantial leverage on the basis of their reputation for quality or their niche within a particular geographic area.

Many respondents in our California study alluded to the high payment rates obtained by Cedars-Sinai Hospital in Los Angeles. Asked why Cedars did not engage in mergers and acquisitions to become a horizontally integrated system, as is common in northern California, a respondent from another area hospital suggested that Cedars can say, - Screw it; we have a strong marketing arm and the [movie] actors, let's grow on campus and they will come to us." As a result, according to another respondent, —Cedars has the highest rates in the world.... The hospitals down the street have no market power. They have to fight for every penny."[11]

Although Miami-Dade County, Fla., has a relatively unconcentrated hospital market, Baptist Health South Florida reportedly has significant leverage because of its reputation for quality and dominant role in the southern part of the county. Some hospitals have leverage on the basis of highly specialized services, such as transplants and trauma or burn care. Children's hospitals are another example of providers with a particular niche gaining significant market power.

Even in markets with dominant health plans, insurers appear unable or unwilling to constrain payment rate increases, because they can pass along higher provider payment rates to employers.

HOSPITAL EMPLOYMENT OF PHYSICIANS

While not new, the pace of hospital employment of physicians has quickened in many communities, according to HSC's 2010 site visits.[12] To date, hospitals' primary motivation for employing physicians has been to gain market share, typically through lucrative service-line strategies encouraged by a fee-for-service payment system that rewards volume. At the same time, stagnant reimbursement rates, coupled with the rising costs of private practice, and a desire for a better work-life balance have contributed to physician interest in hospital employment.

While greater physician alignment with hospitals may ultimately improve quality through better clinical integration and care coordination, hospital employment of physicians does not guarantee clinical integration. The trend of hospital-employed physicians also may increase costs through higher hospital and physician commercial payment rates and hospital pressure on employed physicians to order more expensive care.

Also, hospitals routinely charge facility fees for office visits and procedures performed in formerly independent physicians' offices, where the physicians have converted to hospital employment. In short, it is possible for a physician practice to be acquired by a hospital, not change locations or even practice operations, yet the hospital now receives significantly higher Medicare payments. Often, hospitals apply these billing practices to private insurers as well. Hospitals charging facility fees for physician visits not only results in higher costs for payers, but also for patients because facility fees are subject to deductibles and coinsurance.

OPTIONS TO ADDRESS PROVIDER LEVERAGE

Two broad options are available to address rapidly rising provider payment rates to private insurers—market forces and regulation. The market approach involves changes in insurance products to engage enrollees in selecting providers on the basis of price. One recent trend in coverage offered by small employers is insurance products that have a more limited provider network, excluding providers that insurers believe to be most expensive.

A related approach, which may ultimately have more potential, is tiered-provider networks. The essence of the approach is to offer enrollees incentives in terms of lower patient cost sharing at the point of service—lower deductibles and coinsurance, for example, to choose lower-cost providers. This approach may have more potential because consumers appear more willing to accept incentives to choose certain providers over others more readily than absolute restrictions on choice of providers. However, tiered-provider networks have not gained much traction, particularly because dominant hospitals often refuse to contract with health plans unless placed in the most favorable tier with the least patient cost sharing, effectively circumventing any advantage to the approach. Physicians also have opposed these approaches, typically referred to as high-performance networks, because of concerns about the accuracy of methods used to measure their quality and efficiency, which determines whether they are deemed high performing or not.

Government has some opportunities to support these market approaches. Medicare's development of hospital value-based purchasing and value-based modifiers under the physician fee schedule will advance the state of the art in comparing performance among hospitals and physicians. If private insurers follow Medicare's lead and adopt these approaches, it would send consistent payment signals to providers and increase the credibility of these tools. In addition, regulatory options exist to enhance market forces. For example, Massachusetts has enacted legislation that bans some hospital contracting practices, such as refusal to contract according to placement in tiers. The legislation also bars multihospital systems from requiring that insurers contract with all of their facilities.

Antitrust policy will be an important area where regulation can enhance market forces. In addition to standard reviews of mergers and acquisitions, the Department of Justice and FTC are heavily involved in guiding rules for Medicare accountable care organizations (ACOs) to safeguard against increased provider leverage resulting from greater integration.

Finally, the tax treatment of employer-sponsored health insurance will influence the extent to which market forces can be a countervailing force to provider leverage. Reduced tax subsidies for high-cost health benefits likely will increase the receptivity of employers and employees to insurance products that provide incentives to enrollees to favor lower-cost providers.

The federal and state governments in particular have taken steps to increase the transparency of information on the price and quality of services in hospitals. Much of the available price information is unlikely to have much impact because for insured people, the only prices that matter is what their deductibles, copayments and coinsurance will be if they use different providers.

However, as governments make provider price data available, it is possible that providers with the highest prices will feel public pressure to limit increases. The extensive release of hospital price information by the Massachusetts Attorney General has prompted public scrutiny and perhaps will motivate hospitals, particularly nonprofit hospitals and their trustees, to constrain prices.

The major question with market approaches is how effective they will be. This will depend on the degree to which some markets are already so consolidated that effective competition on the basis of price is not possible. It will also depend on how consumers react to having to focus more on price as they use health care services.

The alternative to market forces is rate review or rate setting by a public entity. This is much more likely to develop at the state rather than the federal level. It could take relatively loose forms, such as a limit based on Medicare payment rates or high rates triggering a review. It could be highly structured, such as the system used in Maryland since the 1970s. A key issue in rate-setting approaches is the extent to which they will foster broader provider payment reforms or accommodate payment innovations.

The topic of increasing consolidation in the health industry is an important one. It certainly has played a role in rising health care spending, especially for services covered by private insurance. But a key role in increasing provider leverage has been broad provider networks and lack of incentives for patients to choose providers that have lower costs. If there is to be a market solution to this problem, it will have to address both the issue of consolidation and engage consumers in ways that they have resisted before.

End Notes

[1] HSC recently completed the seventh round of the Community Tracking Study site visits to 12 nationally representative metropolitan communities: Boston; Cleveland; Greenville, S.C.; Indianapolis; Lansing, Mich.; Little Rock, Ark.; Miami; northern New Jersey; Orange County, Calif.; Phoenix; Seattle; and Syracuse, N.Y. The visits were conducted from March 2010 through October 2010. In each site, researchers interview representatives of major hospital systems and private insurers.

[2] Strunk, Bradley C., Kelly J. Devers and Robert E. Hurley, Health Plan-Provider Showdowns on the Rise, Issue Brief No. 40, Center for Studying Health System Change, Washington, D.C. (June 2001).

[3] Kaiser Family Foundation and Health Research and Educational Trust 2010 Annual Survey of Employer Benefits.

[4] Ginsburg, Paul B., —Cutting Medicare with a Scalpel, The New York Times, (July 11, 2009). Accessed at http://www.nytimes.com/2009/07/12/opinion/12ginsburg.html.

[5] Berenson, Robert A., Paul B. Ginsburg and Nicole Kemper, —Unchecked Provider Clout In California Foreshadows Challenges To Health Reform,|| Health Affairs, Vol. 29, No. 4 (April 2010).

[6] American Hospital Association, TrendWatch Chartbook 2011, Trends in Hospital financing, Chart 4.6: Aggregate Hospital Payment-to-cost Ratios for Private Payers, Medicare, and Medicaid, 1989 – 2009, Chicago (2011).

[7] Ginsburg, Paul B., Wide Variation in Hospital and Physician Payment Rates Evidence of Provider Market Power, Research Brief No. 16, Center for Studying Health system Change, Washington, D.C. (November 2010).

[8] Vogt, William B., and Robert Town, How Has Hospital Consolidation Affected the Price and Quality of Hospital Care, The Synthesis Project, Research Synthesis Report No. 9, Robert Wood Johnson Foundation (February 2006).

[9] Robinson, James, —Hospitals Respond to Medicare Payment Shortfalls by Both Shifting Costs and Cutting Them, Based on Market Concentration," Health Affairs, Vol. 30, No. 7 (July 2011).

[10] Medicare Payment Advisory Commission (MedPAC), Report to the Congress: Medicare Payment Policy, Washington, D.C. (March 2009).

[11] Berenson, Ginsburg and Kemper (April 2010).

[12] O'Malley, Ann S., Amelia M. Bond and Robert A. Berenson, Rising Hospital Employment of Physicians: Better Quality, Higher Costs? Issue Brief No. 135, Center for Studying Health System Change, Washington, D.C. (August 2011).

INDEX

C

I

J

L

M

T

U

V

W

Y